The Perennial Philosophy

Series

T0302581

World Wisdom
The Library of Perennial Philosophy

The Library of Perennial Philosophy is dedicated to the exposition of the timeless Truth underlying the diverse religions. This Truth, often referred to as the *Sophia Perennis*—or Perennial Wisdom—finds its expression in the revealed Scriptures as well as in the writings of the great sages and the artistic creations of the traditional worlds.

Maintaining the Sacred Center: The Bosnian City of Stolac appears as one of our selections in the Perennial Philosophy series.

The Perennial Philosophy Series

In the beginning of the twentieth century, a school of thought arose which has focused on the enunciation and explanation of the Perennial Philosophy. Deeply rooted in the sense of the sacred, the writings of its leading exponents establish an indispensable foundation for understanding the timeless Truth and spiritual practices which live in the heart of all religions. Some of these titles are companion volumes to the Treasures of the World's Religions series, which allows a comparison of the writings of the great sages of the past with the perennialist authors of our time.

Cover:
Stolac, Bosnia,
by Leopold Goldstein, c. 1870

MAINTAINING THE SACRED CENTER

THE BOSNIAN CITY OF STOLAC

Rusmir Mahmutćehajić

Preface by

Seyyed Hossein Nasr

Introduction by

Ivo Banac

World Wisdom

Maintaining the Sacred Center: The Bosnian City of Stolac

Original published as
Stolačka Čaršija: U vidiku perenijalne filozofije
Zagreb: Antibarbarus, 2008

Translation by
Desmond Maurer

Library of Congress Cataloging-in-Publication Data

Mahmutcehajic, Rusmir, 1948-
[Stolacka caršija. English]
Maintaining the sacred center : the Bosnian city of Stolac / Rusmir Mahmutcehajic ; preface by Seyyed Hossein Nasr ; introduction by Ivo Banac.
p. cm. -- (Perennial philosophy series)
Includes bibliographical references and index.
ISBN 978-1-935493-91-4 (pbk. : alk. paper) 1. Islam--Bosnia and Hercegovina. 2. Islamic philosophy--Bosnia and Hercegovina. 3. Stolac (Bosnia and Hercegovina)--Ethnic relations. 4. Stolac (Bosnia and Hercegovina)--History. 5. Stolac (Bosnia and Hercegovina)--Religious life and customs. I. Title.
BP65.B6M3413 2011
297.0949742--dc22

2011015210

Printed on acid-free paper in the United States of America

For information address World Wisdom, Inc.
P.O. Box 2682, Bloomington, Indiana 47402-2682
www.worldwisdom.com

In the name of God,
the All-Merciful, the Ever-Merciful

For my father, Zulfikar

CONTENTS

Preface

I first heard of Rusmir Mahmutćehajić from Titus Burckhardt in the early 1970s. He told me of a young Yugoslav who was devoted to the traditional perspective and who was very familiar with the works of Guénon, Coomaraswamy, Schuon, and himself. Years passed during which momentous political events took place, including the Iranian Revolution of 1979 that caused me to migrate to America and the breakup both of the Soviet Union and Yugoslavia, the latter combined with the worst atrocities in Europe since the Second World War, especially in Bosnia where Rusmir Mahmutćehajić resided and where he was playing a major political as well as intellectual role. Even before these tragedies, that is, in the 1980s, some of my own works began to be translated into Bosnian by such men as Enes Karić, who was both a major traditional scholar and minister of education of Bosnia during the war. As my contact in Bosnia with the newly formed intellectual elite in the Guénonian sense developed, I also began to have direct correspondence with Mahmutćehajić, who was elected Vice-President of the Government of Bosnia-Herzegovina in 1991 and who was playing such a central role in the spiritual and intellectual life of his community. When after the war I visited Sarajevo, whose beautiful green hills were by then covered as far as the eye could see with white tombstones of young men and women killed during the murderous siege of the city, I tried to see him. He was, however, traveling at that time but sent his daughter Fatima to speak to me at my hotel. So we never met in person but I began to read more and more of his many writings.

Since I founded the traditional journal *Sophia*, he has been a regular contributor to it in addition to writing many valuable books and other articles, all of which are based on the principles of the perennial philosophy and in defense of what Schuon has called "the transcendent unity of religions." With remarkable serenity and in writings characterized by literary beauty, Mahmutćehajić defended—even amidst a most cruel war fueled by a strife basing itself on opposition between the Orthodox, the Catholics, and Muslims and the fanning of the fire of the hatred of the religious other—the harmony between Muslims, Christians, and Jews that had existed in Bosnia for centuries, the religious harmony that lies at the heart of the traditional understanding of the perennial philosophy. It is due to him and a number of other traditionalist Bosnian writers and intellectuals that the traditional perspective as understood by Guénon,

Coomaraswamy, Schuon and others occupies today a central position in the intellectual and spiritual arena in Bosnia in a manner that one does not find in any other European or for that matter non-European country. Where else can one walk out of a house of worship, whether it be a mosque, a cathedral, a synagogue, or a temple, and find displayed in the front windows of bookshops in the surrounding area so many books by Guénon, Schuon, Burckhardt, Lings and other traditional authors as one does when walking out of the central mosque of Sarajevo? It is around the principles of Tradition and the perennial philosophy that many are trying to reconstitute the cultural and intellectual life of Bosnia and this reality owes a great deal to Mahmutćehajić as well as to a few other figures such as Enes Karić, Rešid Hafizović and among the younger generation Nevad Kahteran.

In this precious new book Mahmutćehajić turns to the ever-living teachings of the perennial philosophy, as they concern the individual human being, human society, and the cosmos, by studying the tragic history of one Bosnian city, Stolac—the city from which he himself hails. It is, however, a history viewed from the perspective of meta-historical realities and therefore pregnant with universal significance that is of interest far beyond the confines of the history of a city in the Balkans. Stolac and its history serve in this book as a means of expressing abiding truths which should be of interest to all those concerned with the life of the spirit. Even the geography of Stolac, including the sacred center called *čaršija*, is treated by the author in a symbolic manner as sacred geography as are the gardens which are related symbolically to the Garden, *al-Jannah* or *al-Firdaws* of the Quran, that is none other than paradise. It is appropriate to recall here that the word paradise in English is itself related to the Middle Persian word *pardis* meaning garden, a word that is also the origin of the Arabic term *firdaws*. It is remarkable how the author deals with the deepest spiritual realities by drawing upon the sacred geography associated with Stolac and its *čaršija*.

Certain masters of old such as Ibn Arabi have compared the traditional city to the human body. The traditional Islamic city was marked by a sacred center, usually the tomb of a saint or a mosque. The rest of the city was then built around that center as we see in the case of Cairo, Fez, Mashhad and so many other historic cities. In such cities, which could also be called emblematic cities, all the outer parts of the urban area were related to that center and the architectural spaces were created in such a way as to facilitate connection to the center. There was an integrated urban space of which the sacred center was the heart. The whole city, therefore, received the *barakah*, the grace, emanating from that sacred center.

Now, the comparison of such a city with the human body is obvious. At the center of the human body lies the heart, the meeting place of the horizontal and vertical dimensions of reality, the locus of the Divine Presence in the human microcosm. It was to this spiritual and not only physical heart that Christ was referring when he said: "The kingdom of God is within you." So at the center of the heart resides the sacred and the person who through faith, love, and knowledge of God is able to break the hardened walls of the heart—a hardening that is a result of the fall—and realize that he or she indeed possesses a sacred heart at the center of his or her being. Furthermore, the heart governs the flow of blood and therefore life throughout the body and is thereby related in some way to every organ and limb of the body, whether they are near or far. The comparison to the traditional city is obvious.

It was in fact traditional men who created traditional cities, men who were aware of the heart-center within their own body as the spiritual center of their whole being. They had also realized the reality of the microcosmic/macrocosmic correspondences and built cities upon their basis. They built traditional cities always with a center that opened into the transcendent dimension and disseminated the grace of that world beyond to the everyday spaces in which men and women lived. Modern man, who has rebelled against heaven, has no center and possesses a chaotic soul. Naturally he builds the chaotic and centerless urban sprawl of modern cities that now are spread all over the world.

Stolac was, however, a traditional city of historic and architectural significance, set in a beautiful natural surrounding that itself symbolized different Divine Qualities and could be seen as a theophany. This city of exceptional beauty suffered grievously, like so much of Bosnia, throughout the follies of the nineteenth and especially twentieth century leading to its almost complete destruction. Mahmutćehajić paints the suffering of the Bosnian people as a whole through the literary canvas that depicts the history of this tragic city and the deliberate attempt to destroy its sacred center. But in doing so he also teaches the reader much about perennial truths that do not die no matter what the condition of the outer world might be.

The Quran asserts concerning the friends of God (*al-awliya*) or saints: "They fear not; nor does sorrow overtake them." The author approaches his subject with this attitude. In its pages there are to be found words of despair but also of hope and most importantly, beyond the duality of despair and hope, words of truth that should be of great interest to students of the *philosophia perennis* whether they have ever heard of Bosnia or not.

We pray that Stolac will be rebuilt with its sacred center, *čaršija*, and with its rebuilding will come a healing process of which the people of Bosnia who have suffered so much are in such deep need. It is not accidental that there is so much interest in Bosnia today among traditional authors and those in the field of the perennial philosophy. This country is a small but well-educated plural nation in the heart of Europe and a natural bridge between Islam and the West. For centuries it was a land where Muslims, Orthodox, Catholic, and Jewish communities lived side by side for the most part in peace. There are many Bosnian intellectual figures, including the author of this book, who see the destiny of Bosnia as becoming once again a place where these different religions and cultures can live side by side in peace and harmony. And this goal cannot be achieved seriously except on the basis of the teachings of tradition and the perennial philosophy.

In this moving book, Rusmir Mahmutćehajić has taken an important step towards the realization of this goal as well as drawing greater attention to the cultural and spiritual significance of Stolac. We pray and hope that all his tireless and far-reaching efforts, including the writing of this book, will aid in the spiritual, psychological, and physical reconstruction of Bosnia, whose very existence is of much importance to both the Islamic world and the West, and in keeping the torch of the perennial philosophy burning in this beautiful but scarred land that stands as a bridge between these two worlds.

wa-Llahu alam
Seyyed Hossein Nasr
Fair Oaks, California
October 2010

Introduction

Stolac and Its *Čaršija*

Bahadur Shah Zafar II, the last Mughal emperor, composed a *ghazal* for Delhi as it lay in ruins, after the British quashed the Indian Rebellion of 1857.

> Delhi was once a paradise, where Love held sway and reigned; but its charms lie ravished now, and only ruins remain. No tears were shed when, unshrouded, they were laid in common graves; no prayers were read for the noble dead; unmarked remain their graves.

In his book on Stolac and its central public area, the *čaršija*, Rusmir Mahmutćehajić has written a *ghazal* to Stolac in ruins. If it were only a question of lyrical inspiration, prompted by nostalgia for what has been lost, his account would be no less moving, but it would be less inspirational. The key lies not in the loss of the urban order, a signpost towards the center—towards the transcendent—but in the discovery of order within oneself, which enables one to rebuild a destroyed world.

No one has a more powerful vocation than Rusmir Mahmutćehajić to present this knowledge to those who are now on this quest. Scientist, statesman, public figure, and seeker of God, he is the most intellectual representative of the Bosnian generation that has returned to its tradition—as he himself says, to "the 'prevenient idea' that underpins and inspires the entire life of a people." His return is a quest for the lost center that has been obstructed by modern ideologies.

> So long as there is a single seeker in the world who suffers, no one enjoys absolute discovery or liberation. The seeker and the climber may suffer pain and evil, but they always requite it with good: they pray that good may be to everything that is in existence (p. 93).

That the suffering was personal may be seen most vividly from the rejection of our fathers' generation. In his moving Post Scriptum, Rusmir Mahmutćehajić describes the destruction of the Muslim *harem*s (burial grounds) in Stolac during the surge of communist dogmatism in 1949.

> My grandfather Derviš was almost 90 years of age. All his children were communists, building a new world, whose masters had no mercy for anyone on their path and wanted nothing to do with mosques and graveyards (p. 158).

The author reminds us that the destruction of the Stolac *čaršija*, all of the mosques of Stolac, and about two thousand of its houses, as well as the forced expulsion of its entire Muslim population—all carried out by Greater-Croatian nationalists in 1993—was but the *Walpurgisnacht* of an unbroken process that began in the nineteenth century with the demolition of much of the Stolac Fort and the Veli-Dede Mosque, and the laying of roads through the burial grounds with their *stećci* (mediaeval tombstones with enigmatic carvings) in Radimlja and Gorica. Ostensibly acting in the name of "progress" and the struggle against a "dark past," each new regime pulled down yet more public buildings, clock towers, and *mekteb*s (schools). Nor was that all, as the author reminds us: even books fell victim to times of discord and insecurity, buried in the graveyards during the Great Eastern Crisis of 1875 to 1878, the Austro-Hungarian occupation, the establishment of the Kingdom of Serbs, Croats, and Slovenes, World War II, and the early years of communist rule. People, too, were victims of these times, of course. None of this happened by chance, as:

> . . . people do live with distorted and destroyed self-understanding (p. 123).

While:

> Distortion and destruction of the self is the cause of distortion and destruction of the *čaršija* (p. 123).

Rusmir Mahmutćehajić articulates the meaning of the *čaršija* in order to speak of damaged modern man:

> The city is the image of the garden, the garden is the image of Adam, and Adam is God's image. All of God's names are brought together in Adam. But these names have been scattered in the garden. To this scattering across the garden there corresponds the gathering within Adam. The *čaršija* is the focus of the city. Through it we renew our image of the garden and so of ourselves as the focus of all the names (p. 124).

Though the Truth "may be revealed through the uncountable host of signs, from the tiniest to the greatest," modern man lives in a state of distrust and confusion, and for this reason becomes destructive. It was people with damaged selves who laid waste the *čaršija*: not only those who believed that the denigration of the Muslims was necessary for their own "national liberation," but also the true heirs of this traditional garden.

The way out of this state of affairs is in the return to, the quest for the sacred center. The orbs topping the minaret attest to our violation of the center and the necessity of the return:

> When our quest leads us to our goal, which is the Sacred, the city will be restored to its original nature as the garden with the sacred or inviolate tree. The city will become the City. Everything in it will bear witness to the garden of the most beautiful height on which and because of which we were created (p. 94).

This is why the human rights of the people of Stolac could not be restored without the restoration of the central mosque—the Čaršija or Sultan Selim Mosque. Without the restoration of the destroyed heritage, there can be no social cohesion. One of the author's great achievements has been to create the conditions for the people of Stolac who had been driven from their homes to return through the reconstruction of the central symbols of their identity—mosques and *mektebs*—exactly as they had been. They were destroyed by nationalists and communists; but fundamentalists would have "modernized" them in their falsified center, where God has no abode. Those who base the return of refugees and displaced persons on factories and schools are in error. Without renewing the earthly signs of our human center, we ourselves as humans cannot be renewed, and unless we are renewed, there can be no reconstruction of Bosnia or its society.

Zafar ends his *ghazal*, in the language of his faith, with the words:

> But things cannot remain, O Zafar, thus, for who can tell? Through God's great mercy and the Prophet, all may yet be well.

Stolac is still far from the state of cohesion in which it was before the destruction, dispersion, ideological violence, and hatred. How long will it take? That is the final question Rusmir Mahmutćehajić poses. A boy is holding a piece of

> . . . one of Stolac's thousands of Muslim gravestones. . . . Will he be receptive to this remnant of the book of existence and, through

> it, begin the process of bringing together the dissolute world? (p. 198).

No answer comes, but we know that unless that answer is Yes, neither we nor the world will survive.

Ivo Banac
September 20, 2007
Bradford Durfee Professor of History
Yale University

Come out of the city by the east come out of her by the
west
Build a city in thyself and turn thy face towards thy city
For the time is at hand

Mak Dizdar, "The Garland"

Foreword

To belong to a people whose members have been humiliated, persecuted, and killed for centuries, to see one's country covered by the ruins of the towns and villages they once lived in, to see war cause such devastation during one's own lifetime, and to see members of one's own people play a more or less willing role in it—only two words can describe this: "loss" and "confusion."

Worse than such loss, however, is failing to understand that what has been lost can be recovered. Those who have suffered loss can also benefit from it. We must find the justice in what has happened. Nothing can stop us judging ourselves and others or sifting the false from the true. Nothing can stop us showing and speaking the truth. That is all justice is. In the teeth of humiliation, persecution, killing, destruction, and recrimination, it is the only way to pay the debt we owe ourselves and others.

The world's confusion, in which we are immersed, challenges us to turn towards our higher selves and transcend what has happened and is past as part of the world from which we have come, eschewing dreams of an imaginary future pregnant with deception. We must enter the "now," which contains the essence of all that is—truth and wisdom, the first and the last, the in and the out of each thing and all existence.

Any answer to the question of humanity must surely refer to "orientation." Each and every moment of our lives is oriented by death. There are two certainties—our "now" and our death. But if these certainties are absolute, how can there be two? If they are absolute, surely they transcend the finitude of the quantitative world in which and from which our knowledge of them comes?

We can never step outside our "now." Our position in space is different, as we change it all the time. One may say that the present is always with us, but we are always within space. The "now" envelops us, as we journey through night and day and the seasons of the year, from the first to the last hour of life in this world, from our mother's womb to the grave. Our representation of time is inextricably linked to the immeasurably short moment, just as our understanding of space is to the infinitesimally minute point. Any representation of duration takes on the aspect of infinity compared to this moment. The same is true of space: compared to the minute point, any place takes on the aspect of infinity. Contemplating the immeasurably little and small, we experience an intimation of eternity and infinity.

Is it not obvious that the infinitely short moment and the infinitely minute point are the Beginnings or Principles of space and time, respectively, insofar as they are measurable? It is. So obvious that it escapes us, for we dwell amongst their shades, unmindful that traces cannot replace that which left them.

Created upright, we look up from the earth towards the sky, face forward, crown behind. We are split between left and right. We face the heavens, as it were, ahead and to our right, having come from below, behind, and the left. This orientation is informed by polarities: south-north, east-west, and nadir-zenith. Every "here" and "now" finds us approaching one or other of these poles, in an unwavering motion.

Wherever we are, night and day, summer and winter, spring and autumn come and go. But two desires remain constant—life and happiness. Neither being-in-the-moment, which carries us from birth to death, nor being-in-space, which cannot contain us, provides answers on how to approach our goal. Our essence is concentrated in the goal we are trying to reach, which, in its fullness, is both absolutely near and absolutely far. It is represented by the Seat[1] and the Throne of Him[2] who rules over all.

When we focus on our goal and move towards it, our progress on the path brings about change within us, as we rise towards our higher self. This ascent is continuous. As we attain higher levels on our path of ascent, the attributes of our goal become clearer within us. The Seat (*Stolac*) is the name given to that ultimate goal. God speaks of it in the Quran, or Recitation:

> God, there is no god but He, the Living, the Upright. Slumber seizes Him not, neither sleep; to Him belongs all that is in the heavens and the earth. Who is there that shall intercede with Him save by His leave? He knows what lies before them and what is after them, and they comprehend not anything of His knowledge save such as He wills. His Seat comprises the heavens and the earth; the preserving of them oppresses Him not. He is the All-High, the All-Glorious.[3]

Our journey from the lowest depth to the sublime height is necessarily by way of the Seat of the Lord. The Seat is the name for all the worlds together, as they reveal their Creator's sublimity and glory. Through the Seat, we can each transcend worldly existence and our own achievements to realize ourselves fully in the Living and the Upright, to whom all the most beautiful names belong. These names are contained within us, as well as revealed throughout existence. He is hidden, but wills His revelation and so creates. These names become distinct within our own selves, without scattering, as we relate to Him: we become the container and revelation of all the names that pertain to Him and His Seat.

We are the being in which God focuses the totality of His creation. Consequently, we are above the angels, even though we are created of earth and they of light. This is confirmed in the Recitation, where God teaches Adam the names. Perfect, Adam knew them.[4] This is why both names and things connect us to God, our Creator and Teacher, and to His desire to be known fully—even in what He knows and the angels do not.

Discovering the original and authentic meaning of the names is our means of self-realization and our path back to God. Everything in existence has its own name. When we, as knowing subjects, imbue things and names with a meaning other than their proper reference to God, then they are no longer taken as His signs and the names are deformed. On the Day of Debt, when the truth of creation is revealed in full, the false teachers shall deny their false teachings, and the lack of fit between things and the names we have given them, beyond their role in revealing their Creator, shall be revealed.[5] Then the Real shall shine, thanks to the purity of the things it contains and that which they reveal. This is (up)right being, which was ours at the beginning and may be again before the end.

The Bosnian noun *stolac*, translated here as "seat," is commonly used to refer to a place of power or judgment, normally carved in stone.[6] It is a common enough name for a place of settlement,[7] the best known being the southern Bosnian city of Stolac. The name is inseparable from its connotations, and the Seat is a key term in any discourse on God. These considerations have stimulated us to explore the case of the city of the seat, Stolac, from the perspective of perennial philosophy. Our purpose is to demonstrate how this perspective has become distorted within us and so in our acts, particularly between the end of the nineteenth and the end of the twentieth century. In doing so, we hope to be able to provide a tentative answer to the crucial question: Where are we, the people of this age, headed?

The city of Stolac is given shape by its valley and the slopes of its five stony hills. Its location, orientation, and forms afford ample recognition to our relationship with "everything that is in the heavens and on the earth." The proof is in the gradual and harmonious development of the central public area of the town, known in Bosnia as the *čaršija*, as an affirmation of the Sacred, a point at which the four cardinal points meet to reveal a sacred center that acts as focus for whatever is in our selves and our worlds. Why was this endeavor given the name of Stolac, which is to say the Seat?

The nineteen chapters of this book present various aspects of this complex whole, informed by and oriented towards Unity. We cannot orientate ourselves as human beings, without taking into account existence as a whole and every aspect of our own selves. Knowledge of the cosmos is knowledge of the self, and vice versa—knowledge of the human self is knowledge of the cosmos.

Taken overall, the Stolac *čaršija* is an act of witness of our relationship to the cosmos. Through it, we recognize and determine our place in relation to the cosmic whole. Nothing, however great or small, escapes that relationship. Within it, we can pursue our quest to unfold our sublime and beautiful potential, to be guided by our higher self.

An accelerated "disenchantment" of the world and of human being began at the end of the nineteenth century, when the cosmos and the human self ceased to be two sides of a single whole. They were presented as independent and opposed. We came to believe ourselves called upon to bring order to this wild and savage world through our action. We privileged our action over knowledge, but action without knowledge is simply violence. It was precisely such action without knowledge that initiated the destruction of the Stolac *čaršija*, destruction that culminated around the middle of the twentieth century. That was when the final destruction of Stolac's Muslim graveyards took place, an affirmation of the unconditional power and rights of the living over the entirely helpless and disenfranchised dead. This act was considered a victory for the "New Man" in building the "New World" without God. The final destruction of the *čaršija* and the expulsion of its Muslim heirs at the end of the twentieth century should be viewed as an inexorable extension of this inner destruction of the self.[8]

This book investigates the relationship between knowledge of the cosmos and knowledge of the self. Conclusions are drawn regarding ignorance as a source of corruption, expulsion, and murder on the basis of the case of the Stolac *čaršija*, how it came into existence, how it developed as a reflection of the inner life of its people, and the destruction it suffered during the twentieth century. Our original dignity cannot be restored until the relationship between knowledge of the cosmos and knowledge of the self is recognized within a discourse of the eternal principle of all existence. This is so because there is nothing in the world whose being is not in some way for us. Unless we discover that purpose, we cannot find ourselves.

The forms and contents of the Stolac *čaršija*, whose destruction began at the end of the nineteenth century, are here viewed from the perspective of perennial philosophy. There are two reasons for having chosen this approach.

The first is that the Stolac *čaršija* cannot be understood in whole or in part so long as one ignores prophecy and revelation as sources of knowledge.

This neglect is a crucial element of all modern philosophy, which looks to modern science for the only undeniable source of knowledge. It was precisely this approach that informed the ideological image of the world of the "revolutionary movements" whose adherents destroyed the *čaršija*.

The second is that any approach based on the modern image of the world assumes the principle that what cannot be quantified does not exist. Modern science recognizes no worlds that are not subject to measurement, making comparison and analytical reason the highest principles of learning. This rules out of court any human tendency to transcend the limits of the quantifiable world. Consequently, there is no room to recognize knowledge sent down by God as His discourse in human language: prophets and prophecy cannot be recognized as what they claim to be. But, like every other form of sacred tradition, the Stolac *čaršija* can only be understood if we transcend that boundary forbidding access to the Principle and accept our debt towards It, if we continue to hope that we may find the world's end and the way beyond it.

We are in the world. But our world is fully comprehended by God's Seat (*stolac*). In comparison to His Seat, the totality of existence is a ring tossed into infinite space.[9]

A Note on Anthropological and Cosmological Premises

Many traditional towns and cities suffered ruin and destruction during the twentieth century. This destruction passed largely without notice or understanding. These towns were built and developed on the traditional view of the world. The disappearance of this traditional worldview and its replacement by the worldview of modernity is the main cause of their destruction. The destroyers thought to expunge the traditional form from material and spiritual existence. This book is about one such town, in which the author grew up and which shaped him and his approach to the world.

We human beings are the only beings in existence that are at once active and passive and nothing serves quite so well as the city to stimulate our fantasies of independence through unbridled action or to cause us to forget the passive and receptive aspect of our nature. This forgetfulness culminates in destruction. It causes us to view ourselves as masters of space and time and to misconstrue our constructive capacity. Our lives involve both building up and tearing down. When we build, we reveal our Lord as the Builder. When we tear down, we are ruled by death.

The leading Bosnian poet of the twentieth century, Mak Dizdar,[1] was born in this same traditional town. It was there that he "foresaw" his own destiny in his *ars poetica*, a destiny whereby humanity has been cut off from heaven and relies on action out of little knowledge and great ignorance. He knew that town as a revelation of indestructible unity, present in the self, which first receives and then gives, and consequently out of the reach of the destroyer. At the end of a poem on destruction and killing, he turned from the self to the denier:

> So
> Come on then
>
> I've long grown used to your ravages
> As if to the throes
> Of a disease from far away
>
> As to the icy waters swept savagely along
> By this night river of darkness that grows
> Ever more swift

And strong
"Message"[2]

Out of the darkness of existence, from the bottom of the valley, the poet knows the river, which comprehends every glimpse of the One and all of the self from its lowest depth to its most beautiful height. He acknowledges the river, confirming his own self-realization by passage over it. We are always at the edge or in the depth, but also always able to turn towards the center, our highest moment, so that from the bank of existence we may cross over the river that is everything through which Unity reveals Itself. Between the edge or depth and the center or height lie the heavens, the earth, and everything between them, and higher and farther—the blue river of the unseen, of which all the signs within the horizons of the world and within our own selves speak. Seeking ways from edge to center, from depth to height, from body to Spirit, the poet says:

That's where a dark blue river flows
The river that we need to cross
"Blue River"

The wounded town, with its ruins and ashes, and the murdered and exiled, murderous and destructive, wounded and deformed selves of its folk, faces the survivor like a black hole in existence. All the links and relationships in the webs of meaning woven through history are broken. Everything has sunk below the surface, like a corpse under a grave mound. To the living, existence as a whole now presents itself quite differently. Every thread that binds phenomena with meaning passes through the dead and their graves, through wounded and tortured selves, through destroyed buildings and their contents, to find itself in the shadows and light bounded by the earthly horizon and the arch of heaven and all that lies between them. It seems that the fading riches of the way of life of the murdered and their world remain, somehow mysteriously, within that frame.

Do not all things, whether present or absent, reveal the One?

One must state unequivocally that the One is always present, revealed by giving and receiving, passivity and action, heaven and earth, Spirit and body, as only He remains. The world and its contents are a countless multitude in constant flux. We must recognize the limits of this totality, if we are to understand our place in it. Both the world and we reveal the One.

To whom does the One and the Only reveal Himself? What purpose do we serve for Him that is not served by the earth and the heavens and what is in them? Can He be known without us?

These questions and some answers to them may appear to be intimated in the verse on the prostration of everything in existence:

> Hast thou not seen how to God prostrate all who are in the heavens and all who are in the earth, the sun and the moon, the stars and the mountains, the trees and the beasts, and many of mankind?[3]

Everything in existence is, according to the verse, revealed in pairs, strung across the heavens and the earth and everything between. And people are divided into two groups, those who prostrate themselves before God and those who do not.

The many who do are included both individually and as a group in the universal prostration. The state of their selves is revealed and confirmed in the heavens and on the earth and the things in between. That is why they reveal what is within themselves as being in absolute harmony with what is in the heavens and on the earth, for there is no discord in the creation of the heavens and the earth, as God told us through His Messenger, Muhammad, whose name simply means "the Praised":[4]

> Thou seest not in the creation of the All-Merciful any imperfection.[5]

The lack of any imperfection in the creation of the All-Merciful serves to reveal Him as the Truth and Creator. The heavens, the earth, and everything between reveal the Truth, in their own way. We too, as Spirit, soul, and body, are a revelation of the Truth, in our own way. By coming to know the external world, we come to know ourselves, internalizing the external. By coming to know ourselves, we come to know the external world. Everything revealed to us within the horizons of the world is a reminder of the treasure within the treasure chamber of our own hearts. Both the world and we reveal our Master, who is contained by neither the heavens nor the earth, but is comprehended by the heart of His faithful servant.[6]

The world, as the Creator's self-revelation to Himself, shows itself in its perfection to us, as creatures in perfect measure and balance[7] and the epitome of everything that makes up the cosmos. The heavens, the earth, and everything between them are gathered together within the human will, when it is in harmony with the Will of the Creator and so with the will of the perfect exemplar (the Praised). And that will is that God is the Truth and that He has created with Truth, obliging us as knowing subjects to confess the Truth of creaturehood in everything and so His claim on us as the epitome of all existence and bearers of the knowledge of all the names. By this confession, we come to understand ourselves as indebted to God the Indebting. The relationship between us is one of debt. Through this debt, we shape our nature to the attributes of God, to whom the most beautiful names belong. These names include Peace, the Loving, the Knowing, and the Beautiful. Realizing or discovering these names within ourselves through the practices of being-at-peace, loving, knowing, and being and doing in the most beautiful way, we become the peaceful bringers-of-peace, the beloved lovers, the known knowers, the beautiful. First, we discover ourselves in and through our most beautiful moment, our most beautiful sublimity. When the perfect exemplar, in whom are realized both the reception and the return of praise to God, relates to God as the All-Praised[8] through the act of praise, then the self is revealed to itself as its own finest example and highest moment.

When furthest from God, we are in the deepest dark. The Praised leads us thence to the greatest closeness with God, to the furthest mosque. This is passage through all the shadows to the fullness of light; this is return to God. On this path, we cast away all that is "ours" as mere seeming, that we may receive what is real from God. Then, as we prostrate ourselves, the sun appears to us as Intellect, Light, or Spirit, as perfect giving. The moon then becomes for us the sign of perfect reception in the dark of the depth. The stars are signs of the indestructible light in each human self, the mountains of the ascent from dissolute multiplicity towards the focus and the One. The trees signify the axis of the world and the upright path whereby the sundering of the heavens and the earth is brought back to authentic Unity. The beasts are the sign that whatsoever is present on the surface of the earth is connected by common orientation towards the world axis, the upright path, and the watering hole, on whose waters the Spirit descends, that the self may discover and prove itself, confessing that there is no truth but the Truth.

Space and time in both the cosmos and in us exist as flux, with ceaseless going-up and coming-down, darkening and lightening, gathering and dispersion. Such are we in our hours and days, months and years, ages and histories, between our coming into the world and our going out of it. Each individual life is the discovery of how to relate to this flux and the things within it, so that we may discover the first and intrinsic reason of our having arrived in the world and the ultimate and fully extrinsic purpose of our leaving it. The town is the stage on which we as human beings play out the mystery of space and time, open to all sides, oriented within six directions, and included in a calendar determined by the cosmos and the self, but only as the revelation of the One, from whom everything comes and to whom everything returns.

Our central position within existence is a consequence of our willing acceptance of God's offer, which all other beings refused. God speaks of this through the Praised:

> We offered confidence to the heavens and the earth and the mountains, but they refused to carry it and were afraid of it; and man carried it. Surely he is sinful, very foolish.[9]

God's offer and our acceptance of confidence established a relationship between us as faithful and the Faithful. That God is the Faithful entails His absolute knowledge and absolute love of what He knows. Our being faithful, however, is based on little knowledge and love of what can never be fully known to us. Everything in the heavens and on the earth and between them, the entirety of body, soul, and Spirit, simply serves to remind us of the Beloved with whom we wish to be re-united, to attain fullness of knowledge, and to be with face to Face, that we may know ourselves through Him and that He know Himself through us. In this attempt to return to the original Unity, we always find ourselves between two extremes—the most sublime sweetness and the worst bitterness, the illumined height and the dark depth. The heavenly and earthly prospects are scattered with signs of the whole which we seek in ourselves, through our return:

> By the fig and the olive and the Mount Sinai and this land faithful! We indeed created man in the fairest uprightness, then We restored him the lowest of the low—save those who believe, and do righteous deeds.[10]

Even behind the bitterness of the fruit of the olive tree and the dead land, which signify our being the lowest of the low, there is light and faithfulness and an indestructible link to the full sweetness of the fig and the mountain height on which all roads meet and become one, in the original fullness or creaturehood of humanity, "in the fairest uprightness." They remain, no matter how far we stray from the One, for *nothing* is mere appearance. Wherever we are, we do not lack ample opportunity for full return to our original perfection. When we resolve to act in the nadir of all existence, when we are one of those "who believe, and do righteous deeds," then we are transported above the bitterness of the world, the harshness of the material, and we are the bearer of heaven's presence on the surface of the earth, in its matter. For, we are God's vicars on earth.[11] God created us and what we do.[12] In us and with us, the Word descends and ascends. We are the focus of all existence on earth and the confession of the Principle's constant and subtle action within the horizons of the world and in our own selves. When this connection is shown in its authentic perfection, we receive and we give in the fairest fashion, and we leave behind us the revelation of love as the connection between one who loves God and God who loves back. God spoke of this relationship with us through the Praised:

> My servant draws near to Me through nothing I love more than that which I have made obligatory for him. My servant never ceases drawing near to Me through supererogatory works until I love him. Then, when I love him, I am his hearing through which he hears, his sight through which he sees, his hand through which he grasps, and his foot through which he walks.[13]

Nowhere is our active relationship with the Creator, and so with the totality of the heavens, the earth, and everything in between, shown so clearly as in the coming-into-being and continued existence of the traditional city. We descended from Unity and revealed ourselves through externalization in the things of the world and the self. Being in the city, involving ourselves in its continued existence and transformation, it is within this constructed externalization, this anthropo-cosmic harmony, that we search for the primary center of the self. The town is in our image and we are the focus of everything to be seen in the heavens, earth, or between them. Whenever this relationship of showing and the shown is cut, we lose insight into the ways and passages from the center to the edge and back towards the Principle, revealed by existence and everything in it. Having taken our little knowledge for a sufficiency, we act, but as doers of violence and destruction in a world of perfect order. This is how we seem on our historical stage to the choir of angels in the heavens, who ask the Creator:

> What, wilt Thou set therein one who will do corruption there, and shed blood, while we proclaim Thy praise and call Thee Holy?[14]

To limited knowledge, the relationship of God and humanity as mutually faithful can only appear such as the angels saw it. In relationship with God, we appear perfect builders of the city, who focus the order of the heavens and the earth. But we are not infrequently also destroyers of that in which we are set, as those who do not prostrate themselves.

How are these two possibilities to be explained from the perspective of absolute knowledge? Who shall comprehend them, other than He who says: "Assuredly I know that you know not"?[15]

We bear the burden of confidence which we accepted when God offered it. Must we also know the justification for the consequences of our all too frequent failure to take responsibility for what we have received?

Locating Bosnia in Europe
Russia
Belarus
United Kingdom
Poland
Germany
Ukraine
Czech Republic
Slovakia
Austria
Hungary
France
Romania
Switzerland
Slovenia
Croatia
Bosnia
Serbia
Bulgaria
Italy
Montenegro
Macedonia
Turkey
Albania
Spain
Greece

Locating Bosnia for the American Reader

That each individual is equivalent in value to the human race as a whole is a sublime truth. The reason is that we all comprehend existence as a whole. We do not always actively reveal existence in its totality, however. For that we must travel a path on which we may discover and realize the innate perfection that is in every self. These paths both traverse and transcend time and place—earth, and heaven, and all that lies between.

These paths are the ways followed by each individual through life in quest of meaning; they are the ways of living well and properly, of living justly and being justified in the eyes of our God. Each such path begins on earth, with all its regions and all the peoples who have lived on it, from beginning to end. Each such path provides an orientation and a perspective that leads our vision from the earth to our common goal. It is on our path that we each find our own personal perspective, persist in it, and mature. This is why the self, however infinite, is bound up in the concrete perspective of the individual. Earthly humanity participates in all the things that belong to it—the sun and the moon, the stars and the mountains, the trees and the animals. We create the spaces within which the shapes, boundaries, languages, and histories of our societies and states are formed, the spaces within which we are ourselves formed as beings capable of following a path to the common goal, as moral and ethical beings capable of justice to ourselves and each other, and of injustice in the name of justice.

The beginning of the twentieth century was marked by one such act of injustice in the name of justice, the assassination of the Austrian Archduke Franz Ferdinand and his wife, Sophie, in the center of Sarajevo, the capital city of Bosnia. The killer and his accomplices were motivated by a desire for "national liberation." The assassination was the occasion for the First World War, a hitherto unimaginable orgy of destruction and human suffering. The same century came to a close with another act of injustice, the 44 month-long siege of the same city. Her inhabitants were starved, tortured, and killed. Similar and even worse things were taking place across the country—expulsions and destruction, mass slaughter and genocide. And again, these crimes were committed for the sake of "national liberation," which the predominant ideological worldviews cannot think except through the figure of the "other" as enemy, subject to annihilation. This would be reason enough to admit that the question of human destiny necessarily involves the question of Bosnia. The Bosnian poet Mak Dizdar put it as follows:

Once upon a time a worthy questioner asked:
Forgive me who is this what is this
Where is this
Tell me
Whence and
Whither
Is this
Bosnia

"A Text about a Country"[1]

This Bosnia is a European country, part of Europe, just as Europe is part of it. It lies in the hinterland of the Adriatic and forms the central country of the Slavic south—south of Hungary and northern Croatia, but north of the Dalmatian parts of Croatia and west of Serbia and Montenegro. It is a forested and mountainous land, with rivers that flow in all directions. For as long as it has existed, it has been suspended between the Latin south-west, the world of German culture to the north-west, and the ethnic and cultural mosaic of the Balkan peninsula, with its combination of Hellenic, Slavic, and Turkish cultures. For most of its history, it has been the meeting point of empires: first the western and eastern Roman Empires, later the Venetian Republic, the Austrian Empire, and the Ottoman Empire. During the twentieth century, it formed the heartland, both physically and symbolically, of the common state of the southern Slavs, Yugoslavia. Unfortunately, even fatally, then, as in the preceding centuries, the centers of power were elsewhere, creating tensions that tore apart, rather than commonalities that might bind and heal.

Bosnia is the heartland of Europe, at its cultural crossroads. It brings together and holds together all the diversity that Europe contains. It is the most westerly point of eastern Christianity, the most easterly of western Christianity, as well as an area of Muslim and Jewish presence. It has also been the playground of the ideologies of European modernity: Fascism, Communism, and Liberalism. At all the periods of this country's history, individuals and families from these groups and communities, with their different religions but common tongue, have coexisted as neighbors, all aiming, more or less consciously, at the same goal, human perfectibility, albeit by different paths. There have been those, too, who attained the nadir of human imperfection, but the story of Bosnia is not their story.

Bosnia's existence has always been interwoven in complex ways with its environment. An inland country, the roads that cross it have continuously brought peoples and cultural influences that have combined to shape individual and collective identities here. It is worth recalling that the Slavs who form the majority of the population of the Balkan peninsula are no more autochthonous than any other European people. They came here as a result of the great migrations that marked the twilight of the western Roman Empire. The inhabitants before them were Illyrians, tribes whose relationship to the Indo-European family of peoples and languages is unknown, but who were influenced first by Greek culture and then incorporated and assimilated by the Roman Empire. Many of the cities and towns of Bosnia, including Stolac itself, were Illyrian and Roman foundations. To what extent this Illyrian and Roman stock remains the ethnic basis of the population is unknown, perhaps unknowable. What we do know is that the arrival of the Slavs was gradual and that they became the dominant cultural and social force by a process of assimilation. When the Roman Empire split, the faultline passed through what would later be Bosnia. To the west, there was the ferment of transformation, as the incoming Goths, Visigoths, Lombards, Franks, and others created new states out of the dying empire, providing fertile soil for the Universal Church of Rome, the primary centralizing and cultural force of the Latin middle ages, a force that saw itself as transcending mere states and nations. To the east, there was retrenchment and consolidation, as Byzantium forged a new alliance between state and church that would form the basis for a new cultural synthesis, Orthodox Christianity in the service of the state. The border lands between these powers were ignored in times of weakness, fought over in times of recovery. The cities of the Dalmatian coast, still largely inhabited by the pre-Slavic populations, retained a somewhat formal allegiance to the Emperor in Constantinople, while the Slavic tribes of the hinterland went about their business as tribes are wont to do. The names of some of these tribal groups—Croats and Serbs—have come down to us by the accidents of history as the designations for states and for nations that incorporate far more than just the direct descendents of the original bearers of those names. Other areas and states have preserved the more general ethnic name of Slav (Slovenia, Slavonia, Slovakia), while yet others take their name from geographical territories and features (Bosnia, Montenegro, which means the Black Mountain, and Kosovo). This reflects the complex ways in which states and peoples are formed and the fictional basis of any attempt to trace their origins back to a single primordial and pure original people.

When states did begin to develop in the region, they were, as elsewhere in Europe, centered on dynasties and the pattern of feudal relations, with fluid borders and highly variable territories. Those to the east, Doclea and Rascia, were at first clients and later rather underpowered rivals of the

Byzantine Empire, humbled as it was by the combined incursions of the Muslim and the Frank. They formed the nucleus of the later medieval state of Serbia, whose integrative principle was the Nemanjid dynasty. Towards the end of its two hundred years of existence, Nemanjid Serbia did become a power of sorts, expanding southwards into mainland Greece. The end of the dynasty was the end of the state, however, and caused a vacuum in the central Balkan regions into which the Ottoman Turks stepped. The entire region would remain under Turkish rule until the nineteenth century, when, in the aftermath of the French Revolution, new nations based on inconsistent principles of ethnicity and territory sprang up across Turkey-in-Europe. These were states whose homogeneity was founded on the mass expulsion of the Muslim inhabitants of the region, a pattern that was to be repeated at various critical points over the following 150 years and to which modern Turkey would respond with the expulsion and worse of non-Turks. This new nationalism also adopted another feature of Ottoman administration as a founding principle, namely the identification of peoples and religious confessions—the so-called Millet system, whereby subject peoples were ruled through their religious representatives. As a result, all Orthodox southern Slavs (with the significant exception of the Bulgarians) were identified as Serbs, and Serbdom with Slavic Orthodoxy. This provided a mechanism for the identification as Serbs of Orthodox southern Slavs living outside the new kingdom, like the Montenegrins, the Slavic Macedonians, or the Orthodox inhabitants of Bosnia and Croatia. The new kingdom of Serbia soon settled, like its new neighbors, into a pattern of irredentist expansion, chipping away at the remaining Ottoman territories on the basis of the restoration of "ancient national states," as the dynastic empires of the medieval period were re-imagined. In reality, the new Serbia had as little to do with its medieval homonym, Nemanjid Serbia, as the new Kingdom of Greece with the Byzantine Empire or the Greece of Homer, Pericles, and Alexander. This was nineteenth century historicist nationalism's search for legitimation in a glorious past and invented tradition. Under its cover, Serbia had an altogether more modern model in mind, however—the goal was less to recover the southern Balkan lands of Tsar Dušan's empire than to establish Serbia as the Piedmont of the southern Slavs and, just as Piedmont had acted as the nucleus around which Italian unification had been orchestrated, so Serbia would promote the unification of the southern Slavs in a single state under Serbian leadership. Whether this would be achieved by promoting a common Yugoslav identity or by expanding the definition of Serb to include southern Slavs of different religious persuasions was a matter of debate. The distinction was, for many, tactical rather than essential. In the event it was the Yugoslav option that was brought into being by the trauma of the First World War, a war that Serbian irredentist ambitions had done so much to start.

The situation to the north and west of Bosnia was not dissimilar. A kingdom of Croatia developed in the early middle ages to the west, which, as it grew, sparred with Byzantium and Venice for hegemony over the cities of the Dalmatian coast, while to the north a Banate of Slavonia came into being that passed back and forth between the Croatian and the Hungarian crowns, until the extinction of Croatia's royal house and the personal union of the crowns of Hungary and Croatia in the twelfth century rendered the matter moot. Croatia continued to be a possession of the Hungarian kings until the Ottoman victory at the battle of Mohacs in 1526 resulted in the extinction of the Hungarian royal line and the incorporation of the greatest part of Hungary and Croatia into the Ottoman Empire. The rump of both kingdoms became possessions of the house of Austria, who would spend the next hundred and fifty years fighting a rear-guard action, followed by a *reconquista* that would eventually establish their control over the former territories of the Hungarian crown. As they did, they expelled the Muslim inhabitants, erasing all evidence of the Ottoman presence and of Muslim culture, and resettling them with Christians, often Serbs who had migrated out of the Ottoman Empire and were employed to man the militarized border areas in eastern Hungary, Croatia, and Slavonia. Recognition of the exiled Serbian Orthodox Patriarchate (established at Karlovci by the Austrians) helped promote the process whereby all the Orthodox inhabitants of the southern Slav Habsburg lands came to identify and be identified as Serbs, though many of them were not even Slavs.

Croatia would never form a united political entity under the Habsburg crown, however, even when all the territories of the medieval kingdom had been "recovered." There was a threefold division. The coastal territories had passed under the control of Venice, with the exception of the independent city-state or republic of Dubrovnik, and remained so until the defeat of Napoleon led to the incorporation of Venice, its Dalmatian territories, and Dubrovnik into the Habsburg Empire. They were, however, kept administratively separate from the inland territories of Croatia proper and Slavonia, which were themselves split between a militarized border area under martial law and Civil Croatia. Unification of all the areas of present-day Croatia would only come with the demise of the House of Austria and the creation of the Kingdom of the Serbs, Croats, and Slovenes after the First World War. It was not for want of trying, however. Croatia had maintained its formal separation from Hungary and had accepted Habsburg suzerainty by an act of its own *sabor*, or parliament. The Croatian notables continued to insist on their autonomy, their ancient "state rights," but they came under increasing pressure during the nineteenth century from a restored and resurgent Hungary, which attempted to absorb Croatia and Slavonia as provinces. This process came to a head after the Compromise of 1867, which split the empire into an Austrian half and a Hungarian half, with Croatia and Slavonia belonging to the latter, Dalmatia to the former. One response was a narrow Croat nationalism, the other an attempt to construct a common southern Slav or Yugoslav identity to act as the basis for a new tripartite settlement of the Empire into German, Hungarian, and southern Slav thirds. When the First World War made it impossible to do so within the Empire, the proponents of the Yugoslav idea looked outside and particularly at the prospect of some form of federal union with Serbia.

These convergent processes took place around a central area within which the medieval Banate of Bosnia and the associated southern principalities of Zachumlia or Hum and Terbunia developed. Hum and Terbunia would later be joined and receive the appellation of Herzegovina (the Dukedom), after their most famous ruler, the Herzeg Stjepan (Duke Stephen). Bosnia arrived on the scene later than the kingdoms of Croatia and Rascia, but its growth from a central area around the river Bosnia was steady and it came to occupy the entire territory of modern-day Bosnia and Herzegovina, as well as large parts of the Dalmatian coast. For most of medieval Bosnia's existence, its ruler, the Ban or King, was formally a vassal of the king of Hungary. Relations between the notables and royal family of Bosnia, the Kotromanićs, with the royal families and major feudal magnates to both east and west were close and complex. At the height of its expansion, under Tvrtko I, who was closely related to both the Arpad line of Hungary and the Nemanjić line of Serbia, the banate became a kingdom. Tvrtko also claimed the crown of Serbia by inheritance and declared himself King of both Bosnia and Serbia, amongst other possessions. After his death in 1391, a further nine kings of Bosnia followed, with a turbulent relationship with their Hungarian cousins and overlords and under increasing pressure from the Ottomans in the east. Bosnia was conquered by the Ottomans in 1463, Herzegovina in 1482, as part of the consolidation of Ottoman power in Europe after the fall of Constantinople and the ending of the dying Byzantine Empire in 1453. Unlike Serbia and Croatia, Bosnia's territorial integrity and political continuity was in large measure preserved under Ottoman rule, as it became a *sanjak* and latter a *vilayet* (different forms of province), to which *pasha*s were appointed as governors.

The Ottomans founded most of what are now the main towns of Bosnia, including Sarajevo and Mostar, and built a network of roads and bridges which are still in use, the most famous being the Old Bridge at Mostar and Mehmed Pasha Sokolović's bridge over the river Drina at Višegrad. They also established mosques and endowments throughout the country and promoted acceptance of the Muslim creed amongst the Slavic population. As in the rest of the Ottoman world, non-Muslims were second-class citizens, but they were tolerated and accorded freedom of religion and conscience. This was the reason why emigration to Ottoman territories was so attractive to the Jews of Europe, particularly after the expulsion of Jews and Moriscos from Spain by their Most Catholic Majesties in 1492. Many of these Sephardic Jews from Iberia came to Sarajevo and the other new cities of Ottoman Bosnia, establishing a major Jewish presence in the country that would last until the Second World War.

The Ottoman conquest of Slavonia and Hungary meant that Bosnia was an internal province of the Empire until the eighteenth century, with the exception of the southern borders it shared with the Venetian possessions and Dubrovnik on the Adriatic coast. The spread of the Muslim faith in Bosnia, as well as in other parts of the Balkans, meant that many of the Slavic inhabitants could be integrated into the ruling class on the basis of conversion. Many were also "recruited" to imperial service through the institution of the *devshirme*, a practice whereby Christian boys were taken from their families and brought up as Muslims and servants of the Sultan. The leading administrators of the Ottoman Empire were often chosen from this group, as were the dreaded Janissary corps. They did not necessarily lose their connections with their families, however, and were often among the greatest benefactors of their original communities, as founders of public buildings and works and endowers of mosques and even of churches.

The idea that Ottoman rule was a period of despotic misrule is therefore mistaken. For Bosnia, it provided a four-hundred year period of relative peace, broken by the occasional incursion, as when Prince Eugene of Savoy, following up on his success at Zenta, burned Sarajevo in 1697, or the occasional rebellion, like that of the Dragon of Bosnia, a Muslim magnate, in 1831, and the Christian-led Herzegovinian revolt in 1875, which provided the excuse for the occupation of Bosnia and Herzegovina by Austria-Hungary in 1878. During the first two hundred and fifty years of this period, Bosnia benefited from administration that was as good as any in the Europe of the day and Christian *raya* (subjects) were no worse off than serfs in the other Slavic lands of eastern Europe. As the Ottoman Empire stagnated, falling further and further behind the powers of Europe, whose economic and social development was spurred on by the Enlightenment, so the quality of Ottoman administration in Bosnia declined by comparison.

The Habsburg roll-back of the Ottoman presence in Hungary and Croatia in the late seventeenth and early eighteenth centuries and the creation of new nations in the eastern and southern Balkans during the early nineteenth century left Bosnia an Ottoman outpost connected by an ever thinner strip of land with the main area of the Empire. Bosnia's neighbors, the new kingdom of Serbia and Austria-Hungary, increasingly eyed it as a "natural" acquisition. Great power politics meant that it would be ailing Austria-Hungary that would occupy and later annex the country, rather than Serbia. Austria-Hungary would rule Bosnia as a separate province until the First World War, which put an end to the Empire itself and allowed Serbian ambitions to be fulfilled, as Bosnia and Herzegovina became the central area of the new Kingdom of the Serbs, Croats, and Slovenes. While many of the Muslim inhabitants of Bosnia did emigrate to Turkey proper during the 40 years of Habsburg rule, many remained and Bosnia did not undergo, at that time, the ethnic cleansing or forced population exchanges that characterized all the other new nations of the Balkans well into the 1920s.

Bosnia was left, alongside Albania, as the only Balkan country with a significant Muslim population who could not be ignored or dismissed as a mere minority. There was, however, a general denigration of Bosnia's Muslim heritage and history as alien and backward. Progress became synonymous with eradication of Muslim culture, a view many Bosnians of Muslim background also accepted, their faces turned towards the future. The impressive modernization project embarked upon by Austria, which included electrification and railways and major building programs, entailed the destruction of much of what the previous society had created, but it was under the Kingdom of the Serbs, Croats, and Slovenes that Bosnia's integrity was violated to the core, with the denial of Bosnian identity, culminating with the division of its territory between the Croatian and the Serbian halves of the kingdom under the Cvetković-Maček Agreement and its later absorption into the fascist or Ustaša Independent State of Croatia, during World War Two.

Resistance to the fascists came primarily from two groups: the Serbian Četniks and the Communist partisans. The former group was made up of loyalists, dedicated to the Serbian royal family, but increasingly committed to a Greater Serbian ideology, which was as intent on the assimilation or dismantling of Bosnia into Serb and Croat halves as were the Croat Ustaša, and by means just as brutal. The partisans were committed not just to resisting fascism, but also to an internationalist perspective that saw a future for Yugoslavia as a federation of equal, constituent peoples. Their struggle against the German occupier was concentrated on the territory of Bosnia and Herzegovina and it was in Bosnia that the Anti-Fascist Council of the People's Liberation of Yugoslavia was convened as a provisional government of post-war Yugoslavia, one of whose constituent republics would be Bosnia and Herzegovina, with the same borders as it had had throughout the Ottoman and Austrian periods, the same borders it now has. The nationality of Bosnian was not recognized, however, and it was only in 1971 that a new official category was created for those who were reluctant to identify as Serb, Croat, or Yugoslav. This status was Muslim, the only religious category in an otherwise ethnic system.

The twentieth century thus saw the systematic official denigration and denial of Bosnian identity to favor the spread of identification with Serbia and Croatia amongst Bosnia's Catholic and Orthodox populations, while denying the Muslim population of Bosnia any ethnic identity at all. In fact, as Muslims they were often characterized as alien, a remnant of foreign occupation, at best blood traitors who had abandoned their "native" culture. Along with this went the continued destruction by neglect and redevelopment of the remaining Muslim heritage of the country, entailing the rejection of the combined product of more than 450 years of the country's history as foreign and worthless. This process culminated in the wars of Yugoslav succession. Without the denial of Bosnia, the peaceful dissolution of the federation into its constituent republics might have been possible, each republic being in nature a multi-ethnic community to a greater or lesser degree. The revival of the irredentist programs of the Serbian nationalists, who were the main movers behind the dissolution, with its paler Croatian echo, entailed, however, the denial of Bosnia as an artificial construct, a state without a corresponding nation. In this reading, Bosnia was a prison for members of the "authentic" nations of Serbs and Croats and an obstacle to the establishment of their national states within their "natural borders." The establishment of a Greater Serbia meant absorbing large parts of Bosnia, just as the establishment of one state for all Croats did. Serbia might claim some areas of Croatia as well, but a settlement and exchange of territories could be negotiated between the two. No such settlement was possible or necessary with Bosnia. The leaders of Croatia and Serbia, Franjo Tuđman and Slobodan Milošević, were explicit about this. Their dreams threw into relief the problem of the Muslim population of Bosnia and Herzegovina, for whom there was no place left in the scheme. They were surplus to requirements and could expect at best the future of a tolerated minority, at worst the fate of a minority for whom no tolerance is shown. It was this that made war over Bosnia inevitable and it was this that made the defense of Bosnia and Herzegovina as an integral sovereign territory and as a cultural ideal of coexistence so important.

The remainder of the story is no doubt familiar to the reader. The war that broke out in Croatia in 1991 provided cover for the beginning of militia activity and ethnic cleansing in Bosnia, processes that were conducted by an organized radical minority and the victims of which were predominantly Bosnians who happened to be Muslims. The vast majority of the population was surprised by events and felt caught up by them. Some followed the siren songs of nationalist solidarity and sought refuge in the herd. Many, however, from all the religious confessions and ethnic groups, stood by their Republic and the Bosnian ideal. In the end, and despite terrible hardships, they prevailed. The settlement agreed at Dayton, with US mediation, was far from perfect and far from just. It has left the country with a broke-back constitution, practically no central or state-level government, and allowed the gains of ethnic cleansing to be preserved and the injustices it imposed to be perpetuated. It has, however, left the country; rebuilding and the restoration of community is taking place. It is no exaggeration to say that behind all the destruction and the tragedy suffered by this country there survives within its still-beating heart a sublime model for Europe and the world—the gathering of what is dispersed and the lighting of a lamp that reveals the diversity of the world against the monotony of the dark.

To take just the last ten centuries of Bosnia's existence in history, we find traces of the use of Greek, and Latin, and Glagolitic, and Cyrillic, and Hebrew, and Arabic scripts. The actors of these ten centuries of history in this country inherited elements of civilization that link them back to the most ancient times, but it was from the tenth century on that a culture developed on the territory of Bosnia that differed from those around it, while nonetheless sharing much with them.

The Slavs were and are no more "naturally" Christian than they are "naturally" Muslim. Christianity came to them as a revelation of a path. In fact, it came as several paths, thanks to the divisions to which Christianity has always been prone, like any other great faith. These Christianities were fully absorbed by the Slavonic languages, providing the quest for human perfection within Bosnia with symbolic and ritual form, myths, and systems of initiation. As a result, against the background of the various political arrangements and exposure to the imperial aspirations discussed above, a conviction took root in the country and survived through the centuries that there are different paths to the one God, whom we know, if we know ourselves. From the Bosnian perspective, these paths may be Jewish, Christian, or Muslim, each with its own variegated history, replete with similarities to and differences from each of the others, and each an advocate of the inalienable right to dignity in difference.

The reception in the Balkans of the joyful news of the Anointed One [the Christ], who announced the revelation of the heavenly kingdom within the human self, came to be inextricably linked to the question of allegiance to the Churches of Rome or Byzantium, and so to the secular authority connected with each church. In Bosnia and Dalmatia, Rome and Byzantium met, mingled, and fought. It was in the split thus opened up that a Bosnian Christianity, Bosnian faith, and Bosnian church came into being that differed from both these dominant forms. Bosnian Christianity took shape as a unique spiritual current, in opposition to these external systems. Bosnian Christians (who referred to themselves as *krstjani*) stressed, like all other Christians, that they were the heirs to the true apostolic faith, in which they were truly reborn in the Holy Spirit, descending from above. Their fellow Christians of Roman Catholic and Orthodox persuasion saw in them heretics and apostates, in their practices and beliefs the products of diabolical inspiration. It was reported that they belonged to the Manichaean heresy, as part of the band linking the Bulgarian Bogomils to the Cathars of Provence, and they were treated accordingly. For more than 300 years, the Bosnian Church and its freethinking members were subject to inquisition, abusive practices, and extreme pressure to "return to the fold." By the fifteenth century, the decline of Byzantium, the pressure of the Ottoman advance, and the intransigence of the Catholic West, who admitted no compromise with the Orthodox, never mind alleged Manichees, left the kings and notables of Bosnia with little choice. They bowed to Rome, and the internal persecution, however half-hearted, of the home-grown Bosnian Church began.

It was this alienation due to persecution by their fellow Christians and their own rulers and erstwhile co-religionists that created the fertile ground for the seed of another form of faith to grow, and that allowed the Bosnians of the fifteenth century to recognize in the Muslim way a path they too might follow. As early as the seventh century there had been, on all the southern and on large parts of the eastern and western shores of the Mediterranean sea, a dramatic transformation of the various Christian forms of witness of the Anointed and the Virgin, with a turn towards the revelation of the Word by the Seal of the Prophets [the revelation of the Quran by Muhammad]. According to this revelation, "the Praised," a title which simply serves to translate the meaning of the Arabic name Muhammad, came as the Seal of prophecy, representing the maternal principle of prophecy, a mercy to the worlds, and the most beautiful example of and for human existence. His coming was expected by all times. All the prophets had announced and borne witness to him as the first thing of all creation, the keystone of the world, as mentioned in all the revealed books. According to the testimony of this revelation's followers, the Praised was closest of all to the Anointed, the Christ, the son of the Virgin. This is why they bore mutual witness: the Anointed announced the

Praised, while the Praised bore witness of the Anointed.

Abiding with their neighbors and relatives who accepted the joyful news of the Anointed and continued to bear witness to it in the same way as before, the Bosnian *krstjani*, like many of their neighbors who belonged to those foreign churches, accepted the news of the apostolate of the Praised as the rediscovery of that which they already were and which they already contained within themselves, in their sacred books, and in their sacred tradition as a whole. It was through their love for the Anointed, the son of the Virgin, that the Praised was revealed to them. Thus, in what they had as love for God, a way opened up to follow the Praised as the most precious and most sublime exemplar of humanity. They found that as Christians they had always already been Muslims.

Thus it is that neither the Christians nor the Muslims in Bosnia come from somewhere else. They are simply each on their own path towards the possibility of perfection. When the truth of this presence in the self, which has every right to take a different path towards a common goal of perfection, is distorted, then the other and the different are figured as strangers and intruders. National liberation always presents such a construction.

The Bosnian Muslim community continued to take shape in the period after the fifteenth century, as political relations altered after the fall of the kingdom in which the Bosnian *krstjani* had for some decades already been denied the right to follow their own course. Bosnia remained a country with a single language, but became a protected area in which different paths towards God and different interpretations of the Anointed coexisted. The churches and monasteries and synagogues and mosques are a constant reminder of this. This orientation of ordinary Bosnians towards our sublime potential as human beings acts as the measure of our very humanity: our attitude to the other and the different is the measure of our own ethical nature. Being on the path towards the discovery of this perfection places us under an obligation of unconditionally doing what is good and beautiful, and rejecting what is evil and ugly.

Like every other form of orientation towards the perfection we enjoyed in paradise, the Bosnian form takes place in the world of reality, amongst people who are on the path, which is to say both those who are focused on the goal and those who are wandering, both good and evil people, the repentant and sinners. There is nothing good or beautiful that is not measured against what is evil and ugly. Evidence of this sacred orientation of humanity is to be seen across the Bosnian landscape—in the synagogues, churches, and mosques, as well as the killing fields, the graveyards, and the ruins. At different times, the Bosnian paradigm of self-realization in perfection on the basis of a multiplicity of paths has been lived with varying degrees of commitment, clarity, and success. At times, it has appeared to suffer complete defeat, only to resurface in all its strength, bearing witness that nothing is capable of truly destroying the truth, which is the expression of our right to survive and be happy.

Today, Bosnia is a weak, enfeebled, and fragile state. Ranked against it and the lofty ideal it embodies are individuals and groups and organizations and states whose activities are informed by the modern ideologies of nation and national state. No matter how numerous the external enemies of Bosnia, however, the ideal is invulnerable, so long as the people of this country remain conscious of it as their sacred testament. From the point of view of this ideal's enemies, Bosnian unity was not possible. This is because it contained religious difference. And yet, this religious difference is the condition of its continued existence.

This is why the threat to Bosnia as a country that survived the incursions of the Inquisition, the Crusades, imperial occupation, and the ambitions of its closest neighbors, with its unity intact, is in fact a threat to the world. Whenever they fail to find reasons for goodwill towards the other and the different, the people of the different religions betray their witness that the God of all people is one and that nothing can justify betrayal of our responsibility towards Him. The persecution of Bosnians because of their beliefs, the seizure and destruction of their property, the burning of books, and their prosecution before courts and by militias may be primarily a matter for this country and its people, but it affects all others.

If Bosnia is no longer possible as unity in difference, then what is the outlook for the world, which is constituted out of difference?

In the Bosnian ideal taken as a whole, however helpless, feeble, small, and fragile it may appear, we find the promise made to each individual without which no sense or meaning can be attributed to our having come into the world. The poet Mak Dizdar provides his answer to the question of Bosnia, pointing to that invincible ideal:

> The questioned swiftly replied in this wise:
> Forgive me there is a country called Bosnia
> A footsore a frosty a
> Fasting a drossy a
> Country for sure
> Forgive me
> That's cussed
> After
> Sleep
>
> "A Text about a Country"[2]

Bosnian towns and villages came into being out of the striving for unity in difference. The most beautiful forms they contain, their synagogues, churches, and mosques, public buildings and private houses, streets and squares, and the high points and holy meadows that serve their people as places for individual and collective prayer are treasure houses of the riches left by our highest aspirations, the victory of good over evil, of beauty over ugliness. But, hundreds of these towns and thousands of villages across Bosnia have been destroyed in a process that has lasted more than one hundred years. They were turned into spaces where the other and the different were made to choose—convert, leave, or die. Such fatal decisions were made on the grounds that, so long as they are powerless, the other and the different are wrong. These fatal decisions have their roots in ignorance. Who knows not the other, cannot know him- or herself. Who knows not the self, acts out of violence and does evil.

Stolac was one such Bosnian town, and it is the ideal that town embodied and the story of its degradation, which is told in this book. It is a small town in a valley, between stony hills, on the shores of a river flowing west. It is about 30 km from the sea. It contains and is surrounded by traces of culture going back to the Paleolithic. It is possible to trace their course from the Paleolithic drawing of a horse in a cave not far from Stolac down to the present, through the forts of the Illyrian tribes, with their imposing buildings and works of art, the Roman fortifications and villas, with their elaborate mosaics, the medieval castles and stone tombs, with their links to the Bosnian kingdom and its autocephalous, but esoteric church, the taking root and flowering of the Muslim tradition in both existing and new layers, and the modern restructuring of society along rationalist and nationalist lines. The sacred center of Stolac brought together this luxuriant diversity, manifesting it, and guaranteeing it.

All the most important elements of pluralism in Stolac, as a typical Bosnian town, which were liable to interpretation as Muslim, were destroyed in 1993. The entire Muslim population was expelled from the city in brutal fashion. Many were killed, while many others succumbed to the hardships of exile. The mosques were destroyed, as were houses with their furnishings, books, and works of art, a treasure built up over centuries. As soon as they could, a large number of those who had been expelled returned to the town, to their burnt-out ruins, and the graves of their ancestors, to search for what had been lost and to rebuild what had been destroyed. Today, it is possible once again to see in the town the indomitability of the belief that there is no redemption for humanity except on the basis of goodness and beauty, and that to search for and bear witness of them is an unconditional good. It is possible to see this once again, in spite of the resistance and the threats of ignorance and the fears it inspires.

For Further Reading

Ivo Banac, *The National Question in Yugoslavia: Origins, History, Politics.*
Ivo Goldstein, *Croatia: A History.*
Marko Attila Hoare, *The History of Bosnia: From the Middle Ages to the Present Day.*
Tim Judah, *The Serbs: History, Myth and the Destruction of Yugoslavia.*
Noel Malcolm, *Bosnia: A Short History.*
Mark Mazower, *The Balkans: A Short History.*
Stevan Pavlowitch, *Serbia: The History of an Idea.*
L. S. Stavrianos, *The Balkans since 1453.*
Marcus Tanner, *Croatia: A Nation Forged in War.*

1. *Philosophia Perennis*

Compared to the world as a whole, human beings appear infinitely petty. This relationship can be reversed: the world as a whole can be presented from the human point of view as lacking consciousness, as material for human shaping and, consequently, far more petty in principle than we are. From either of these perspectives, humanity and the world are two distinct things. In truth, however, the world cannot exist without us, nor we without the world. Everything in the world is also in us, always and forever.

For us to become wise—which is our constant wish—we need the whole world. Human wisdom lies in our relationship to the world and to our selves. Wisdom is given to the world as a whole as well as to us. God is Wise and His wisdom is apparent in every created thing. Something of Divine wisdom passes into every thing in creation, while wisdom is how we, its recipients and passers-on, relate to God the Wise, who gives reality to everything.

For us to be properly wise, we must deny all wisdom except God's, confessing that only the Wise is wise. This confession leads us to union with the Wise as our Beloved. None of us lacks this desire in our being. Love of the Wise is philosophy. And the philosophy that finds and tests every thesis against the Eternal is eternal—the *philosophia perennis.*[1] No change in us or the world, in its ceaseless flux, excludes the presence or attraction of this wisdom.

The world as a whole is the revelation of the Wise. He apportions Himself from above, through the multiple levels of being. We too are so apportioned. The levels of the world are reflected within us and both we and the world are organized from lowest to highest. When we turn towards the world, we have two options. We can accept the world as orderly, good, and beautiful and desire to explore it as such, revealing both it and ourselves as the word of God. Or we can find it disorderly, wild, and ugly and desire to bend it to ourselves, remaking it after our own images.

Applying the first attitude to the hills around Stolac and the area between them, all is comprehended as order, goodness, and beauty that reveal the All-Merciful. Everything done in the place discloses and confirms the infinite variety of the perfect whole. But this requires a comprehensive metaphysical, cosmological, anthropological, and psychological understanding.[2] Being guided or living by such an understanding of the world means constantly reconciling two wills, ours and God's. It is not for us to impose our will on God, however. We face a constant struggle to subordinate our will and reconcile it with God's and to bear witness in whatever we do that everything comes from God and everything returns to Him, to strive to be poor in spirit, that as such we may receive everything from God the All-Sufficient and, above all, be joined with Him in being-at-peace, which means both being peaceful and a bringer of peace.

Bosnian unity-in-plurality is fully disclosed in these towns and cities.[3] Each town is a hub with a number of smaller and larger settlements connected to it. These networks between towns and their hinterlands weave the complex web of the Bosnian whole. Nearly all Bosnian towns or cities have developed on or near rivers. Bosnian rivers mostly flow through valleys surrounded by hills, while the towns tend to spread out along the river banks and up the slopes of the hills. As a result, crossing over, going up, coming down, flowing downstream from the source and towards the estuary are all important symbolic vectors of urban space, determining how the town and life in it are felt and understood.

Earthly locations are bounded by the lines of the horizon and the points where the hilltops touch the sky. Seen in this way, town and sky touch. This simultaneous distinction and connection between earth and heaven has its analogy in the distinctions that bind body to Spirit in us. These links between heaven and earth and what lies between them, on the one hand, and body and Spirit and what lies between them, on the other, are a very important aspect of the development of Bosnian towns as centers of life. Nothing in this integrated habitat, from the stitch on a scarf to the edge of the leaf atop the minaret, is without meaning for the teaching of our journey from and back to perfection.

Everything in the world or in us functions as a sign in the ongoing discourse of our return to perfection. This discourse comprehends the revelation sent down by God to us as His Word in human speech. This revelation is the basis of all human knowledge. Only through it can we and the world open up to higher levels, above and beyond the limits of the phenomenal. We, the world, and the revelation reveal the One in the many. In Bosnian tradition, the town and its dwellings are open to the sky, reflecting our endeavor to be open to the Spirit and to return to our moment of perfection.

Whatever our condition, it reflects the condition of our knowledge of the world and ourselves. Whenever we assume the final sufficiency of the world and the body, we lose our ability to understand, keep to, or affirm the path on which we face the Most Beautiful at all times and in all our works. We lose the skills of inheriting and passing-on in ways informed by reason and a purpose above and beyond mere finitude. Inheriting and passing on mean finding full reasons and fullness of purpose in everything. When we no longer know how to inherit and pass on the gifts of creation, the horizons of our world and our own selves shrink and the idea of salvation in perfection wanes.

Old Bosnian towns and their traditional elements have become practically incomprehensible to the modern worldview. The process of reshaping and tearing out their guts has lasted for more than a century. The cardinal points of the world meet in the human self, regardless of how enlightened or how obscured it may be. The equivalent in the traditional Bosnian town is the *čaršija*, the central public area, where markets were held, which was equivalent in many ways to the Roman forum. It was the sacred, as well as the commercial and social center of the town and normally contained the main town mosque and public buildings whose functions were rooted in the sacred, as the legitimating force connecting life as lived to the cosmic order and orienting all human activity towards the task of self-realization through return to the One. The word refers to the four sides of the world, its cardinal directions. The condition of the town's *čaršija* mirrors our condition as human beings.

There can be no transition from chaos and destruction to order and renewal without first investigating the causes and consequences of the changes that blight our towns. Human self-realization is possible only on the basis of a total teaching that transcends mere human achievement. This teaching follows its own path, on which everything in the world or the self has meaning. We find ourselves on that road, when we recall perfection as the reason and purpose of our existence. Doctrine, the way, and virtue evoke the irreducible potential in each of us. Virtue has meaning, so long as it is practiced on the path to perfection. This path leads to perfection, so long as the traveler recognizes it as the goal, as the source of knowledge, and as the prospect of finding a way out of the disorder in which we are confounded.

Today, only parts of most Bosnian towns have been preserved, but even they bear witness to how the long process of their development was grounded in traditional teaching, within the framework of the perennial love for wisdom. The inheritors of these remnants rarely know anything of this teaching or the way and the virtue which shaped their towns. Given that the modern world-image has an entirely different train from that of traditional teaching, the remnants of these former urban wholes generally meet with incomprehension from their contemporary heirs.

Stolac is the urban center of one of these Bosnian networks of minor settlements. It grew in a valley with three legs, on the banks of a river and the slopes of the surrounding hills. Its center is the *čaršija*, which comprises a number of architectural elements, including the mosque, the *mekteb* or school, the *musafirhana* or guesthouse, the *kiraethana* or reading room, the *sahat-kula* or clock tower, a number of shops, the weighing place or *tepa*, which was also used for other public purposes, and a number of *harems* or burial areas.[4] The Stolac *čaršija* was one of the best preserved right up until the recent war against Bosnia. Study of its parts and the meanings associated with them in holistic sacred teaching may contribute to an understanding of the general context within which Bosnian towns developed, as well as to determining those aspects of the modern worldview that reinforce our incomprehension and enmity towards this heritage.

Most towns of the Ancient World developed within the context of a sacred teaching and holy art. For all their unique features, urban units contained sacred art that reflected sacred teaching. The *čaršija* both takes and gives, bringing people and their actions together and sending them out into the world. There is a ceaseless coming and going of people in the places and times of our everyday lives, as well as beyond them: we cannot offer any answers regarding the reason and purpose of human life if we ignore or deny the boundaries beyond which it comes and goes. In this complex flux of life, the arts and skills of giving and receiving are always present.

The *čaršija* is unimaginable without traditional art and crafts.[5] Whatever passes through the shops or is prepared in them for sale is drawn from existence as a whole. These flows are framed by traditional social order and traditional architecture.[6] We have nothing that has not been given to us; even what we do can be understood only on the basis of its absolute dependence on what has been given and done before it. For us being in the *čaršija* means divining the spiritual aspect of each of its elements. First, we discover the meanings of the occupations, whose symbolism preserves traditional teaching. Then, and more importantly, these occupations can help us, on the basis of their meanings, in our own spiritual development and reception of Divine mercy.

Paths cross in the *čaršija*, dividing space into four. These paths cross at an invisible point, which might be any place. When one says that two paths cross in the *čaršija* or that the four cardinal points meet, it means that we are in the world and that the world confronts us, both as center and periphery. We and the world are two sides of one and the same revelation of the Creator.

Each one of us contains all of humanity. But all of humanity is what each individual is. And more. As both center and goal, the human being is not finite: what neither the heavens nor the earth may comprehend, the human heart can.[7] This is why the *čaršija* is another name for our individual capacity for fullness of experience. We offer ourselves to each other as both listeners and recipients. By listening and receiving, we take on an obligation or debt to everyone else with regard to their speaking and giving. This open interplay of individuals requires a world of openness.

Human beings and the world bring together a mutable order of signs. The key question is therefore: How can these signs in the world and in us be taught or learned as a discourse on the earth and the heavens and what lies between, as well as of the body and the Spirit and what lies between? Moreover, how can that teaching help us regain our most beautiful (up)rightness and how may it be realized in relation to the Most Beautiful?

Answering these questions involves three inextricable aspects. First, everything that can be experienced within the world reveals Unity. Second, both we and the world require a perfect Principle as beginning and end. Third, both we and the world return to that Principle. Both we and the world have received and reveal God through His most beautiful names. Possessor of the most beautiful names, God is Most Beautiful. As the recipients of these names, we are expected to do everything in the most beautiful manner, making real the name of the Most Beautiful. The concentration of our capacity to give and receive within the *čaršija* can only reveal the beauty of our actions so long as our skills and knowledge are connected to the confession of Unity and recollection of the One.

Everything that comes together in the *čaršija* reflects the principle, *ars sine scientia nihil.*[8] This is true for both *scientia sacra* and *ars sacra.*[9] It is on the basis of these two aspects that everything in the *čaršija* complex is revealed. When skills, doctrine, attitudes, and behavior lose their connection to the Highest Principle and those who share in the life of the *čaršija* become oblivious to the reasons or purpose of humanity, then the destruction and unenlightened alteration of the inherited content of human history begin. The spread of corruption over the earth and the oceans is merely a reflection of the corruption within our own selves, inseparable from the various forms of individual and collective disease. Such disease is inevitable whenever the mosque is separated from the *čaršija* or the *čaršija* from the mosque. For the mosque is the opening up and focus of our transition towards the highest condition of the self, through three degrees—will, love, and knowledge, which may also be termed purification, enlightenment, and union.

Both sacred art and sacred science have their earthly forms, but the beauty and the significance they radiate have been sent down from higher levels of existence. Their role is to raise those of us who live in and by them up towards our highest possibilities.

The *čaršija*, the place in which the four cardinal points of the world are revealed, is a developed social or urban form. Everything in that development reveals the center, which is the Principle as source and refuge of everything. This omnipresent centrality determines the *čaršija* as *ars sacra*. Nothing can deny the presence of the center, nor can anything limit it.

2. The Garden

The *čaršija* lies at the bottom of a valley. Its position emphasizes a pair—depth and height. On entering the *čaršija* and facing the *mihrab* of the mosque, one sees Mount Vrsnik, whose name means the peak. It is the height, a conical hilltop in the air which points to the House in the valley of Becca or Mecca,[1] the center around which the worshipping devout are spread out in infinite circles "described" upon the surface of the earth. This pair, the valley and the mount, is bound by humility in sublimity and sublimity in humility. Humility corresponds to the way in which the manifold comes together in the individual, as it were in a valley or receptacle. The mount corresponds to generosity or the self that shares equally on all sides.

The center of the valley splits in three—left, right, and straight towards the peak. This split gives the *čaršija* its shape.

The peak, a near perfect cone, closes the valley to the south. Down in the valley, facing the peak, one's back is to Ošanići, with Komanje hill to one's left and Križevac to one's right. Had we come down from the Ošanići side, with its many sunny gardens, we would have passed over water, heading towards the *mihrab*. There is the *čaršija*, like a labyrinth to be traversed, with the peak on the other side of the valley.[2] At the highest point on the mount, there is a mosque.[3] Turning to face the *mihrab* entails ascent towards the coming-together-into-unity of everything scattered through existence and seeing it as the revelation of the One and the Only, who is within, and before, and behind all multiplicity.

How is this pair of depth and height related to "the debt of truth,"[4] "the debt of honesty,"[5] or "the debt of (up)rightness"[6]? These three ideas are present in different ways in the revelations of the Torah, the Gospels, and the Quran. Our relationship as debtors of the God who indebts is informed by truth, honesty, and (up)rightness of being as modes of self-realization. The term "debt" signifies our relationship with God the Giver. God reveals himself through the creation of the infinite multitude of beings on earth, in the heavens, and between, each a declaration of one of the names of God.

We are the image of God and all His names gather in us. Nothing is real for us that we have not received from God. Consequently, we only become real ourselves when we recognize our debt towards God. Whatsoever exists within us or the horizons of the world is a sign of God. Recognition of our debt towards God and His claims on us entails recognizing our debt towards the things of the world and their claims upon us. This further entails seeing the truth of creation in everything—facing all things great and small in or outside of us with honesty and desiring to do so while on our path back towards our original (up)rightness of being:

> It is He who has sent His Messenger with the guidance and the debt of truth, that He may uplift it above every debt. God suffices as a witness.[7]
>
> We have sent down to thee the book with the truth; so worship God, making thy debt His sincerely. Belongs not the debt of sincerity to God?[8]
>
> That which you serve, apart from Him, is nothing but names yourselves have named, you and your fathers; God has sent down no authority touching them. Judgment belongs only to God; He has commanded that you shall not serve any but Him. That is the debt of uprightness; but most men know not.[9]

If we are to answer the question of how height and depth are related to the debts of truth, honesty, and (up)right being, we must look at the meaning of two key ideas of the Recitation. These two ideas are major signs in the external world. But no major signs in the external world are without bearing upon our inner world. The first is the Inviolate Mosque in the valley of tears,[10] the second the Further Mosque on Mount Zion. These two mosques, the one on the mount and the other in the valley, face each other on an approximately north-south axis. The ancient Semitic word *masjid*, which lies behind the English mosque and the Bosnian *mesdžid*, has various translations in the languages of the world. Its complex meaning may be teased out using the designation "the place of annihilation or self-abnegation."[11]

The Messenger says that the Inviolate Place of Annihilation was the first to be raised, the Further Place of Annihilation the second. In the words of Abu Dharr,

> I said: "O God's apostle! Which mosque was first built on the surface of the earth?"
> He said: "The Inviolate Mosque."
> I said: "Which was built next?"
> He replied: "The Further Mosque."
> I said: "What was the period of construction between the two?"
> He said: "Forty years."

> He added: "Whenever the prayer time becomes due, perform the prayer there, for the best thing is to do so."[12]

These two mosques were our first abodes in our new station on earth. They signify the temporary nature of our stay here and our return to our original condition. That original condition was the garden, everything in which was given to us by God: the truth of everything clearly seen, absolute honesty between us, and most beautiful (up)rightness of being. Images of all the attributes of God were brought together within us. We were fully given over to the contemplation of God as the All-Praised, and it was through praise that we related to Him—for we, who had received everything from God, were praised as God was All-Praised, to whom all things belong and who gives to whom He will.

The second mosque, the one on the mount, corresponds to our original location in paradise, where we were allowed everything except one tree. Whatsoever we wanted was God's will, just as it was His will that one tree be inviolate. Being in paradise made everything, the world and us, a revelation of the Creator. Nothing could be added or taken away. Nothing depended on human action: all was pure and perfect. And it was kept so by the sanctity and inviolate nature of that one tree as its center. The authentic model of creation was also realized in and through us, namely the Messenger, whose name means "the Praised," the first of the people of peace, the most beautiful example, the lamp which shines as a mercy unto the worlds. As denizens of paradise, we were perfect images of the Praised, who is our reason and goal.

When we broke God's injunction not to will differently than His will and stretched our hands towards the inviolate tree, all became inverted: We descended from the beauties of the sublime to the lowest depth, as God says:

> We indeed created Man in the most beautiful uprightness, then we restored him the lowest of the low—save those who believe, and do righteous deeds; they shall have a wage unfailing.[13]

There in the depths, the nadir of existence, in the valley of tears, we discovered the difference between our original and our new condition and all our desire was to return to find what we had lost. Repentance was our first step in turning from the depth to the height. For this, however, we had to understand the depth to which we had arrived. Our return is the discovery in ourselves of the Praised as our guide on the journey back, our discovery of the best model in mercy and in the light of the shining lamp.

The Praised is a crucial promise to us who have fallen. The words which God gave us, as we turned to Him in our fall, crying out to Him our confession of sin, having violated that which God had made inviolate, themselves bear witness to the Praised. At our lowest point, we require him as guide. Through him we may come to understand our level and the way out of it. Out of this coming-to-understand, God's call rings out through the Praised:

> We have seen thee turning thy face about in the heaven; now We will surely turn thee to a direction that shall satisfy thee. Turn thy face towards the Inviolate Mosque; and wherever you are, turn your faces towards it. Those who have been given the Book know it is the truth from their Lord.[14]

Turning to face the Inviolate Mosque is intimately entwined with confessing our insult against that which was inviolate and redeeming that insult through our understanding that we may regain our lost condition through repentance and observance of the inviolate and sacred nature of our ritual and the signs or symbols associated with it.

The house at the bottom of the valley is a symbol of building, of culture, and of civilization. No perfect cube is to be found on earth or in the heavens, or anywhere between them. The house therefore symbolizes the work of our hands and so the culture of the town which we brought into being after the fall. But the culture of the town aims at the garden—that is its original burden. In the beginning, everything, whether in ourselves or the world around us, bore witness to the Unity of the Creator. Alone inviolate and inedible, the holy tree at the center gave meaning to human will, which found peace in everything and so gave us a reason for loving what we knew. There was nothing uneven, or sharp, or burning, or bitter. All was harmony and to hand. Such was the place God gave to us to dwell as His revelation of Himself to Himself.

Our beginning was this creaturehood in most beautiful sublimity. But we lost our original position and came to know it from the aspect of the fall, from the bottom of the valley. On the flanks of the mount, plant and fruit blossom show themselves to us in our new condition, but always on a bed of sharp stones and thorns and surrounded by wild animals. Nothing is to be had without toil and cultivation, remembrance of what we have lost, and repentance for the urge to touch what was not to be touched, to violate the inviolate, to taste what was not to be tasted.

No flower or fruit, however beautiful, is more than a sign of what we once had and can have again, but only on the basis of a severe and ceaseless testing, of suffering and bitterness, of endurance and exposure, danger and doubt.

Our vision of the great house at the center, the symbol of our return to that original perfection without cut or break, announces the forms of purification, enlightenment, and unification.

Purification means accepting that no condition we have attained offers anything that might be termed an end. Our path remains open and we remain under the obligation to purify ourselves in relation to the world as a whole, all that is in it, and ourselves. We must never accept a path that leads only to a determinate end. We must confess that only the Pure is pure and that, so long as we remain separate from the Pure, our path has not ended, leaving us in need of the relation of purification.

Enlightenment is our relationship to the light in and with each of us. By simply accepting that no light is ever anything other than a sign of the Light, we can initiate a transformation of our darkened obscurity, fanning the light which has remained unextinguished within us, for the Spirit is Light. After He made us from earth, God breathed His Spirit into us. Nor can this process of enlightenment ever come to an end, as there is no light but the Light.

The path of purification and enlightenment is open to each being or thing in existence until the last, which is to say that nothing attains its goal or purpose except by unification with Him who is revealed and to whom all things return. In the end, the town shapes our endeavor at the bottom of the valley, as we bring together square and circle—the square that symbolizes our responsibility to curb our wills to our awareness that we tend to the inviolate and forbidden—as through the circles of circumambulation we realize the fullness of the seven heavens within our selves, hoping to restore that original condition in which garden and town were one: when no human hand was needed for perfection, as everything bore witness to the hand of God. We wanted our hands and our will to be independent of God, and this wish was given to us: if we are to return to the original and perfect condition, divine and human hand must come together, with the divine always the upper hand.

Every form in the *čaršija* bears witness to the house. Two trees predominate—the male and female cypresses, with the occasional bitter almond, barren fig, or hackberry. The cypress gives bitter, hard, inedible fruit, but its dignity and endurance recall our lost relation to the tree in the center of the garden. As do the apples atop the minarets. We are given to chance upon the inviolate, the sacred, and the inedible within the labyrinth of the world, as a way of happening upon and reaching for what we have lost. We need only think of the inedible barren fig, the malodorous tree of heaven, the ivy, the hackberry, and the bitter almond, even the sparse rosehip, the vine, the rose bush, and the box hedge. In this range from the lofty tips of the cypresses down to the surface of the grave we may perhaps also glimpse a certain reflection of the heavenly recesses, in the flowers of the hyacinth, the lily, the sage, and the heather that grow amongst the headstones.

The entire view of the town is framed by hills. Their flanks pass from craggy tops into gardens separated by heaps of cracked and scattered rock. The gardens are walled and marked off with this rock. And as the hillside comes down towards the houses, the walls show evidence of increasing workmanship. One might say that in the architecture of Stolac stone and the uses to which it has been put represent our quest for Unity. Stone appears as both cohesion and dispersion. Overall, the architecture of Stolac represents an attempt to gather together by our work what was scattered and to put to rest the startled stone shapes we find around us and employ in our constructive effort in ways that are not in conflict with the world as we have received it, so that our world is not damaged or wounded by our presence and work, but discovered as the revelation of the One in the many and the many in the One. The buildings of Stolac were originally made entirely of stone: from the retaining walls and garden walls, made of stone picked from the hills and arranged without mortar, to the courtyards and house walls, made of stone handpicked to be dressed and bound in lime mortar, to the paving of the courtyards and the streets, pieced together from stones gathered from the hillside scree and the riverbeds, to the basins and sinks and thresholds and columns and window jams and arches carved of the hard local bedrock or of the grainstone we call *tenelija*, to the headstones, shoeing stones, and the decorated or inscribed plates carved from those same stones or from the marlstone we call *miljevina*. Such too were the ashlar uprights of the minarets and the clock towers, each block dressed for its place in the whole. Such were the vaults of the water cisterns, outhouses, and roofs.

Every stone put in place, from the dry wall of the garden to the capstone of the cistern vault or the gateway arch, is an inscription of human presence and our quest to become one with and return to Unity. It was brought into the building process from the world as the Creator laid it out for us. Wherever such a stone exists, it speaks of us, but also of its existence before it came into the builder's hands and took the place a master gave it. Every stone thus bears witness that the world and we who build within it and everything we do are all works of the Creator.

The roofs of the houses of Stolac are made of stone slabs extracted from the earth. This stone, that paves the courtyards and the streets and is in the walls of the gardens, courtyards, and houses, in the cisterns, bridges, and minarets, in the covers and vaults of the cisterns and outhouses, confirms the durability of the cold and stony passivity with which human persistence is received. The stone's cold passivity is bounded by the warm passivity of the wood from which the doors and windows, the awnings and the pillars, thc rafters and the eaves, the stairs and the railings are made. These two predominant forms of durability of *čaršija* architecture—cold stone and warm wood—frame our quest for inner harmony, in which the town reveals the accessible and nourishing aspect of the lost garden and the blessed tree at its center that gave meaning to it all.

3. The Town

Original or first humanity was placed in the garden on the height. This was our creation in most beautiful (up)rightness of being. As recipients, we refract the garden, which is shown to us from its center or highest point to the infinite reaches of the plain below. We are the link between the heavens and the earth.[1] All that we have is from above and we pass on that "all" through our knowledge to the lower levels as multiplicity. We are fully balanced between giving and receiving, between male and female principles.

After the center or the highest point was violated, we fell to the lowest point of existence, the lowest depth. And there we wept. Our tears made of the valley the sign that our downward path was over and that the path back had begun.

From the valley of tears, that moment when we recalled God, who created the world and its seven heavens, through which we return to our authentic condition of most beautiful (up)rightness of being, the Prophet brought his people to the north, towards the most beautiful height. God said to him:

> Say, "If you love God, follow me, and God will love you."[2]

And the faithful followed him on the road toward the north, toward the Further Mosque. They dwelt with him in the fertile valley of Yathrib, which God had shown him in a dream, and he said:

> In a dream I saw myself on the way from Mecca to a place with many date trees. I thought that it was Al-Yamama or Hajar, but it was Medina, i.e. Yathrib.[3]

This move from the infertile valley with the Inviolate Mosque at its bottom towards the Further Mosque on the mount via the Prophet's Mosque at the fertile oasis is the pattern of our path of ascent and return. The Prophet said of the three mosques:

> Do not set out on a journey except for three mosques—the Inviolate Mosque, the Mosque of God's Messenger, and the Further Mosque.[4]

This journey from the lowest depth towards most beautiful (up)rightness of being is the way of every prophet as an image of the Praised. On this journey, which is only marked out in the external world—whether as crossing over the earth's surface from the Inviolate Mosque to the Further Mosque or ascending from the earth through all seven heavens—we discover the Spirit breathed into us by God as our uncreated essence. Perfecting ourselves through the Spirit, we perfect our understanding that there is no god but God and the Praised is His servant and His Messenger.

God speaks in the Psalms of this journey in the valley, the place of turning towards God after our sin against Him and of weeping in sorrow for the place we have lost in the garden height, of crying out for joy over the promise of return symbolized by Sinin or Zion:

> Blessed are those who find their strength in You; whose hearts are set on pilgrimage. As they pass through the valley of Becca [Mecca], they make there a water hole, and—a further blessing—early rain fills it. They make their way from height to height. God shows himself to them in Zion.[5]

The traveler confirms the valley as a place of remorse and weeping. One ascends from it, from height to height, towards Zion. This is the attainment of "most beautiful (up)rightness of being" after the "most beautiful example." Trouble and joy, bitterness and sweetness on that path confirm the link between valley and mount:

> By the fig and the olive and the Mount Sinai and this land faithful! We indeed created Man in the most beautiful uprightness, then We relegated him the lowest of the low—save those who believe, and do righteous deeds; they shall have a wage unfailing.[6]

Thanks to our violation of the forbidden center of the garden, which was inviolate and not to be eaten of, both the world and we ourselves are inverted: the height has become a valley and the body the cloak of the spirit. The garden has been transformed into the town, given to us that, in virtue, ritual, and knowledge, or purification, enlightenment, and unification, we may find what we have lost and return to our original perfection. This means transforming into a garden the town in which we, as the epitome of the world, have been placed. This is our return from the lowest depth to the most beautiful height. We had a garden, but it was turned into a town, symbolized by the house in the valley. We have been offered a chance to realize our original covenant with God, our acceptance of the confidence that was offered and of our oath to the Praised in pre-existence, by returning from the depth to the height. This self-realization includes following the Praised and swearing to him under the tree in reaffirmation of the original covenant with God.[7]

The Praised was, or had existence, even before we were in the garden. He said of this: "I was a prophet when Adam was between clay and water."[8] The Praised is thus a perfect model for all of us. He is the reality of the garden, spread through all its manifestations as the fullness of relation with God, who is praised by praise. In the garden on the height, Adam was the perfect image. But when Adam found himself at the lowest depth or the lower boundary of our fall it was the Praised who provided the image of perfection or archetype for Adam, the image that would lead him back towards the most beautiful height.

To realize humanity in one self is to reach the goal by following the Praised. This is our love of God and God's love of us. God is the Light. The Praised is His revelation, for it is through him (or them) that God has sent down His light.[9]

That Adam broke God's commandment regarding the inviolate tree means that he lost absolute nearness to the Praised; a split took place between his self-understanding as transgressor and his self-understanding as authentic follower. No matter where we may be, the presence of the Praised within us cannot be eradicated: even at the lowest depth the Praised serves as our most beautiful example, as he is mercy to the worlds and God's mercy comprehends all.

Our fall to the position of the lowest of the low, signified by the bottom of the valley, becomes an upward journey thanks to the turn towards God. This is why we are always somewhere between the bottom and the most beautiful (up)rightness of being: we can either fall or rise. Wheresoever we find ourselves, this is symbolized to us by the Inviolate Mosque or place of self-abnegation, which corresponds on earth to the inviolate tree in heaven. Confession that the Praised is God's servant and His Messenger is also affirmation that we are in the position of the lowest of the low and turning towards God. With the Praised, we turn towards the north, each of us conscious of our place of debt: in so turning, we are constantly aware of two things—the inviolate place of self-abnegation and the further place of self-abnegation, which symbolize the centrality of the inviolate tree at the center of the garden—for we are always between them, on the upward path of return, following the Praised.

> It is not for the people of the city and for the Arabs who dwell around them to stay behind God's Messenger, and prefer their

> lives to his: that is because they are smitten neither by thirst, nor fatigue, nor emptiness in the way of God, neither tread they any tread enraging the unbelievers, nor gain they any gain from any enemy, but a righteous deed is thereby written to their account.[10]

Within himself, the Praised experienced both the most beautiful height and the lowest depth, but as one whose will is entirely God's. He repeated the seven circuits around the inviolate place of self-abnegation, as we must cross the seven heavens on our return to God. In the valley, the Praised resolved the relationship of earth, as the square symbolized by the house, and the heavens, as the sphere symbolized by the circuits around the House and by the Further Mosque, with its octagonal base a transitional form towards the circle and its golden dome a symbol of the return to perfection.

Through the Praised, God calls on us to turn to the inviolate place of self-abnegation, of which the Praised is the center, as both God's servant and His Messenger.[11] He entered the House and prostrated himself before God. But he then passed from that place of self-abnegation to the Further Mosque, which is to say from the body to the Spirit, from earth to heaven, from the things of the world to the lotus-tree of the final boundary, and beyond.[12]

This relationship of the valley, our new home, and the mount, the place we once were and to which we desire to return, marks the distance between heaven and earth in the outer world and between body and Spirit in the human soul. The best we can do in our low condition is to turn to God, repent, and weep like Adam in the valley.

When he reached the position of the lowest of the low, at the bottom of the valley in the middle of the desert, fully opposite to the garden on the most beautiful height, Adam could clearly see the consequences of violating the inviolate tree. He could see the consequences of his will to act according to his own reason or evaluation, without taking due account of God's command. In the garden, everything was made for him in the most beautiful way: the work of God's hands was before him and he had it for himself in silence and quiet; nothing that he could have added with his own work was lacking; wherever he might turn, the perfection of the garden spoke to him of the Gardener, who appeared through that perfection as in a mirror in which all that beauty gazed at itself.

At the bottom of the dry and infertile valley, lined by dark stony hills, Adam turned, from below, from the depths to which he had come, towards God; he repented and wept bitterly:

> Adam's tears over his nakedness are a powerful sign of "divorce," not only from the lush garden of Eden but from a state of grace with God; "Woe is me! . . . Now I am an exile from glory." One has lost communion with one's Creator, is "cut off," and there can be no more profound loss than this. Adam grieves the lost shared love: "My soul wearies for the Lord, and I seek him in tears. How should I not seek Him? . . . I cannot forget Him for a single moment, and my soul languishes after Him, and from the multitude of my afflictions I lift up my voice and cry: 'Have mercy upon me, O God, have mercy on my fallen creature.'" Thus did Adam lament, and the tears streamed down his face unto his beard, onto the ground beneath his feet, and the whole desert heard the sound of his moaning. The beast and the birds were hushed in grief; while Adam wept because peace and love were lost to all men on account of his sin.[13]

The signs are in the world and in the self. Nothing has any meaning except as a sign of the Truth. That is why every valley-mount pair is a sign of our descent from our original condition to the bottom of the valley, but also a sign of our ascent by following the Praised as the best example. In doing so, we realize our authentic and most beautiful (up)rightness of being.

We fell from the garden to the town. The garden signifies our original most beautiful (up)rightness of being, while the town signifies the lowest depth. From that lowest depth, from that new condition, whose name is the town, and which is signified by the house at the bottom of the valley, we may return to perfection by transforming the earthly town into a heavenly one, which will correspond to the original garden:

> And he showed me a pure river of water of life, clear as crystal, proceeding out of the throne of God and of the Lamb. In the midst of the street of it, and on either side of the river, was there the tree of life, which bare 12 manner of fruits, and yielded her fruit every month: and the leaves of the tree were for the healing of the nations. And there shall be no more curse: but the throne of God and of the Lamb shall be in it; and His servants shall serve Him: and they shall see His face.[14]

The town, as the work of human hands, both hides and discloses the center for which we are seeking. Many roads from all four sides of the world meet in the *čaršija* to announce this center. Everything on the road towards the town, the labyrinth that hides the center, has its meaning. When we learn to read these signs, then any movement around the *čaršija* or towards it, all our contacts with other people, all the things we do and all the things that affect us announce in one way or another the center we seek in ourselves and through everything that is gathered in the world, the town, and the *čaršija.* While both the world and its people are constantly coming and going in what appears an incomprehensible flux, our approach to the entirety of the world and self remains informed by the knowledge of unity, the unity of knowledge, and our love of both.

We have within ourselves the possibility of two points of view. The first is recollection of the most beautiful height on which we were created and from which we regarded the whole world laid out before us. This was a panorama over all of existence, a view over the expanses of the earth from the peak of the highest mountain. In this view, we were the perfect vicar of the Creator over all existence. We understood both ourselves and the world as two sides of one and the same image of the All-Merciful. The second perspective is from below, from the surface of the earth towards heaven, up from the valley along the hillsides that surround it. This is the view from the depths. From this perspective, the world is revealed to us as an undeniably contradictory multitude.

Return to our original perfection means starting from within the totality of existence and facing the constant challenge of looking for the unity or center in everything. On this quest, we must give multiplicity its due. We and the world are open only in so far as the darkness inside ourselves is removed. We are preconfigured for such discovery. This preconfiguration comprises two confessions—that there is no god but God and that the Praised is His Messenger. But there is no confession that does not include thought and the entirety of being. Discussion of the town as the context of our return to most beautiful (up)rightness of being presupposes certain thoughts regarding the Real and the reality of thought. If the town is a labyrinth, then such thought may be a map to lead us to the center.

Two questions are decisive for all thinking. The first is: "Is that?" The second is "What is that?"

What-it-is-not accompanies, but cannot determine what-it-is. What-it-is does not limit or determine its what-being. There are countless forms in which essential being may be revealed, but essential being does not depend on any one of them.

Being is not determined by anything else. It is all that can be found. Everything through which Being reveals itself ex-ists (stands out). But Being as such does not ex-ist. Being is.

Being is praised. This quality of being praised is not received; it simply is and reveals itself in ex-istence. All things partake of essential being, substance, and praise. All of ex-istence is praised, but as recipient and revelation of the Being of the All-Praised.

Ex-istence, as the revelation of Being as All-Praised, is praised. The relationship of all ex-istence to What Is is all the levels of being from nothingness to Being as Necessary Being. All being is praised as the recipient and revelation of Necessary Being as Necessarily Praised.

All ex-istence is, accordingly, to-be-praised. Here we are complete, as the revelation of the Necessarily Praised. The totality of the to-be-praised is the totality of being, which is the Praised. All ex-istence, the limitless and illimitable flow of the revelation of the Necessarily Praised in the to-be-praised, comes together in perfect humanity or our highest condition. The Necessarily Praised is the All-Sufficient. This sufficiency is absolute. But all ex-istence is poor. This poverty is absolute. There is nothing in ex-istence that does not derive from What Is. It is the gift to the entirely impoverished from the absolutely sufficient. Everything the to-be-praised has was given by the All-Praised. Admitting what we have received, what the Praised owes to the All-Praised, means turning towards Him as the All-Praised and returning what we have received to all ex-istence. This is why all ex-istence and perfect human being, as to-be-praised and as beings which admit and return their debt to the All-Praised by praising Him, are two sides of one and the same ex-istence and one and the same condition of being to-be-praised.

4. The *Mihrab*

Human existence may be said always to take place between two extremes. The first is the authentic perfection of the garden, the other the lowest depth. At a basic level, this is the human town in its permanent struggle to become the heavenly city and our growing consciousness of return to our original condition as our goal. Both these extremes and everything between them are, as it were, veils through which the Essence reveals Itself, at once concealed and revealed.

The presence of a veil naturally entails two sides, a human and a divine. God is never hidden. He is always revealed and His face is on all sides. We are hidden, insofar as we do not clearly see God as present and revealed in the world. Our return to God and self-discovery in Him involve drawing back these veils, as we approach and ascend towards that which they reveal and which has always been in our hearts.

This return is possible, so long as we can overcome resistance, in the endless battle against whatever threatens our self-realization and recovery of original perfection. In the town, we are like travelers in a labyrinth, seeking the center. That center corresponds to the doors we must pass through to our salvation, to attain the condition of perfection.

In order that everything everywhere may affirm the presence of the center, the *čaršija* is oriented on the mosque. Everything that makes up or belongs to the *čaršija* proceeds from the mosque as its center. This reflects our own orientation towards the mosque and the *mihrab* as the arena of repentance and of overcoming resistance on the path towards perfection, which is why we are in the world. The mosque is the place of prostration and the willing subordination of everything we have to Him from whom we received it. It is the confession of humanity as poverty in comparison to the All-Sufficient. Acknowledging this, we open ourselves up to giving and receiving.

Imam Ali, the son of Husayn, made the following prayer:

> My God,
> I have no mediation with Thee
> but the tender acts of Thy clemency,
> nor any way to come to Thee
> but the gentle favors of Thy mercy
> and the intercession of Thy Prophet,

the Prophet of mercy,
who rescued the community from confusion![1]

To say that the mosque is the center of the *čaršija* is the same as saying that each human being is the center of the world. The central significance of the mosque is only meaningful if one accepts that each of us is on a ceaseless quest for our highest mode of existence. The mosque is the means for this journey to the form of self that acts to focus heaven and earth and what is between.

While the earth's surface makes up the first level of the *čaršija*, its horizontal and vertical surfaces, its doors and windows, its external and internal planes all testify to the interrelationship of the heavens and the earth. We think of the earth's surface as extending in four directions—south, north, east, and west. These cardinal points have their analogues in the four seasons of the year—summer, winter, spring, and autumn. Constantly applying these distinctions, we constantly rediscover our own centrality. This is the discovery of our purpose: always approaching it, we can never attain it, so long as we remain other and separate from it. Space and time are both expressions of infinity and eternity: our desire is to escape our finitude for that absolute freedom which is God alone.

Analogous to the four cardinal points and the four seasons of the year, a properly organized *čaršija* has four entrances and four exits. In the case of the Stolac *čaršija*, the four entry-exits are situated in relation to the other elements forming the *čaršija*. The first entry is from the north, between the shops and the *kiraethana*. The second is from the south, between the *mekteb* and the *musafirhana*. The third is from the east, between the shops and the forge. The fourth is from the west, between the shops and the *musafirhana*.

The *čaršija* proper is the focus of the town, its inner core. And the town is the focus of the world as a whole (for its inhabitants). There are four ways into the valley, to which correspond the four gates of the *čaršija*—the first from the east, along the river; the second from the south, along Vrsnik Peak; the third from the north along Ošanići Hill; and the fourth from the west, along the river and across the fields.

These four directions and four entrances announce a fifth entrance or gate. Our openness towards the Most High and so orientation towards the sky makes clear the existence of this fifth gate, to which the *čaršija* bears witness in all its parts. Whatever gate one uses to enter the *čaršija* area bounded by the *musafirhana*, the shops, and the *mekteb*, one further gate stands out among the others.[2] This is the entry into the *čaršija* mosque. To it lead the major roads and the many secondary ones between them: there are, they say, 19 such roads, which makes clear that they are all merely instances of the One. To these 19 roads corresponds an equal number of water cisterns. Each road has its own water cistern, according to Stolac tradition, in memory of one of the 19 guardians of the town. These were the good grandfathers, friends of God.[3] There are a number of traditions as to their names, one of which lists them as: Muharem, Hajdar, Ali, Šačir, Salih, Mahmud, Selman, Husein, Ibrahim, Sirija, Sulejman, Adem, Ćamil, Mustafa, Mehmed, Ismail, Ishak, Velija, and Jahja.

The row of shops to the north has two sides—one towards the *tepa* and the other towards the street. On the external north-eastern corner of the *čaršija* is the *kiraethana* or "house of reading." To the south, there is a row of shops facing the *tepa*, with their backs to the mosque. They are an extension of the mosque courtyard in the direction of the *tepa* or the external world. This link signifies the interconnection of all levels of existence and life. At the western corner of this row of shops, towards the *musafirhana*, is the *mekteb* or "place of the Book." These shops along the mosque courtyard are split in the middle by the gate. The common Bosnian word for a major or congregational mosque, *džamija*, is derived from the Arabic and means "place of gathering." In the garden, our original station, we served as the focus of everything in existence: everything within the horizons of the world had a clear representation within our consciousness that spoke plainly of God. Moreover, the garden was originally on the top of the mount: it was proximity to the One and the One's revelation in the multiplicity that is descent and decline.

With the violation of the inviolate, this order was scattered, placing us on the downward path and distancing us from the One. God explained to us our new condition of no longer acting as the cosmic epitome, since our hearts had been diverted:

> Nigh unto men has drawn their reckoning, while they in heedlessness are yet turning away; no Remembrance from their Lord comes to them lately renewed, but they listen to it yet playing, diverted their hearts.[4]

The single-fronted shops in front of the mosque, the *mekteb*, the *musafirhana*, the double-fronted shops, the *kiraethana*, the forge, and the bakery line the trapezoidal surface of the *tepa*. The dimensions of the trapezoid are 16m by 27.5m by 25m by 27.5m. The interior area of the *čaršija* is connected with the mosque through a gate, and it is this link that determines the relationship between the outer and inner orders of the *čaršija*. No relationship in the world, however, has any meaning except through its significance in *scientia sacra.* When that is forgotten, perfect order takes on the appearance of disorder. And *vice versa*, those who discover order in themselves will find it in the world.

The world was created in six days and in six dimensions (the four cardinal directions and up and down). Everything that was dispersed through the creation of the heavens and the earth and what lies between them came together in the creation of humankind. We, as the completion of creation, were placed as the seal on each determinate thing, while also acting as the opening towards the seventh heaven or Peace from which and towards which all the worlds proceed. This is why prostration is our most sublime or highest station. Prostration is the confession of the seventh heaven as Peace. This is the meaning of the seven points of contact in prostration: the forehead, the two palms, the two knees, and the toes on both feet.

We were created as the completion of six days and six heavens. This is why we are called to the act of focusing as our real essence:[5]

> O believers, when proclamation is made for prayer on the Day of Congregation, hasten to God's remembrance and leave trafficking aside; that is better for you, did you but know. Then, when the prayer is finished, scatter in the land and seek God's bounty, and remember God frequently; haply you will prosper.[6]

This act of focusing has two aspects—the low point of the valley as the symbol of the bringing together of what is scattered and the peak as the original human condition and the highest proximity to the One.

Responding to this call, sent out to us by God that through worship on each sixth day we might in remembrance of our creation fulfill our role as the epitome of creation, we confirm our ability to expand our own selves to embrace all things and every person. Recalling God, we discover the meaning of all the signs in the world and in our own selves. Our nature is revealed in the ability to distinguish truth and lie, recognize beauty and good, and to cleave to truth and beauty. Whether focused on the fullness of our own selves or at large within the horizons of the world, we have the Messenger as our most beautiful example:

> But when they see merchandise or diversion they scatter off to it, and they leave thee standing. Say: "what is with God is better than diversion and merchandise. God is the best of providers."[7]

All the worlds come together in us. This includes their manifestation in the six days and six dimensions as horizons before us. We set off through these horizons as travelers returning home. The *čaršija* is the image of coming and going and gathering and dispersion. The Messenger is our highest, and that means our original and ultimate, possibility. All searching within the self brings us upwards towards him. On that path, we form ourselves by overcoming the obstacles which are on all paths.

A question is repeatedly asked of us in the mosque, the center of the *čaršija*:

> Hast thou not seen how to God prostrate all those who are in the heavens and all who are in the earth, the sun and the moon, the stars and the mountains, the trees and the beasts, and many of mankind?[8]

The mosque is our invitation to join "those many" who accept the revelation of doctrine and the way, affirming it through virtue. They relate to themselves and to others and to the world by submission to God, which they confess through humility and generosity. Justice is simply showing what is in proportion and measure, in harmony and beauty.

Our original condition was the garden, the clear and complete manifestation of God as Peace. Our perfect relationship with God, as the Creator and Ruler of all existence, in the garden appeared in our condition of being-at-peace as people of peace. The inviolate nature of the central tree in the garden maintained our peaceful relationship with God as Peace. The fruit of the tree was not to be eaten of, but it was central nonetheless. It designated as such the Word which binds us to most beautiful (up)rightness and authentic dignity. The voluntary confession of the centrality of the inviolate tree reflects our position at the peak of creation, in our original (up)rightness of being.

After it was violated, the garden was scattered amongst the valleys and the hills of the world, amongst the islands in the seas and the oases in the deserts. The height with the garden at its peak was inverted: the peak became the bottom of the valley. Everything became different in the new human condition. If we are to attain anything that we have lost in the world and in ourselves, we must battle against everything in our selves which keeps us in the condition of separation from God. And so the *mihrab*, "the battlefield," is the center of the mosque, itself the kernel of the *čaršija*.[9]

Any journey through ourselves leads us to the *čaršija*. The *mihrab* is the place at which we may attain what we lost through violation of the forbidden tree in the paradisiacal center. For this to happen we must accept to shape our will to God's as Peace, to become peaceful and peaceable, and to accept being-at-peace as our essential obligation towards God. The world is split into earth and heaven, as the self is split between body and Spirit, and it confronts us constantly, hiding what is lost from us and making it hard to attain: it appears to us that our bodies are real, and the Spirit far and obscure.

In this vicious war, which brings us to the fullness of being, we are expected calmly to overcome the infinite multitude of enemies who threaten us on our path towards the Holy. They threaten us, for the most part, with poverty and suffering, sickness and death. They offer us an infinity of earthly goals, to turn us from connection with God as Peace, to hide from us and deny us the Spirit as the uncreated core of our being, to violate the inviolate, and to have us eat that which must not be eaten. These enemies, who lie in ambush for us and attack us on all our paths, tried to show the town or city as unconnected in any way to the garden and the garden as independent of the city, while connection with Peace allows us to see that city and garden are merely two sides of one and the same existence, which is distorted in the human self. Is this not what the good model Ali said, when he told his companions:

> Live in great cities because they are places where the people of peace congregate. Avoid places of neglect and wickedness and places where there are few who assist in obedience to God. Confine your thinking to matters that concern you. Do not sit in the markets, because they are rendezvous of temptation and targets of mischief. Reflect often on those over whom you enjoy superiority, because this is a way of thanksgiving. Do not journey on the day of congregation until you have attended common prayers, except when you are going in the way of God or on an excusable matter. Thank God in all your affairs because obedience to God has precedence over all other things. Entice your heart into worshipping God, persuade it, do not force it. Engage it when it is free and merry, except in necessary things enjoined upon you, for they should not be neglected and must be performed at the appointed times. Be on guard lest death come down upon you when you are far from God in search of worldly pleasure. Avoid company of the vicious because vice enjoins vice. Know that God is great and love His lovers. Keep off anger because it is a great one of the Tempter's armies.[10]

5. From Left to Right

The mosque gate links the two areas of the *čaršija*, the one around the *tepa* or the place of hospitality, negotiation, and measurement, and the other around the *mihrab*, where oblivion and errancy are conquered through recollection and return. It is a part of the *čaršija*, forming a barrier between two seas, one salt and the other sweet.[1]

Human beings are split between earth and heaven, body and spirit, darkness and light. This division runs through our whole being. Every division requires a barrier. Self-realization involves ascent from barrier to barrier, from below upwards, from the dark to the light, from the body to the Spirit. This inner ascent has its strict analogue in the upward journey from heaven to heaven of the external world, as one veil after another is removed.

The traveler passes "over water" from the barrier within the *čaršija* represented by the entrance into the mosque courtyard to the *mihrab*, the symbol of the "heavenly gates." Life in this world only has meaning if we confess that the other world is higher. Everything in the world and our own selves reveals that other world.

As human beings, we are always between two worlds. Our self-realization requires that we ascend from the lower to the higher. This outer journey of return cannot end in any form of imperfection. Only unity of knowledge and being can bring us satisfaction. Only then can we become what we love. Only then is the goal of our journey within our grasp. Then we can say: I am what I know and I know what I am. That is why the heavenly gates open to those who know and testify to the signs of God: "Those that cry lies to Our signs and wax proud against them—the gates of heaven shall not be opened to them."[2] These are the gates through which we remove ourselves from duality and move towards Unity. Our goal can be attained only by transcending duality and by enacting the confession that there is none but He.

All aspects of earthly existence are brought together in the *čaršija*, and the *čaršija* is focused on the mosque or "place of prostration." The mosque is focused on the *mihrab*, the battlefield on which we overcome the obstacles on the path back to that self which lies at the innermost core of our being, that self which languished in the shadows after the violation of the inviolate tree and was wrapped in the veils of existence at the bottom of the valley. The focal point of humanity lies within our heart. Only within it is self-realization or unification possible with that which bears witness out of the duality which is the world. That is why the mosque belongs to the *čaršija*. And why the *čaršija* belongs to the mosque. Whenever this pair is split asunder, confusion enters the world and us. The mosque is a higher level of whatsoever visible is oriented towards the Principle that is its origin and its goal. The *čaršija* gathers in the mosque, with constant movement to and from it. The central part of the *čaršija* mosque is the battlefield of the *mihrab*. There is as much peace in the world as in people. Peace is infinitely close to each of us. This is because God is Peace.[3] He says: "I am near to answer the call of the caller, when he calls to Me."[4] But, we are always less than and somehow removed from Peace. Appearances call us to the multitude and to action based on less knowledge and on free will that holds itself sufficient and independent of the Will.

Connecting with and approaching Peace is the upward journey from the lower to the higher levels, the war against that in us that tempts us to evil.[5] In this war, we shall accept no side as final, but open ourselves to the confession that there is no god but God and that the Praised is His servant and His Messenger. Confessing this, we meet our debt to ourselves and to others in the world around us and to the world itself, recognizing the claims of all that is. Recognizing the claims of all things, we accept our debt regarding everything we have received in our poverty from the All-Sufficient. Since everything in the world was created with Truth, our debt regarding all things is pregnant with truth. We can repay our debt to God only by means of His creation. He made Himself known through His creation. His desire to be known took on form as the world, as the earth and the heavens and all they comprehend, as the macrocosm and as the human being, its perfect epitome. This is why our return to God is in recognition of our debt for all that is. For only in this way can we know Him we love. This is how we relate to God and it is necessarily through the Praised as the perfect example. There is nothing, however great or small, however close or far, on any of the four sides of the world, that is unrelated to the self's pursuit of Peace. God is Peace (*Salam*). To receive Peace, we must pass on what we have received. Our connection to God must be being-at-peace. Being–at-peace, as our basic attitude towards God, is our only debt or obligation. The best example, our best model, is the Praised as the first of the people of peace.[6]

All the ways of humankind in and through and towards the *čaršija* involve deviation and backtracking. No goal can be attained without crossing and re-crossing the same point from different directions. Only by turning to the mosque gates and passing through them to the *mihrab* do we choose an orientation and approach a center we believe somehow preserves what we are looking for, what we seek. This is ascent or return from the bottom of the valley, up the steep path, to the peak, and so the gathering of the multitude that is in the One.

On the path, we are aware of crossing over water on our way to our goal, marked by the House in the holy valley of Mecca. That House is in turn a sign of God's Seat and of the human heart, which comprehends everything, as God says through the Praised: "My earth and my heaven comprehend me not, but the heart of my believing servant does comprehend me."[7] This path ends when the goal is reached, as left and right disappear, and Unity is.

So long as we remain travelers, we move from left to right, seeking full return and union. When we turn towards the house, the *čaršija*, its contents, and what lies beyond them are to our left, delineating for us the path we have taken and what still lies before us. A careful look at the shape of the space in front of the mosque courtyard gate reveals that its left side, with the *sahat kula* (clock tower), *kiraethana* (reading room), bakery, and forge, is narrower than the right, with the *mekteb* (school), porch, and *musafirhana* (guest house). This stresses the aspect of left and right on our road back.

Were the left side of the *čaršija* wider, one might see the river source and canyon. The river approaches the town and the canyon widens. Within the town itself, there are watermills and washing places on that side—places for grinding flour and beating laundry. On that side are the *hammam* (bath house), the *dershana* (house of teaching),[8] the greater graveyard, and the *kiraethana.* These are precisely the elements that mark our growth from insignificance to wholeness on the road back. Gathering the dispersed, liberation through purification, learning through erasure, and so on, these decisive contradictions or contraries are to be found in the beating of a woolen skirt and the milling of grain, in bathing and cleaning, in lecturing (which is one meaning of *ders*, as the discovery and erasure of traces on the path towards Him they announce) and in learning (revealing what was originally in unity). Only through these relations on our path or approach to that which we love because we know it and in coming to know that with which we wish to unite, is it possible to retain or recall unity.

Looking towards the right, the path from the reading room and the clock tower is marked by the *mekteb*, the captain's house, the *muselimat* (town offices), and the fortress to whose gate an upward path leads along the slope of the hill. All these elements are signs of human advancement in knowledge; they belong to the people of the right hand.

Taking a wider view of the valley, the river canyon is to the left, between the hills and the eastern approach to the town. Everything on that side is narrow. Looking from the *čaršija* towards the house, space spreads out in various directions, unfolding. The rich *musafirhana* is to the right, and behind it are the inns, the administrative buildings, the fortress, and the plain. From the north, from Ošanići, a road crawls down to the river. The superiority of the right side is made clear by everything that contributes to its more expansive view. The conical hill, Vrsnik Peak, in front of the worshipper, marks our orientation towards the center and the final purpose of rising up towards the self. In this complex of signs, we see the transformation of the valley into the mount, the depth into the height.

Between these two sides, left and right, we are called forward, towards the *mihrab* or battleground, the gate through which we must pass if we are to return to Peace, to begin our ascent to the peak as the sign of Unity: Unity is non-duality. On that road, we may trust in our right hand, but our goal is to transcend all duality. That is why we confess that there is no god but God. No matter how far we may progress upon this path, we never surpass the best example, who is both in us and before us. We are kept back from him by the forces of duality, as progress towards and return to Unity from the differentiated require us to become warriors and to view our own selves as the battlefield.

Nothing on our road back can surprise us, as God has said to us: "O soul at peace, return unto thy Lord, well pleased, well pleasing!"[9]

Entry into the town, properly speaking, is discovery of the lost garden. It means passing through the graveyard outside the town, so that the good model Ali might point out to the traveler the traps of ignorance, which is revealed through knowledge, and of freedom, which is revealed through service:

> Kumail bin Ziad has said: The Commander of the Faithful [Ali] caught hold of my hand and took me to the graveyard. He breathed a deep sigh and said: O Kumail, our hearts are vessels. The best are those that keep best. So keep well what I say to you. People are of three types. One is the scholar and divine. Another is the seeker of knowledge who is also on the path to deliverance. The last is the common rot who heed every call and bend in the direction of every wind. They seek no light from the lamp of knowledge nor the protection of a reliable support.
>
> O Kumail, knowledge is better than wealth. Knowledge guards you, but you must guard wealth. Spending decreases wealth, but multiplies knowledge. The effect of wealth ceases, once wealth itself dries up.
>
> O Kumail, knowledge is belief that is acted upon. With it, we enjoy peace during our lifetime and a good name after our

> death. Knowledge manages, while wealth is managed. O Kumail, those who amass wealth have already died, even though they may be living, while those endowed with knowledge will live as long as time. Their bodies have gone, but their persons live on in our hearts. Look, here is wealth of knowledge [The Commander of the Faithful pointed to his own bosom]. I seek one who may bear it. Should I seek one whose wits are quick, but is not to be relied upon, who would use faith for worldly gain and God's favors to attain dominion over His servants and God's proofs to hold sway over His friends?[10]

The center of the valley is the *čaršija;* the center of the *čaršija* is the mosque; and the center of the mosque, the *mihrab.* The center of the world is the human being; the center of the human being is the heart; and the center of the heart is Intellect or Spirit. Almost everything in the valley has sharp edges. This sharpness sets apart the house as a sign of the world we seek to leave, but the *mihrab* stands out from these flat surfaces and sharp edges so as to recall the tree which determined our original perfection and our fall to the lowest depth.

In our quest for passage towards the reality of perfection in the garden, there is a clear unfolding from left to right, from the narrow canyon to the expanse of the plain, from the penury of the hillside and the insecurity of the narrow passages towards the solidity of the fortress, from the rigors of travel towards the *hammam* and *musafirhana.*

This development from left to right does not cut our connection to the surface of the earth. We cannot ascend the upright path or the path of the fortunate without first liberating ourselves from the superficial and transcending it. In all that unfolds upon the surface of the earth, from weakness to power, from dispersion to union, we seek passage that is neither left nor right, neither before nor behind. This is ascent from the body to the heart and from the heart to the Spirit. Then, the upper and lower arches of existence may be discerned. The sky and the mount mark the upper arch, while the earth and the valley mark the lower arch. They meet at a barely discernible line along the hilltops, below which the variety of plant life, both edible and inedible, becomes thicker and thicker as one travels down towards the center of the valley. And always there are the thorns and brambles to hinder access. But, when the flowers of the wild rose and the rosehip and the almond blossom appear in this wilderness, and the flowers of the wild orchid and violet appear in the rock under the thorn, it all comes to signify, together with the birdsong, the Mystery that is both covered and revealed by the veils of the world. It marks the finitude of space against infinity and the ephemeral nature of time against eternity.

What was lost is nowhere to be found. We yearn endlessly for our desire, as all sweetness is tinged with bitterness, all happiness with suffering.

6. The Call

We are at the lowest depth. This is not our original condition or goal. We can ascend, but must first discover fullness of self and return to the original purpose of our creation. Regardless of our condition, we human beings never lose our essence, the authentic and uncreated Spirit of the All-Merciful. Nor is the presence of this uncreated Spirit ever in doubt.

In the reality of every moment, life appears as reality itself to us. At the same time, our highest, authentic moment calls to us, when we remember our lost condition for which we mourn and yearn. These two shape our selves—the manifestation of the reality of the present, flanked by past and future, on the one hand, and remembrance that authentic and most beautiful sublimity is possible, on the other. This is the essence of God's call to us. He calls on us to see all the signs in the world around us and in ourselves, all of existence, as presenting Him, since none of it means anything without Him, "here" and "now," and not at some past or future time.

Our position at the lowest depth, at the bottom of the valley, is transformed by regret and hearing the call of the Most High into a turn towards most beautiful sublimity. This call transforms the bottom of the valley into the city, behind which lie the images of the garden and of woman.[1] Relating to the house at the bottom of the valley and to woman as our other half, we come to realize that "no associate has He."[2] Having discovered unity in duality and sublimity in the depth, we follow our possibility of perfection, our most beautiful example. This call, sent down to the bottom of the valley to bring about the enlightenment of its inhabitants through knowledge, ritual, and virtue, guides us in transforming its infertility[3] into the profusion of the garden and the apparent into the Real.

The Praised, who is the Messenger, is an act of mercy to the world, as he encompasses every moment of humanity; from the lowest depth to the most beautiful height. His perfection gathers in the "immense magnitude of [his] nature,"[4] shaped as it is by the confession that there is no god but God and that the Praised is His servant and His Messenger, providing every one of us with our "finest example" and every town with the "Mother of Cities." There, in the mother of all other cities, the valley floor marks the lowest depth and so the place the Book was sent down to as "a warning to the worlds,"[5] into the heart of the Praised,[6] who was born there:

> This is a Book We have sent down, blessed and confirming that which was before it, and for thee to warn the Mother of Cities and those about her; and those who believe in the world to come believe in it, and watch over their prayers.[7]

Confidence is the relationship of God the All-Faithful and the individual of faith. The All-Faithful is one of the most beautiful names of God.[8] God's fidelity is absolute, as His knowledge and mercy comprehend everything. But human knowledge is limited and always little. Our confidence, in relation to God, is perfected only through love of Him. God offered confidence to us, despite our weakness and the limits to our knowledge. We in return have offered ourselves such as we are to Him. To the extent that we bring together love and knowledge in our faith, we follow the Praised as the finest example. Then we love God and God loves us.

Confidence is part of human nature and is open to us all. When we decline the confidence offered us by another, we deny our own nature, which is shaped by the acceptance of the confidence God offers us. There can be no relationships between people without confidence. God enjoins us:

> Return what is given in confidence to its owners; and when you judge between people, judge with justice. Good is the admonition God gives you; God is All-Hearing, All-Seeing.[9]

This demand to judge justly is unconditional: to judge justly means to confess the full truth of creation, which is beyond mere appearance:

> O believers, be you securers of justice, witnesses for God, even though it be against yourselves, or your parents and kinsmen, whether the man be rich or poor; God stands closest to either. Then follow not caprice, so as to swerve; for if you twist or turn, God is aware of the things you do.[10]

To judge justly, we must confess and point out the truth in all things. As bearers of confidence received initially from God, we have a responsibility. It is our debt to God. Each and every one of us is a bearer of this confidence. If we are to confess our debt to God, we must recognize the same debt is owed by others. This is why offering and receiving confidence is the means of realizing relationship to God.

Confidence is the highest modality for all relationships in the *čaršija*. We are each expected to offer and receive it and to test ourselves and each other as worthy bearers of confidence. This testing is a judgment in justice, and justice is, it will bear repeating, the disclosure of Truth in everything. We have a standing debt towards the Truth. That debt towards the Truth of all creation furnishes us with our one and only irrevocable right—life without end in happiness, both here and now and after death and all deprivation.

We can meet our debt to the Truth only in relation to the world as a whole and to ourselves as whole. None of our knowledge is sufficient to raise us above other people, nor sufficiently deficient to prevent us from loving them. To judge justly requires that we confess Truth, but also that we love whatever reveals the All-Merciful.

We always know the other less well. We know less about others than about ourselves, which is why we have a debt to listen to the other, so as to learn more and to judge rightly. Recognizing the others' right to speak and placing ourselves under an obligation to listen to any who address us, we come to know ourselves as both hosts and guests. We are never simply host or simply guest. We are always both. This is why the individual does not exist towards whom we have no debt, against whom we have no claim. Each of us is at the same time guest and host. Our duty as host and our claim as guest are different, however. They differ from hour to hour and from place to place. When the guest/host stands in the *čaršija*, facing the *musafirhana*, it is not difficult to recognize the principle of the upraised hand as the basis for the overall construction of the whole. This principle even runs through the architectural plan of the *čaršija* mosque.

The right hand, open palm, raised level with the face, signifies the union of will and knowledge.[11] Everything we do is done on the basis of little knowledge, or even none, and on the basis of impulse and fear. All true knowledge is received, and, for that to be possible, we are expected to be-at-peace, quiet in our attitude towards both ourselves and the world. How far we may receive is determined by the tranquility through which God reveals Himself to us as Peace. Both the world and the self announce God as Peace: for the people of peace relate to God as Peace through being-at-peace. This is our debt towards God:

> Today I have perfected your debt for you, and I have completed My blessing upon you, and I have approved being-at-peace for your debt.[12]

Through this relationship, we receive peace and are at peace, and whosoever gives what they have received is a person of peace—a peace-bringer. That which we have received becomes the principle of our relationship with everything in existence.

Being-at-peace is a form of relation to our selves and to our world and so to the signs through which God reveals Himself. It is orientation towards the Principle and openness to It, but in our inner world, which is a mirror of all existence:

> Whomsoever God desires to guide, he expands his breast for being-at-peace.[13]

Given such tranquility and divine guidance, a little knowledge may reveal itself to the person of peace as the face of God: we are in the labyrinth of the world, but the face of God is always and everywhere before us as we strive to approach Him, for everything which we know intimates a revelation of Him and we love Him through His creation.

Whatsoever is in existence finds meaning in and through this orientation. But orientation entails awareness of the complement—of descent and wandering, of left and right, of duality and unity. Our love for God is subject to constant testing:

> And who does greater evil than he who forges against God falsehood, when he has been called unto being-at-peace?[14]

Faith is knowledge regarding the Creator through His creation and love of Him as the truth of everything in existence. The face signifies will, love, and knowledge, while the right-hand is the sign of power. The unification of will and power and love and knowledge is presented as the doing of what is good and fine, and whosoever does good and fine things serves God as if he saw Him.

There are five pillars to both the left and the right of the mosque entrance, four wooden ones and the final wall. These pillars or supports correspond to the fingers of the hand. In total there are ten pillars and nine passages. Between the five pillars to both left and right of the entrance there are doors, and beyond them the *mihrab*. The apex of our ascent on this path is prayer in prostration: both right and left arm extended and the head between them, signifying the One and our return to Him.

This principle of the two hands with the head between them is also applied in the *musafirhana* and on all of the clusters of shops. The guest house also has 10 pillars, marking off four shops to the right and four to the left of the entrance, thus creating nine entrances. The number nine corresponds symbolically to the heavens, revealing to us the perfect harmony of all creation.[15]

The significance of the numbers, four, five, eight, nine, 11, and 12 for the layout of the Stolac *čaršija* may be traced throughout the sacred complex. Here we trace in simplified form the significance of the number five and the "principle of the upraised hand," testified to by its use in traditional Bosnian greetings.

Human life overall can be presented in terms of four levels: the will or action; belief or faith, as the unity of knowledge and love; perfection or always acting well and beautifully; and recognition of the hour, as both the immediate and deferred realization of the confession of unity. These are the four important aspects of our debt to God—being-at-peace (*islam*), faith (*iman*), beauty (*ihsan*), and the hour (*saa*).

We are expected to bring everything we do into line with the will of our Lord, the All-Merciful, the Ever-Merciful, the King of the Day of Debt. By acting in the world in this way, we attain the level of "companions of the right hand,"[16] those who affirm their beliefs, and so their knowledge and their love, by doing whatever they do in the best possible way and as if the hour were nigh. The greatest achievement of such people may be said to be their becoming what they know and knowing what they are. They are symbolized by an individual with an upraised and open right hand.

The loftiest condition to which they can attain is *sedžda* or prostration. In this position, their condition of being is marked out, that is their being what they know and knowing what they are. Then, their open hands are raised beside their faces, so that one can say that their will is gathered in love for One whom they know through Him. One may also say that then He loves them:

> And the most beloved things with which My servant comes nearer to Me is that which I have enjoined upon him; and My servant keeps coming closer to me through supererogatory works, until I love him, so I become his hearing with which he hears, and his sight with which he sees, and his hand with which he grips, and his leg with which he walks; and if he asks Me, I will give him, and if he asks My protection, I will protect him.[17]

This coming together of the two wills, the human and the divine, is possible at any moment and in any place. This is the confidence of the faithful with God the Faithful. Under such circumstances, we are satisfied with what we have received, and so we satisfy Him who impregnates everything with reality.

When different wills are gathered together in the *čaršija* in their various searches for their various paths to redemption, each self faces ascent by the pillars of confession that there is no self except the Self and adherence to the Praised on the road to God.

This is why the *čaršija* is the scene of the salvation and liberation of each individual, regardless of their affiliation or lack of affiliation. The *philosophia perennis* inheres within every sacred tradition or teaching. But it is more than that: it is a possibility within each of us. For each of us who applies this always present and possible love of wisdom in our life, the return to original or authentic loftiness is not deferral of redemption from this world to some future date. For those of us, the possibility is alive in every "now" and every "here." We strive to redeem ourselves from a condition of severed consciousness in time and to raise ourselves to the eternity to be found in conscious communion with the Principle. Given that the principle can and should be known through confession of Unity in this life—for that is the reason and the purpose of life—attaining authentic perfection and returning to the most beautiful (up)rightness of being is not bound behind the doors of the grave. The redeemed individual is simply one who has left behind the illusions of yesterday and tomorrow for the fullness of their "now," a redemption signified by the 8 wooden pillars on the outside edge of the mosque porch.

The first pillar signifies witness to Unity. This is the confession that there is no god but God. Through it we distinguish selfhood from the Self, renouncing the first and opening up to the latter. In this way, we recognize the Self as our reason and our purpose.

The second pillar signifies the Praised. Everything we encounter reveals God as All-Praised, and the world is praised as the recipient of praise from the All-Praised. When we have emptied ourselves of everything but the Self, the totality of existence gathers in us as in the Praised. And that is our highest moment: the Praised is sent unto us like a shining lamp, the most beautiful example, and the "immense magnitude of his nature."

The third pillar signifies the will of the self for extinction and subordination to the will of the Self, which involves turning towards the Self, centering oneself upon Him and embracing Him.

The fourth pillar signifies our orientation towards the All-Praised as Peace through the actions of praise and of being-at-peace. This is the act of loving Him, whom we know, and of yearning to come close to and to unite with Him.

The fifth pillar signifies doing what we know and love, in such a way that we are governed by the will of the Self: so that we exist as an expression of the Beloved.

The sixth pillar signifies that we are "sons of the hour." The real for us exists neither yesterday nor tomorrow: Everything we need for salvation is in the here and the now, everything we need may be found in the Self and through Him.

The seventh pillar is to see and to act in accordance with the recognition of the rights of all things: to do nothing in or through ignorance and in no way to inflict pain or evil. To know the proper place for all things in the world and in our selves.

The eighth pillar signifies death before death: then all appearance of selfhood outside the Self is gone. Whatever we see is nothing but the Self: we are in the house and His face is what we see.

7. The Hour

Even in the lowest depth, at the bottom of the valley, we have every convenience for ascent. This is not a journey towards some distinct or definite goal: that beautiful height, the confession that there is no god except God, is a plenitude in which all appearance and all duality disappear.[1] Perfection, which includes the earth, the heavens, and all that lies between them, transcends all limits. This is the meaning of the confession that the Praised is "a mercy unto the worlds," "a shining lamp," and "the most beautiful example." At no point between the lowest depth and the beautiful height do we lose our need for the Praised and his call, for as the perfect recipient he responds to the Lord:

> Call thou to the way of thy Lord with wisdom and good admonition and dispute with them in the better way.[2]

This call to the way of the Lord comes in the finite world, but is directed at no one but the Caller, who encompasses all with His knowledge and His mercy. Responding to this call involves a path that begins at "the lowest depth," by the "inviolate place of self-abnegation," and whose goal is "the beautiful height," "the further place of self-abnegation."

This path is determined by Unity, which endows this world with significance as the image of the other, higher world. Our conscious openness towards perfection, which includes the earth and the heavens, and all between them, and the six days and the seven heavens, is possible only on the basis of this distinction between this world as image and the higher world as its model. Only on the basis of this distinction can we ascend from the lowest depth to the beautiful height on the upright road, on which the Praised always precedes us as the gentle and patient issuer and interpreter of the Call:

> Assuredly, thou art calling them to an upright path; and surely they that believe not in the world to come are deviating from that path.[3]

> For, the Prophet is dearer to the faithful than their own selves.[4]

This being "ahead" and "dearer" relates primarily to our struggle to free ourselves from the violence of the conscious self as appearance and ignorance and to see the sublime potential we always have to open ourselves to the Self and find ourselves in Him by following the Praised on the pathway back. This is signified by the relationship between the two final stone pillars on the porch of the mosque and the eight wooden pillars between them. Stone has a cold patience. Wood is patient and receptive too, but warm. The wooden pillars, as symbols on our path of self-discovery, begin from cold patience and end with it. Does this not signify our desire to return to Peace, with which we are satisfied and which satisfies?

Climbing this upright path allows the traveler to recognize the Truth in every sign around or within him or her, liberating the self from appearances and the finite, as "all things perish, except His face."[5] For that Face is always before us. It is not and cannot be hidden, for there is nothing real but Him. Our inability to see the Face in everything is part of our being covered in obscurity, and if we are to discover our uncreated essence we must free ourselves from that which covers us, so that we may gaze upon the Face of the Beloved in all that there is to see.

This discovery of the truth of existence in everything allows us to free ourselves of ignorance and the violence it brings about: "His is the Judgment, and unto Him you shall be returned."[6] But this return is not to someplace different from that in which we spend every moment, regardless of how it may seem to us that our ignorance and suffering can only be resolved somewhere beyond our "here and now." The horizons of the world stand before us, that we may confess that there is no self but the Self. Nothing in the outer world makes any sense without that confession. And that is so, because there is no now but the Now.

Responding to God in His Now means orienting and opening the self towards the reality of the Day or the Hour. This is our highest state, in which the Praised is revealed in us as the perfect fulfillment of our debt towards God. Our intercourse with others must obey the command sent down by God through the Holy Spirit:

> Say: "Let you be stones, or iron, or some creation yet more monstrous in your minds!" Then they will say, "Who will bring us back?" Say: "He who originated you the first time." Then they will shake their heads at thee, and they will say, "When will it be?" Say: "It is possible that it may be nigh, on the day when He will call you, and you will answer praising Him, and you will think you have but tarried a little."[7]

Praising God requires absolute confession of His Unity, which transcends all finitude. In the ascent from the many to the One and the discovery of the Reality of all existence in the confession that there is no god but God, we discover our responsibility for every atom of good and every atom of evil that we have done.[8] Nothing exists within the horizon of the world or in the human self but it does so with Truth: Justice is the recognition and bringing to light of this.

When we relate to the signs in the world and in ourselves by recognizing their claims, we bear witness that there is no truth except the Truth and that God is Truth.[9] This means: the truth of each now, from which we can never escape, except into illusion, which is the acceptance of some form of self outside of the Self.

For the Truth is our goal. Only it can satisfy us. Just as Truth may be revealed through an uncountable host of signs, from the tiniest to the greatest, from the closest to the furthest, it is only with Truth that they abide: signs fade, that the Truth may be revealed as Unity. This is the means of our, humanity's, ascent through the world and beyond it, through the signs in the outer world and within ourselves, and beyond them. Unity encompasses our realization towards and by the goal to which the upright path leads, in the *anastasis* after death, namely that the Truth of everything be shown: the confession of Unity cannot be separated from the perfection of character through virtue. This is so because of the relationship between this and the other world:

> The present life is naught but a sport and a diversion; surely the Last Abode is better for those that are God-fearing. What, do you not understand?[10]

When our struggle to ascend through the exercise of our will in ritual is done, then the mountains themselves will disappear in sign of our return to our authentic condition, as God says:

> When the Terror descends (and none denies its descending), abasing, exalting, when the earth shall be rocked and the mountains crumbled and become a dust scattered and you shall be three bands—Companions of the Right (O Companions of the Right!), Companions of the Left (O Companions of the Left!), and the Foremost: the Foremost, those are they brought nigh the throne, in the gardens of delight.[11]

That each mountaintop is only a sign of our origin and the possibility of return and that truth, honesty, and the upright confession that there is no god but God exclude the possibility of taking any sign in place of the

Signified is indicated by the claim that the mountains will disappear due to their dependence on the Hour:

> And thou shalt see the mountains, that thou supposest fixed, passing by like clouds—God's handiwork, who has created everything very well.[12]

For, even the mountains as signs of (up)rightness and ascent are nothing but traces of Him who is both Near and Far and Alike and Incomparable. Our task at any given moment is to seek for His traces and their passing in all that is—that they might not be taken in place of Him, for He who has revealed Himself in all existence is not absent: He is close and to hand, wherever we turn.

In our relationship with the world, which means with ourselves, the most obvious principle is the unity of Truth. This principle extends over everything—both the infinitely near and infinitely far, and it is explicit in the testimony or confession that there is no god but God. Given that God is Truth, this is also witness to the unity of Truth. Everything in existence is derived from Truth, and returns with It to It. So it is with laughter and tears, with life and death, as God says in the Recitation:

> And that is He who makes to laugh, and that makes to weep.[13]

> Who created death and life.[14]

> And He appointed the shadows and light.[15]

Given that it was God who gave us these pairs—laughter and tears, life and death, light and dark—the question arises as to whether they exist in the Divine Reality itself or merely in the created world. We may add a further two pairs of decisive importance—time and eternity and space and infinity. It is easy on the basis of the prophetic tradition to show that God laughs, but no proof is known of His tears.[16] There is a clear difference between laughter and tears. The first is an attribute of God, the other is not. Both, however, are attributes of created humankind.

Given that God does laugh, we may derive three of His names: He who Laughs, the Giver of Laughter, and the Giver of Tears. In a similar way, we may discern another three of His names: the Living, the Giver of Life, and the Giver of Death.

God is He who Lives and never Dies. But everything in existence is in a ceaseless cycle of living and dying. Life and consciousness are the sources of everything, and one can find them everywhere and always in their different forms. Similarly, God is He who laughs but never cries. Everything in existence is in a ceaseless cycle of laughter and tears. Thus, God is the light of the heavens and the earth.[17] He made darkness and light.[18] The Recitation says: "A Book We have sent down to thee that thou mayest bring forth mankind from the shadows to the light,"[19] which means from death to life, from ignorance to knowledge, from tears to laughter. Only by returning to God can death, sorrow, and suffering be overcome.

If tradition presents tears as more suitable for the soul than laughter, the reason is our separation from God following the loss of the garden and our arrival on earth, which is our submersion in death and darkness. Weeping is a natural response to our realization of distance from the Creator, who is the source of all being, all good, all consciousness, and all laughter. Those despised in this world, who suffer and cry, will be happy, blessed, and smiling in the next. And conversely, those who are happy here and laughing may be despised in the next and be those who weep.

Weeping may be caused by sorrow and suffering, but also by mercy and happiness. God did send the Praised as a mercy to the worlds.[20] His mercy is all-embracing.[21] Seeing human suffering, the Praised wept, for he was merciful towards all creation.[22]

It should be stressed that in the Recitation, God reveals His attributes in us, but not the reverse, human attributes in Himself. This is so because everything created is mortal. Each prophet has said: "I am only a mortal the like of you."[23] It is true that the Praised revealed the divine attribute of mercy, but God has not shown the entirely human weakness of tears. The oppositions between anger-mercy, fire-garden, darkness-light, and weeping-laughter will be resolved on our return to God, so that, in line with the principle inscribed on His Throne that "My mercy surpasses My wrath," the fullness of mercy, the garden, light, and laughter will prevail.

The *sahat-kula* or clock tower in the *čaršija* announces God's creation at every moment, which is equivalent to God's constant proximity and remoteness. God is closer to us than the jugular vein.[24] He is not comparable to anything.[25] The clock tower is the other upright in the *čaršija*. It is outside the mosque complex. Although lower than the minaret, its role is to overtop the plane of the *čaršija*, to be visible from all sides, so that the striking of its hourly bell is audible throughout the town.

The visibility of the clock tower reminds us of the Hour as the Real and Its revelation. The possibility of our return is never to be deferred, any more than the absence of the truth. All we have is our "now," as both past and present are illusions which conceal our essence or heart, as this veil seems to us to be a product of creation itself and not of our own confusion.

Seeing that clock on the tower and hearing it mark the hour remind us of our "now." And with this reminder, which is the highest moment of humanity, we are also offered virtue, the way, and knowledge as means of liberation from the violence of the self and of salvation through the mercy of the Self.[26]

Fires are lit on the minaret and calls sent out from it at times connected with the positions of the sun and the moon. Responding to these calls involves us in the order of existence and the universal worship of God, offered by the sun and moon and the stars and the mountains and the trees and the beasts. Every second reveals God, so that the clock on the tower and its bell are reminders of God:

> Whithersoever you turn there is the face of God.[27]

> And God summons to the abode of peace and he guides whomsoever he will to an upright path.[28]

With its marking of the hour and its hands, the clock tower bears witness to the cosmic order as God's speech to humanity. It is located in the north-east corner of the *čaršija*. It brings about a conversation between the shops and the reading room, on the one hand, and the mosque with the *mekteb* and the *musafirhana*, on the other. What the clock tower announces as the cosmic order, the muezzin expresses in doctrinal terms. The horizons, with everything they embrace, ceaselessly pass from one to the other condition. They stand opposite us, who must take them into our hearts. The things in the world and in ourselves become signs on our path of self-realization in goodness and beauty. All things in this world have their models or exemplars in the higher world. Awareness of the links between the lower and higher levels of the world reflects the connection between human presence on the surface of the earth, the upright of the minaret, and that of the clock tower turned towards heaven. Of this, the trees and the hills and the birds and the clouds and the sun and the moon also speak.

Time is measured on the Stolac clock tower on the assumption that the day ends and begins with the going down of the sun. This manner of calculating time is to be found in the Gospels and Quran. The Bosnian word *sahat* corresponds to Arabic *saa*, Hebrew *moed*, Aramaic *šaa*, and Greek *hora*. There is a significant vocal resemblance between the Arabic *saa* and the Slavic *sad*, the English for which is now.

Raising the clock on the tower, so that it may be seen from anywhere in the town and heard from everywhere, contributes to our awareness of the reality of the Hour and the foolishness of flight from it.

> "For the hour is coming," said Jesus the son of Mary, "in the which all that are in their graves shall hear his voice, and shall come forth."[29]

> As God says in the Recitation:

> Lost indeed are they that cried lies to the encounter with God, so that when the Hour comes to them suddenly they shall say, "Alas for us, that we neglected it!" On their backs they shall be bearing their loads; O, how evil the loads they bear![30]

8. The Guest

The *musafirhana* or guest house signifies the nature of our station in the world. We are guests here, and God is our host. The highest expression of how we relate as guests to God as Host is the affirmation of poverty and plenitude. Human beings are poor, but God is All-Sufficient. This is why human dignity is poverty in the face of the All-Sufficient. We experience satisfaction in knowing our own poverty, because of the plenty we have received, in which there is nothing lacking.

God has sent us down the world as our banquet, and we who serve our guests in His name are His vicars on earth. All we have or can have we have received from our Lord. Wherever we are, we ask God: "Lead me on the upright path, the path of the fortunate!" God is on that path. All we want is His gift of Himself, for He alone is that perfect sufficiency that enriches the poor.

Each merchant is a host, a guest at God's table who has received from Him that which he may use in his traffic with others who have need of it. His customer is his guest. The merchant should never forget these roles of host and guest, recalling the perfect example of the Messenger in all human relations, rejecting the chorus that accuses:

> What ails this Messenger that he eats food, and goes in the market?[1]

For, God commanded the Messenger, who was among men:

> Say: "Come, I will recite what your Lord has forbidden you: that you associate not anything with Him, and to be good to your parents, and not to slay your children because of poverty; We will provide you and them; and that you approach not any indecency outward or inward, and that you slay not the soul God has forbidden, except by right. That then He has charged you with; haply you will understand. And that you approach not the property of the orphan save in the fairer manner, until he is of age. And fill up the measure and the balance with justice. We charge not any soul save to its capacity. And when you speak, be just, even if it should be to a near kinsman. And fulfill God's covenant. That then He has charged you with; haply you will remember."[2]

Whatever our condition, we tend towards that which sustains life and happiness, but the world offers no guarantees we will find what we are looking for. Neither the things in the world nor the world itself are Unity: the things of the world and the self merely reveal Him, and He alone serves for us to find satisfaction.

There is always some knowledge involved in what we do. But knowledge and action are darkness and violence, unless their possession is confirmed by virtue, which is humility and generosity to all. The weaker and the poorer the things in existence, the greater our debt to them and our obligation to generous humility. Nothing is weaker or poorer than the dead. All living things have a duty of care towards them and their places of burial. The Prophet would address those gathered around a new grave:

> Forgive your brother and pray for his existence, for now he is put to the question.[3]

Following the Prophet's invocation, Imam Ali, the son of Abu Talib, used to pray:

> My God, Your servant, the son of Your servant, is Your guest, for You are the best of hosts. Of the dead we know only good, but You know him best. He confessed that there is no god but God, and that the Praised is the Messenger of God and Peace, and the way to It. Forgive him his sin and extend him passage![4]

Our obligations or debts towards the living can only be met, if we meet our debt to the dead unreservedly. The dead have no power, so their claim on us is absolute. This is the basis for our absolute debt or claim on the living. We must understand and accept our link with the powerless as the starting point of relationships amongst the living: the power of the living is dependent and weak, but even it is received from the Absolutely Powerful and Eternal. We are guests of this Eternal Power and must approach existence as such. We cannot even admit the honor shown to us by God as His guest, unless we love His honor as mercy to the worlds. Of this relationship to others, the Praised said:

> Whoever believes in God and the Last Day should speak good or be silent. Whoever believes in God and the Last Day should be generous to his neighbors. Whoever believes in God and the Last Day should be generous to his guest. His welcome is for a day and a night, and his hospitality is for three days. Whatever is more than

> that is charity. It is not permissible for a guest to stay with a man until he becomes a burden.[5]

Each of us is obliged to speak good and be generous to both neighbor and guest to affirm our faith in God and the Day of Resurrection. This is not to repay others for what they have done for us, but because our debt to God and so to each of His creations is unending.[6] The guest has a claim on the host,[7] and God is the true Host. He comprehends everything in knowledge and mercy, which informs our own claim to want that which God wants—knowledge and mercy which comprehend all.

Each of us is obliged to be a good guest. This shows in our relationships to others. House and family provide the first arena for expressing and affirming this decisive virtue, but the *čaršija* is where individuals and households congregate to exchange debts, obligations, rights, and claims. The presence of the *musafirhana* confirms in its every detail the inviolate nature of the guest and the guest's claim on the town and its people. This explains why its form is as an ordinary house of the region, and so of the *stećak*, the house-shaped mediaeval tombstone peculiar to Bosnia which represents our home in the world to which we return.

The *musafirhana* is the most lavish building in the *čaršija*. Its position and size confirm the right hand as the sign of power received and the oath made to God and the Praised. It mirrors the *stećak*, as the house whereby the living secure a fine house once dead, a house in this world which provides and secures a house in the other.

Fortress and plain, like every expanse around the *musafirhana*, confirm its position. Protecting the town and its order is a responsibility before God. We are all His guests, and the most powerless—the dead and children, orphans and the sick, travelers and the elderly—have an inviolate claim on us all. Whatever food we gather comes as a gift from God and we hold it in trust to share with all who have a claim on it.

Waking reality and the dream are two experiential levels of existence. They are similar, but also differ. The world and our selves appear in both as images. Our I participates in waking reality as a free image of its own free will, a free will which is lacking in the dream as image of our world. Still, we want more than these images. We want fullness of life and happiness, always and everywhere. We cannot transcend poverty existing only on these two levels, for the images can never be the image maker.

These images both reveal and conceal. By confessing our poverty, we reveal ourselves as beggars before the All-Sufficient, who reveals Himself through the infinite stream of images of both the waking world and the dream. Through the Praised, God is revealed to us in our own language:

> Lo, there you are; you are called upon to expend in God's way, and some of you are niggardly. Whoso is niggardly is niggardly only to his own soul. God is the All-Sufficient; you are the needy ones.[8]

Our neediness is the failure to acknowledge what we have received. This neediness spurs us to rise above the semblance of property that belongs to us alone. This is pride, the opposite of humility. Pride denies life, as the gift of the Living.

The *čaršija* is a gathering in the center of the valley. This gathering leads towards a hidden core, the human heart, which is like a vessel,[9] as the valley is an external image of the human heart. To recognize the claims of all things means to affirm that the heart is a vessel. It contains only what it has received from God. Fully receptive, the heart confirms its poverty, which allows of no change in comparison to the all-sufficiency of God. To become fully human requires purity and openness, because the self is realized through return. This return always has three aspects: knowledge and love of our goal; knowledge of the path back to Him whom we know and love; and virtue, as confirmation that we are on the path towards the Beloved.

Virtue has the aspect of humility and generosity. Humility does not mean hiding our talents or virtues, any more than thinking of ourselves as bad or ordinary. Humility lies in the clear knowledge of what we lack as human beings and not glorying in what we do have, because we have it only as a gift from God, in His mercy.

Even with all His gifts, we remain poor, but our openness and gratitude for the eternal donation is one way of showing that we are on the path back. Regardless of how far we have progressed on that path, we remain poor, albeit in clear consciousness: we see ever more clearly that we have nothing we did not receive and the desire comes upon us to cleanse ourselves of all that is not Him as the Received.

As recipients, we confirm our poverty and our openness. The manifold reveals Unity, gathering in us through the act of reception. What we have received and gathered we can share, bearing witness to Unity as the core of our being. That is the generosity inseparable from humility. This is the meaning of the Prophet's prayer: "O my Lord, increase me in knowledge!"[10]

What comes to us in dream does not depend on our will. But, waking, our will participates actively in reception and our ascent from willed receptiveness to unwilled receptiveness is a sign of the essential reality that there is no will but the Will.

The sensible world is the revelation of its higher levels and death may be understood as a higher station on our path towards the Living, as Jesus, the son of Mary, said:

> For whosoever will save his life shall lose it; but whosoever shall lose his life for my sake and the gospel's, the same shall save it.[11]

The inevitability of death simply means that there is no life except in the Living and that the final meaning of humanity and all our experiences lies in return to God. The Lord stands revealed to those who share this understanding of existence through His most beautiful names and the various levels of the imaginal, the least of which is the world of sensory perception. In the cycle of fall and rise, God's Face is on all sides and every sign in the world or the self reveals Him. This revelation is a discourse directed towards us, but also through us. There is nothing real to discourse that does not have being in and through the Good and All-Sufficient. The Messenger says:

> Whoever believes in God and the Last Day should talk what is good or keep quiet.[12]

We relate to the All-Sufficient as Peace through being-at-peace and have a debt to admit our own poverty through the claims of others in need. Meeting their claims is part payment of our debt to God the Provider:

> A man once asked the Prophet: "Whose practice in peace is good?" The Prophet replied: "One who feeds others and greets those whom he knows and those whom he does not know."[13]

This principle leads us to see the dignity in our poverty in relation to God the All-Sufficient and to do so by giving to the poor. Being–at-peace is being in relation to the Peace in each of us. If we want Peace as our starting place and refuge, we must recognize Him and will Peace in all of us. If we deny another food, we deny it ourselves; if we deny Peace, we deny it ourselves. Insisting on what is "ours" and denying that it has been given us as an obligation, we take our own self for our God. Then, the self is expressed in passion, and it is when it acts under the guidance of passion that it is in error, as God says:

> Hast thou seen him who has taken his caprice to be his god, and God has led him astray out of a knowledge, and set a seal upon his hearing and his heart, and laid a covering on his eyes?[14]

Whenever we are with others, we are both host and guest. The balance depends on us and them, which means on everyone, both living and dead, both past and to come. We, so long as we have life, will, power, knowledge, speech, hearing, and sight, have a debt to all, as all have a claim on us, insofar as we have received from God. For, truly, those to whom God gives are always poor.

So long as we remain in the world, we are strangers and guests. But were we to go to the House of Peace, that most beautiful height on which we were created, were we to return there from the lowest depth we reached, we would surely be host to the Praised as the most beautiful example and the lamp which shines. The Praised is our living guest and always closer than our own selves: "The Prophet is nearer to the believers than their selves."[15] This is so because there is no path towards God as the All-Praised without cleaving to His revelation through the Praised, His servant and His Messenger.

The Praised is, accordingly, the highest possibility of every self. All of God's prophets have spoken of this moment, as witnesses of the Praised, and the faithful relate to God the Faithful through confidence or faith. The faithful are always open, in ceaseless progress towards the Faithful and discovery of Him. Their desire to unite with the Faithful is their love of Him, and the Praised is our guide on that path. This is because the path of liberation is straight, from any point towards the absolute. On that path, the Praised is always in front of us, always on that point towards which the traveler is rising. Regardless of how high the self has risen, the Praised remains a higher moment or possibility. Wherever we may have come to, the Praised remains above us, closer to God who is on the upright path, but as its destination. Love of the Praised is the love of God, as he says:

> None of you is a believer till I am dearer to him than his child, his father and the whole of mankind.[16]

The guesthouse occupies the entire right side of the *čaršija* proper, as a reminder of how we relate to God through the most beautiful example of the Praised. God invites us to the feast, but the Messenger is the invitation. Whenever we invite and entertain a guest of our own, we are following God's call and the example of the Praised, who said, after a vision in his sleep:

> It was said to me: "The Master built a house, arranged a feast and sent someone to issue invitations. He who responded to the host entered the house, ate the feast and the Master was well pleased with him. He who did not respond to the host, neither entered the house nor ate the feast and the Master was annoyed with him."

He explained: "God is the Master; the Praised is the one who extends the invitation; the house is being-at-peace and the feast is paradise."[17]

9. The Market-Square

People gather in the *čaršija* from all sides and leave it. This act of coming together is oriented by a focal point, a central point that is in the world, but also in each of us. The world involves both visible and invisible existence and cannot be separated from us. Our abilities and needs are brought together in this one place, with its four sides and invisible center. It is a stage on which our various needs are met—a place for us to offer and seek their satisfaction. It all recalls our poverty: there is always something lacking for which we seek. Happiness and suffering lie in finding or not finding it. The *čaršija* is the great representation of our needs and our desire to meet them.

Order is preserved in this space by all those present, both as hosts and guests—butchers and bakers, cooks and coffeemakers, cobblers and tailors, blacksmiths and locksmiths, coppersmiths and goldsmiths, pack makers and saddlers, bridlemakers and silkmakers, greengrocers and barbers, heralds and basket weavers, coopers and cartwrights, potters and pastry makers, porters and garbage men.[1] All of them are in the same need of salvation, which runs through the multiplicity of the world and transcends it and so, in the final analysis, paradise or hell.

Every transaction or obligation in the *čaršija* carries the expectation of perfection, and that on three inseparable levels—the will and action; faith as love and knowledge; and doing what is good and beautiful throughout being.

The will, love, and knowledge, three levels of the self, are laid bare in their double distinctions: the will is to want or not to want, to take or not to take, to attack or to flee; love is relaxation or bliss with regard to a revelation of beauty, inaction in the face of something which reveals itself as a treasure of the self; but love is also a desire for that which is revealed and which attracts as it relaxes and calms, a burning desire that it be grasped, to unite with it; knowledge is the distinction between the knower and what is known, but also the knower's desire to be what is known. These are the six distinctions of our self in our desire to attain or grasp the beauty of being in the being of beauty as Peace or the Seven.[2]

Rising through these stations of the will, love, and knowledge, we attain the realization of beauty, which the Praised expresses as follows:

> Doing what is good and beautiful is worshipping God as if you saw Him, for though you don't see Him, He, verily, sees you.[3]

The *čaršija* is a market or public area. Looking at the area bounded by the shops, the *musafirhana*, the *mekteb*, and the other buildings, it has an irregular four-sided shape, visibly wider on the left than on the right. The *čaršija* includes the entire market square and endows it with meaning from the lowest to the highest point, from the earth to the heavens, from outside in, and from the corporeal to the spiritual. Market is a name for everything that can be bought or sold, for the totality of buying and selling, and for the place where it is done. The market as a whole includes our relationships to each other, both as individuals and to people as a whole. But this relationship, in so far as it involves the swearing of oaths and the making of contracts is never without the presence of God. Every market belongs to God, sooner or later, inside and out. The teaching of the *čaršija*, how to be within it and the virtue of being so, is contained in "the Opening": "In the name of God, the All-Merciful, the Ever-Merciful! Praise belongs to God, the Lord of all Being, the All-Merciful, the Ever-Merciful, the Master of the Day of the Debt. And Thee only we serve; to Thee alone we pray for succor. Guide us in the upright path, the path of those whom Thou hast blessed, not of those against whom Thou art wrathful, nor of those who are astray!"[4]

God is the King of everything on earth, in the heavens, or in between. That is why they are peaceful: their will is entirely God's.[5] We become peaceful when we make our interior, which means our will, love, and knowledge, into His kingdom and so render our hearts inviolate as His House. Only with God's kingdom in all things and in our hearts can we realize beauty. Once God is King of the human heart, all other domination within or over us becomes impossible. And so, we join in the worship offered by everything on the earth, in the heavens, or between them.

The heart is the native country of faith. It is the core and essence of each human being, the place of intellection, the understanding, and of all good human characteristics. Neglect and sickness of the heart lead to ignorance, covering over of what is known, and invalid attributes of character. Faith in the heart cannot be separated from knowledge and nobility of nature. The Prophet says: "Faith is knowledge that is in the heart, pronouncing with the tongue, and acting with the limbs."[6]

Faith transcends action, but includes it. Action without faith has no value. "Those who cry lies to Our signs, and the encounter in the world to come—their works have failed."[7] Action without faith is possible, but faith without action is not. It is the essence of faith to know that something is the truth and to confess the truth in both words and actions. That is why faith is primarily a way of relating to the Truth and of knowing It, as we want to be what we know and so to become one with the Truth. Love is our connection with the Truth and our effort to unite with It.

We become people of peace through the voluntary acceptance of God's commands. The higher level of this is faith, while doing what is good and beautiful is a condition of the self which includes both faith and being-at-peace. The Prophet says that bringing about the beautiful is the highest level of faith.[8] "And who is there that has a fairer debt than he who submits his will to God, being a doer of the good and beautiful."[9] "God loves the doers of the good and the beautiful."[10] "Surely the mercy of God is nigh to the doers of the good and the beautiful."[11] "God is with the doers of the good and the beautiful."[12]

Doing what is good and beautiful is the way in which to realize our humanity, no matter what the place, time, or situation. For there is no place or time or situation in which we may find ourselves, but God is with us. God is nearer to us than the jugular vein[13] and He is with us wherever we may be.[14] And as follows from the confession that there is no god but God, whatsoever is good and beautiful belongs to God. This is why doing what is good and beautiful is applying and realizing God's goodness and beauty, real goodness and beauty within the self and the world.

Attaining human perfection means practicing the attributes of God, which form the core of the human self, in our actions. This is realization in God's love. There is no area of human action on the stage of the world where such realization of the self cannot take place, so long as we admit our debt to God.

The *čaršija* is a concentration of the world stage. We are expected to pass the test in our self and ascend towards our most beautiful sublimity, which is nothing other than the Self. In the Self all of existence comes together. Only with Him can we encompass everything and be everything. Without Him we are always more or less ignorant and violent.

In the *čaršija*, we are both part of and faced with a multitude of others and the different. In our relationships with them, we are searching for ourselves, for which we require knowledge. Each individual has a duty to search for knowledge on the upward path towards a better and more beautiful level of the self. This is clearly indicated by the clock tower and the minaret, and the *mekteb* and the *kiraethana*, but also all the shops with their different wares and skills. The area of the *čaršija*, bounded by the *musafirhana*, the *mekteb*, and the shops, contains only one roof on four pillars. Under it are the scales and the weights. We bear witness to justice when we measure honestly what we give and what we receive. It is impossible for us to cheat God, so every false measurement is an act against ourselves and no profit may ever come from it.

No matter how well we may come to know the signs in the world or within ourselves, our knowledge is small. "We raise in rank whom we wish; over every man of knowledge is one who knows more."[15] The steps of finding and discovering ourselves have no discernible end. Return is to God. This is why we are strangers in every one of the situations we find ourselves in. This is what our experience in the *čaršija* tells us. We always know less about those we meet than they know about themselves. The individual's right to protect his or her dignity cannot be realized unless we recognize that all of us are strangers in the world and as such sacred.

Expanding the self through knowledge, as the Prophet requests of God,[16] is inseparable from knowledge of the most beautiful names of God. His names are the original models of everything in existence. Knowledge of these names and their consequences brings about the goodness and beauty they require. If we serve God as though we saw Him, become God's vicar, and realize His names within ourselves and the world, we purge ourselves of everything except His Throne: our existence is testimony that there is no will but the Will. We follow the Praised as the most beautiful example, responding to God's Commandment: "Recite: in the name of thy Lord who created, created Man of a blood clot!"[17]

The entire *čaršija* is bounded both within and without by four measurements which correspond to the earth. Our presence in it is a fifth measurement. Our openness to perfection and the realization of our original and most beautiful authenticity appear as the possibility of bringing together and joining heaven and earth and whatever lies between. We contain the six days of creation and the six dimensions of space, so that we are both within them and outside of them. Our goal is worship and Peace, and the number seven is the sign of worship and Peace.

For our relationship to the world to appear in doctrine as a debt to the Truth, we must constantly confess both theocentricity and anthropocentricity, as well as Unity in diversity. The confession of Unity brings everything in existence into connection with God. But, what does this mean to us, to whom the Revelation has been sent down? The Revelation was sent down to us that we might be led towards the light and happiness.

Learning about God's works and discussing them helps us answer the question: why were we, human beings, chosen for the Revelation? No full answer can be given to this question unless we recognize the comprehensive nature of humanity. We have within ourselves something from all the worlds. This means that we have something of both the visible and the invisible world, of light and darkness, and of all that lies between them.

The cosmos is everything other than God. It is the sum of all God's works, and God reveals His most beautiful names through these works on earth and in the heavens and whatever lies between. This is why the cosmos as a whole is a revelation and image of God. Just so, each human being is also His revelation or image. This is why we contain within ourselves all His names: "And He taught Adam the names, all of them."[18]

Human beings have been allocated the position of God's vicar in the world. To be able to govern the world in the name of God, we must subordinate our will to God's, relating purely as servant and Master, poor and All-Sufficient, beggar and Provider. Some interpretations say that the names God taught to Adam were in fact the Divine names. Through them, Adam knew everything God used to describe Himself. This is why by coming to know those names, we come to know ourselves and, consequently, God. It is precisely this knowledge that constitutes human perfection and self-realization takes place in and through it.

We are perfect vicars only as perfect servants. The imperfection of servants, which leads to the imperfection of our vicariate, appears as rottenness in the self and consequently rottenness in the home, the *čaršija*, and the world as a whole.

The only way out of this condition of rottenness is to turn towards what we can be in our most sublime moment, towards the human being as God's perfect work:

> But the most marvelous, wonderful, mighty, and perfect divine act is the human being, who is compounded of all worlds. Everything that is scattered throughout the two engendered worlds is brought together within him. He is the vicegerent of God, the shadow of the divinity, and the epitome and quintessence of the engendered things. Everything created was created to perfect his level. When he attains completion and returns to his own world, the heavens will be rolled up. On that day the bodies will be lost within the spirits, just as today the spirits are lost within the bodies.[19]

In the *čaršija*, as the stage of coming together and departing, we appear as both givers and takers. And such we are, givers and takers in relation to the world as a whole and to our own selves. All of existence—the earth, the heavens, and everything between—is a market. We may participate successfully in that market—in everything that is for sale or purchase, in all acts of selling and buying, and in the times and places thereof—so long as we accept that every trade is a response to God's invitation or call:

> God has bought from the believers their selves and their possessions against the gift of paradise; they fight in the way of God; they kill, and are killed; that is a promise binding upon God in the To-

> rah, and the Gospel, and Quran; and who fulfils his covenant truer than God? So rejoice in the bargain you have made with Him; that is the mighty triumph.[20]

This call by God that we kill and be killed should be considered in terms of the self and the market. The self is divided up in a more complex way than even the most lavish of markets: it has an infinite multitude of needs which appear to it in the satisfaction it feels to be lacking. When we see that lack in the world, we desire to take it and make it ours. But the world is unlimited or infinite in both directions, both towards what is less and towards what is greater. In both directions, it reveals itself as unachievable by our desire to have it as such. What the self that desires its own perfection lacks is not the world. Whenever we suppose that it might be that, the world or whatever it contains as a desirable condition, we limit the self and make it a prisoner of the world or its images. Then the market too becomes our prison and not a confirmation of our openness towards the self, which both the world and all its specificities reveal. When a condition of the self is adopted as sufficient and independent it becomes our master and master of the market. The only way to prove the rationality of such a condition is to deny the other and exterminate it: these are false images of the world taken for real.

But God calls on us to murder every condition of the self which transforms our heart into a prison, in which there is no place for the Self.

10. The Book

The *mekteb* is the place of the book. In the Stolac *čaršija*, it is placed so as to form part of the interior and exterior of both *čaršija* and mosque. It is one of the links between the *čaršija* and the mosque, and, so, of the mosque with the *čaršija*. It belongs to the right-hand side. One ascends into it and descends from it. The sacred arts embraced within the *mekteb* are five—silence for listening, listening for speaking, speaking for writing, writing for recitation, and recitation for listening.

The practices of listening, speaking, reading, and writing give us direction and open us up to receive the Revelation brought to us by God's prophets and contained in the Recitation. The Revelation is inseparable from our essence, but that essence is not its source. God sent down the Revelation and the Book into the human heart. This is why self-realization includes the reception of God's Word into our hearts and its delivery in human speech. This process of sending down, reception, and giving always involves two aspects—the One in the many and the many in the One, which in turn involve the simultaneous occurrence of differentiation and gathering together. The Book sent down is a connection with God as both Inner and Outer. It connects us with the totality of existence, the horizons of the world, and our own selves, from our lowest depth to the Spirit. This is why the *mekteb* links the mosque interior with the external world.[1]

We are originally so formed that the world speaks to us in its every sign of God as the Truth. And so long as we listen and look, smell, touch, and taste the things of the world with full recognition that there is no debt except the debt to God, not in anything, great or small, then we will be unable to admit anything other than the Truth with which God created everything and which is in every thing. This is why knowledge and ritual and virtue are simply means of returning to God. Whenever one of them is taken without due regard for that goal of return, they become false association unto God (idolatry) and the self is occluded. Such a self loses heart, as unlimited and illimitable by its grasp, for the Throne of God contains nothing but the heart of those who love God in whatever it is through which they know Him, and in this act of love for the known and in knowledge of what they love, the faithful individual relates to Him as Faithful.

The world is the original Book of God, shown us to make clear the Truth for us, but the world is such only to the perfect individual. Once we lost access to our original perfection and fell into darkness, God in His mercy sent us prophets and through them His Word in the form of the various messages or Books. Every human self has the original capacity to receive the message or Book sent down by God through His chosen heralds. There does not exist a people or a language which has not received its Book.

Once the Word and its recipient have become one, which is our highest moment, then the human self has been brought from darkness to light and the Praised is disclosed in that self as the eternally most beautiful example of our return from the lowest level towards the highest height.

As the reception and revelation of God being praised, the Praised is present in every sign and in all of existence. Given that each human being is in a constant state of change, the Praised has been sent to us in each of our conditions, both of life and death, as our path back towards the Living. The expression "Praise be to God, the Lord of the worlds" comprehends both the inner and the outer: when in the outer world we see the act of praise as connection with God, it becomes our only connection with both the world and with God. In this way, the act of praise shapes our consciousness after the perfect example of the Praised, the perfect individual who in his own poverty of heart and spirit received all this into infinite heart, becoming endowed with "a mighty nature" which made of him a mercy to the worlds and the most beautiful example.

Through the teaching of the books which have been sent down, we discover our original purity and the Praised as the most beautiful example and the light that shines through all the worlds. In this way the signs within the world are revealed to us in their authentic meaning, which corresponds to the most beautiful height of our creation and the purity of our perfect beginning. Humanity's return to God, which is to say our ascent on the upright road that connects the lowest level with the most beautiful height, is made possible by following the most beautiful example of the Praised, who is always on that upright path and is always a shining lamp. There is no condition of humanity in which that lamp may be extinguished and rendered useless.

It is not possible for us to reach some level on the road back and that the Praised not remain our guide and perfect example, for as God says, "We have appointed for every nation a holy rite that they shall perform. Let them not therefore wrangle with thee upon the matter, and do thou summon unto thy Lord; surely thou art upon a straight guidance."[2] The number of peoples is the number of rites. But God is one, and return is to him. No ritual can be the goal, for they are all simply means for us to relate to one and the same goal.

The place and the manner of worship and the place and the recitation of the Book become means for us to discover our authentic condition and to return to it as to a lost treasure. But the greatest treasure we can have is love for God, who created the world out of His love in order to show Himself. Once we recognize the world as God's love revealed, we recognize ourselves as beloved, but also as one who loves, and we recognize the signs in the world and in ourselves as the beauty of the Beloved and His disclosure or unveiling before the Beloved.

When this disclosure of the Word God sent down to us as His mercy is viewed from the point of view of the *čaršija*, it has to be recognized that the entire order which corresponds to the ascent from the depths towards the height is spread out from left to right: when we are turned towards the *mihrab*, the source of the river under the mountain is to our left, as is its entry into the valley, the mills, and the *hammam*, the *dershana* and the graveyard, the *kiraethana* and the clock tower. Like a ladder or steps, it all leads to the *mekteb*, raised on the right corner of the mosque complex and above the southern gates of the *čaršija*.

The Book, which God sent down to the Praised through the Holy Spirit, however, runs from right to left. We, starting from our seed of origin in the merciful womb, rise towards the right. With it and from it, the circle is closed: we learn that the entirety of the external world is inseparable from our interior—the body from the soul, the valley from the mount, the earth from heaven, this world from that, and that the quest for the lost center lies principally within us. Within the self, a great battle rages against that side of the self which is not oriented towards the Holy.

The Praised is the perfect example, as the recipient of everything real from God. That is why listening was his most sublime skill. God sent down His discourse through the Faithful Spirit into the heart of the Praised. This is how God's discourse passed into human speech. After he received it, the Praised passed it on, first to himself, that his self might become its full expression. Then he passed it on to the rest of us, and his discourse is the most beautiful utterance.[3] The Praised's own nature thus became a revelation of the Word.

What is heard or said takes on its most beautiful expression in a beautiful transcription: listening is the most sublime holy art in relation to the Discourse God sent down to the Praised; and from these two holy arts, listening and speaking, is derived a third: the holy art of writing. This is why training people in listening, reciting, and writing books is to raise them to higher levels of the self and map out the path from the depths towards the height. The pen in the hand of the writer is an image of the human being in the hand of God. And when the will of the writer is perfect, the transcription appears as fullness of beauty and a revelation of eternity in finitude, but only God's Will is perfect. The consummate writer is one who confesses that there is no will but the Will. Nor should it be forgotten that the Intellect or firstborn of God's creation is equivalent to the Pen[4] and that the Intellect and Pen are perfectly obedient to God.

The ascent to the *mekteb*, open as it is on three sides to the world—south, west, and north—signifies our ascent from the depth and the darkness towards the height and the light. Both human beings and the world, apart and together, are distinguished into a visible and an invisible side. Whatever may be seen within us or within the world is merely a revelation or a sign of the side that is hidden. Nothing which discloses the Creator is Him. Neither is there anything real, beyond Him. Being in the world and confessing that there is no god but God means believing in the mystery that is constantly both concealing and disclosing itself, both near and far.

These signs are in the world and around us so that we may realize ourselves within all of existence. These signs are shown to us on our path of transcending or resolving duality. While the world always shows itself to us through complementary pairs—body and spirit, valley and mount, earth and heaven, darkness and light, male and female, and so on, we are expected and required to confess that there is no god but God, that He is One, not born and without offspring, as no one is equal unto Him.[5] Confessing Him, we realize His attributes within our own selves, and we come to know His creation of everything as the revelation of non-duality. And this revelation is will, whereby we, as beings of will, are participants in God's revelation of Himself, both as servant and vicar, recipient and giver.

As Creator and Guardian of His creations, God is always with them. They never act, without Him being with them. Moreover, He determines and dictates the rules and purpose of human activity. How knowledge is attained and applied in the relationship between God and humanity requires us to participate in the Recitation of God's Discourse sent down to human speech. This is the Recitation sent down from the highest height to the lowest depth through the Praised as the perfect individual in that depth and so the perfect example to all of us, whatever our condition. He who sent down the Recitation is always present, so that listening and remembering, reciting and writing, looking at and reading His revealed discourse are our way of relating to its Revealer. God is present at every moment and He reveals that through the world, through us, and through the Book.

Consequently, there are three sources of knowledge in everything we have to do with: the world, our being, and the revealed Book. But that Book was sent down via the heart of the Praised. For us to accept it as such requires the constant presence of the Praised within the self as a higher salvific nature, as the grace which gives meaning to everything in the world and which does not allow darkness to overcome the light, or error to lose all connection with the Goal.

The book is present in everything the *čaršija* brings together. That is why the place in which it is recited is like a tower. One enters the *čaršija mekteb* through the southern gate and from the mosque courtyard; it is connected with the *čaršija* complex and with the mosque complex. The *mekteb* has two levels: one on the level of the *čaršija* and the other above it. Access to the Book is everywhere—from the mother's lips above the cradle to the final hour, and even after it, from the mouths of those who bid the dead farewell or visit them. But this is always the disclosure of something that has always been in us, as our oath made to God in pre-existence.[6]

The banqueting table in both of the *mekteb* areas, the lower and the upper, is the Book. Children and adults alike gather around it so that they may shape their selves according to the Word sent down and turn themselves towards the Living and Upright Speaker, who is always with them. Insofar as they are honest servants, receivers and bearers of knowledge, they take responsibility for order within themselves and the world as a whole. They are such that no temptation can turn them from the confession that there is no god but God and that the Praised is His Prophet. They may be a minority, but the truth of creation is focused within them.

Talking generally about people, the Tempter said: "My Lord, for Thy perverting me I shall deck all fair to them in the earth, and I shall pervert them, all together, excepting those Thy servants among them that are devoted."[7] That the majority responded to the Tempter's call is not due to his power over them. It is because they have taken their own will for sufficient guidance within the world that they are the majority. As such, they provide proof for the minority who have rested their will with God's. God says to the Tempter: "Surely over My servants thou shalt have no authority."[8]

The insult to the forbidden or inviolate tree, our transgression of the covenant with God, was a consequence of external temptation and voluntary adherence to it. But this in itself can be made right and healed: it is always in our power to repent and turn to God, whose mercy always exceeds his anger. Our arrival to the lowest depth of our new earthly dwelling place established a new relationship with God: "Thereafter Adam received certain words from his Lord, and He turned towards him; truly He turns, and is All-Compassionate."[9]

Receiving the Word of God is both the condition and the means of our self-realization. It is what makes us God's vicar on earth and so responsible both for ourselves and for the world, for the order in which the inviolate shall be yielded its claim and human memory abide with it. We were at peace in the garden, but nothing there depended on us, nor were we responsible for anything; everything was received and there was nothing for which we were responsible except to obey God's order regarding the inviolability of the tree at the center, to be a pen in which everything was focused and through which everything might be distinguished.

Once we had come to earth, our position of being-at-peace received the supplementary content of peacemaking, as active and responsible vicar on earth. The purpose of our vicariate on earth, the fruit of two wills, ours and God's, is constantly brought into question by "historical events" replete with destruction and killing. Our relationship of confidence with God[10] is, so it seems, dangerous for both sides, both for us as faithful and God as the Faithful. There are signs of this danger which God took on before witnesses at our creation:[11]

> Man was seen by them as a dubious proposition in the divine counsels—too frail to be trusted, too arrogant to be thus empowered, too liable to "shed blood and corrupt in the earth." In this Quranic myth of man-the-liability, history is seen as the sphere of the Satanic determination to prove the accusation valid and the divine risk discredited. The very theme of history is that question-mark of human worth, understood as a vital question-mark of divine wisdom and power. The wisdom of God is staked on the credibility of man as its supreme test and venture. . . . The question for God, we may say, is the question of man. The human is in this way the sphere in which the divine is either acknowledged or belied.[12]

11. "Recite!"

The *kiraethana*, which means "the house of reading and reciting," is the far left boundary of the *čaršija* proper. It is open for all forms of human experience and knowledge, coming from all four sides of the world. This openness to teaching and receiving such knowledge confirms our always being both host and guest.

The *mekteb* is in the right-hand corner of the mosque complex, while the *kiraethana* is in the left rear corner of the *čaršija*. This relationship between them testifies to the link between the revealed Recitation, sent down by God to the heart of the Messenger, and all other knowledge and skill, regardless of how or from whom they are attained. Nor is such a marked relationship possible without turning all earthly bonds towards their highest principle, towards the vertical axis which joins heaven and earth, the material and the spiritual. In the sacred discourse of the *čaršija*, it is the minaret and the clock tower which bear witness to the bond between the earthly horizons and the heavenly height. One may say that the *kiraethana* and *mekteb* are linked on the horizontal level in the same way as the clock tower and the minaret under the sign of verticality. The clock tower is to the *kiraethana*, as the minaret is to the *mekteb*.

The emphasis given to right side of the *čaršija*, by the minaret, the *mekteb*, the *musafirhana*, the captain's house, the Opijač house, and, in time gone, by the Šabić and the Tatarević *han*s or hotels, the Šarić house, and the *muselimat* or town offices, is balanced harmoniously by the clock tower and the *kiraethana* on the left.

In this balancing act, it is well to recognize the relationship between the left side, to which the *kiraethana*, the clock tower, the bakery, and the forge belong, and the right side, whose main markers are the minaret and the *mekteb*, but also the *musafirhana* and the *tepa* or weighing station. These are left and right in relation to the path towards the House in the holy valley of Becca.

The name *kiraethana* refers to the key word of the Revelation: "Recite: in the name of thy Lord, who created, created Man of a blood clot. Recite: and thy Lord is the Most Generous who taught by the Pen, taught Man that he knew not."[1] This is the first revelation to the Praised and his first meeting with the angel Gabriel. This meeting and that revelation took place during the solitude of the Praised in the cave on the Hill of Hira.[2]

This revealed word seemed both to its first recipient, the Praised, and to those to whom he passed it on a small but crucially important beginning. With this revelation, everything in the human self and within the horizons of the world took on a different meaning, as if through it everything to whose concealment we had been accustomed now began to show. This is why the Praised's experience meant the opening of the heavens to our rediscovery of ourselves. Nor is it possible to imagine a more difficult human experience: it affects a single self, but spreads from that self to all the worlds, for that self is a mercy to all, revealing the Self through its self-extinction. The majesty of this experience surpasses all spatial and temporal limits, and it seems that the reason and purpose of all existence are within it.

The location of the *kiraethana* to the far left of the *čaršija* speaks of this beginning and this human essence, which God also mentions in talking of our creation from a blood clot, which is to say the human seed or semen, and of teaching us that which we do not know. The apparent insignificance of the blood clot or seed, which nonetheless contains the entirety of human potential, and the emphasis on our relationship with the Lord, His name, and underscoring by the Pen are offered as a complete teaching of our origin, presence in the world, and return to God. Only thus can we and the world appear as two sides of one and the same revelation of the Creator, in which there is no other goal but Him.

Both we and the world embark on a process of self-realization through the confession that there is no god but God, but there is more to it than that. The reality of the world is at all times and places an inexhaustible flow of praise of God as the All-Praised, and the world which receives this praise also reveals it. This is why the world treats the Praised as both recipient and giver. And the Praised, as the highest example of the human mode of being, is the perfect and concentrated manifestation of the world. The signs of this are always and everywhere in the world and within the human self.

Beyond the *kiraethana*, and actually outside the *čaršija* proper, is the *dershana* or "house of teaching." The basic meaning of the verbal root of the Arabic word *dars* is "the erasure of traces." From this it is clear that learning is in some essential way connected with finding, following, and erasing traces. The signs around us and the world and within our own selves appear as traces of the Creator. We are in constant danger of mistaking the Creator's traces for the Creator Himself or signs in the world and in ourselves for the Signified, and so of forgetting Him. This is why we are expected both to follow the tracks and erase them, for our self-realization depends on nothing but God.

If we are mindful of God, then God is mindful of us.[3] When we are mindful of God, we call Him and He responds to us. God told each of us through the Praised:

> And when My servants question thee concerning Me—I am near to answer the call of the caller, when he calls to Me; so let them respond to Me, and let them believe in Me; haply so they will go aright.[4]

The response to God has two aspects—the call and the caller. Whatsoever exists in the world or in our own selves is a call from God to us. None of it can replace the Caller, however, nor does any of it make any sense without Him.

Erasing the traces from our memory to rid ourselves of forgetfulness of Him who left them and agreeing not to represent Him by any form of character,[5] we are led to the hour in the cave of loneliness, in which God made His revelations through the angel Gabriel to the Praised, and through him to all of us: "Recite, in the name of your Lord!"

Recitation is the discovery of our highest abilities, realization of our original perfection, with which and for which we were created, as was the world, which confesses it in relation to God as the All-Praised: "Praise belongs to God, the Lord of all Being, the All-Merciful, the Ever-Merciful, the King of the Day of Debt!"[6]

Beginning recitation in the name of the Lord is the universal seed both within the world and in ourselves. It is precisely this: His wishing something and His speaking it into being: "His command, when He desires a thing, is to say to it 'be,' and it is."[7] All existence begins with these words and the institution of His discourse with the Praised: it moves or unfolds from Him towards Him, from the source of the river under the mountain, on the left, from the insignificance of the seed which bears within itself all the possibilities of perfect character, all the way to the fullness of return to Him, which is signified by development towards the right—the mosque, the minaret, the *mekteb* and the *musafirhana*, the captain's house and the *muselimat*, the fortress and the mosque on the mount, the field, and the remote estuary towards which the River flows.

Nor should one forget that Stolac fortress itself is also a complex that developed around the cave of Veli Dede, above which the mosque that bears his name was later raised.[8] This is one of six mosques within the Stolac valley.[9] The *čaršija* mosque is central and signifies the dominant role of the human heart. There are a further three in the valley,[10] while the sixth is on the top of Vrsnik. Looking at the position of these six mosques, it becomes clear that the *čaršija* mosque is a sign of uprightness and our self-disclosure in our authentic original stature, as may be seen in our original unity or our ascent towards the Absolute. This is why the *čaršija* and the Vrsnik mosques are directly linked, as two signs linking the lowest depth to the highest height. But the Veli Dede mosque, at the heart of the fortress, has its own valley unknown to the vast majority of the current inhabitants of the town. Beneath this mosque is Veli Dede's lodge: rituals conducted in it were so oriented that the cave and Veli Dede's mosque were above them, marking in that way the ascent from lowliness to most beautiful loftiness.

The *dershana* is a house for the recognition of signs, but not for their own sake: the signs within the horizons of the world and of our own selves reveal the Truth, which is always and everywhere the reason and purpose of that which reveals It. The process of erasing these signs while in the house of teaching entails the confession that there is none but He. Beyond the *dershana* is the *hammam*, the symbol and place of purification: we cannot become clean, so long as we take any of the signs for that which they signify.

Once we have become conscious of the call to associate nothing with God, we find ourselves placed on the circle of the world described around the first house in the holy valley. We are both on that circle and on the line which connects our location with the center. Approaching the *mihrab* and so the gates through which the self transcends the boundary of the world requires that we admit our position on the circle and the line: to our left the river flows from its source under the mountain, running on to the right through the fields, towards its mouth at the sea.

To reach the mosque one has to cross over water, from one side to the other. Our path will take us twice over water. The first time is the river, the second time a branch of it that passes in front of the *hammam*, *dershana*, and the shops by the larger graveyard, then in front of the *kiraethana*, the northern gates, and more shops, and then past the western gates and the *musafirhana*. Going towards the *čaršija* and crossing over to it entails passage over the stream in its stone channel. In this way, purity is demanded of all those who enter the *čaršija* and who may be expected to pass from it into the mosque, where this requirement of passage and purification will receive additional emphasis.

This position on the circle around the house and orientation towards it means that we are faced with a near infinite multitude of signs. They are spread about wherever we look, on the earth, in the sky, and in between. When viewed from the hilltops, they descend towards the center of the valley down the stony slopes and gardens, through the thorny undergrowth and the dangerous rocks. In all this, with the thorns and the stones and the snakes and the beasts, there are nonetheless signs of that for which we yearn: for amongst the stones and the thorns there are fragrant, healing herbs and the beautiful blossoms of the violet and the wild hyacinth; above the brambles, the cornel cherry and the almond tree, the pomegranate and the hawthorn flower. In the courtyard of the mosque, there are both male and female cypresses—dark and imposing, with cones that are pretty, but of no use or benefit.

God does not create anything without purpose. The imposing but barren cypresses in the mosque courtyard refer to our place in this world, the world of life, death, and resurrection: at the very core of our being is uncreated Spirit, which we must find as that which is real within us if we are to return to our authentic original perfection. By endeavoring to consume what was not to be consumed, we brought ourselves into the valley which we must now try to turn into a height. That means that we yearn to transform our suffering into happiness by ascending on the upright path, as God instructed us in the Revelation: "Thee only we serve; to Thee alone we pray for succor. Guide us in the upright path, the path of those whom Thou hast blessed!"[11] And our guide on that path is the Praised.

Having reached the bottom of the valley, the lowest depth, we were introduced to space in its six dimensions, the seventh being the way out of it. Everything we do in the world we view in terms of the walls and the corners of that house. The *čaršija* is a labyrinth of walls and passages between them. The curvature of the labyrinth towards the house in the valley and the measuring of all its directions in terms of it are signs of consciousness of the upward path from the bottom of the valley and the house to the seven heavens and the tree. The Praised, who is the guide of all, makes this clear in his own experience of ascent:

> When the Messenger of God—Peace be with him!—was taken for the Night Journey, he was taken to the lote tree of the furthest boundary, which is situated on the sixth heaven, where terminates everything that ascends from the earth and is held there, and where terminates everything that descends from above it and is held there.[12]

According to another tradition, the Praised once met the prophet Abraham by the Inhabited House in the seventh heaven. God himself swore by that house: "By the mount and a book inscribed in a parchment unrolled, by the house inhabited and the roof uplifted and the sea swarming!"[13] The lote tree of the furthest boundary is in that seventh heaven too,[14] which means that the tree is in both the sixth and the seventh heaven: its branches, leaves, and fruit are the most sublime distinction of Unity. Its roots are in Peace. The seventh heaven unites the house and tree as two revelations of Unity.

The house is the principle of the city or town. Just as the trunk, branches, leaves, and fruit are to the tree as a whole, so the foundations, walls, streets, windows, and doors are to the town as a whole. Moreover, both are given as revelations of the heart and the Spirit. But neither the one nor the other is the purpose or goal of humanity. They and whatsoever they contain are simply signs: the garden is represented by the town or city, so the knowledge of the city is the path back to God through the garden.

Human self-realization is oriented through openness towards the recognition of what we have received: we are indigent, but God is All-Sufficient. If we deny our poverty, then there is nothing for us to receive: our role then is to seize and subject, and on that basis construe our life, will, power, knowledge, speech, sight, and hearing.[15] When our self acts out of such a feeling of independence, it requires fabrications to justify this act of subordination. This is the only way to explain the means, orders, and models which become our goals. Nonetheless, there is nothing in either the world or in our own selves that makes any sense except insofar as it signifies the truth. When we take the signs for that which they signify, we fail to recognize our dependence on the All-Sufficient, while making others dependent on us.

As Jesus, the son of Mary, put it:

> Blessed are the poor in spirit: for theirs is the kingdom of heaven!... Blessed are the pure in heart: for they shall see God! Blessed are the peacemakers: for they shall be called the children of God![16]

Only by recognizing the poverty of the human spirit can we expect to discover it as our own essence. Only by recognizing the poverty in our hearts, can we expect to receive or find mercy and grace within ourselves. In this way, we may turn towards "a city that is set on a hill."[17] This city represents our highest possibility and the most beautiful example towards which we ascend as towards a lighted candle. "Nor does a man light a candle and put it under a bushel, but on a candlestick, and it gives light unto all that are in the house."[18]

This burning candle or shining lamp is before and above us as we climb towards the city. It is never held so high as to overtop the city, which is on the highest place. But we travel towards that city, in truth, for the sake of the One whom it reveals. The perfect city is a garden, and the perfect garden is a city. And just as the city derives from a single house, so the garden from a single tree, and the house corresponds to the tree, and the tree to the house.

The world and the self and the revealed Book are all manifest as many signs. Coming to know them offers us, in the terms used by perennial philosophy, a way of discovering, making true, and bringing to realization that which has always been within us as our essence and our highest possibility. Thus, the goal of human knowledge and of the human being is to focus and become one in that sublime possibility. No knowledge of the external world or the Book, or of that which transcends them as their essence, has any meaning unless it leads towards self-knowledge. This is why the seeker of wisdom finds the path to redemption and happiness through knowledge of his or her own self. The self is unlimited in this quest. It is on the upright path by which Intellect, Spirit, and the Word came down from God and return up towards Him. They, Intellect, Spirit, the Word, and the Light, are in possession of Truth, Right, the Debt, Harmony, and Responsibility. But there is no truth without the Truth. This is why everything that reveals the full Truth also conceals It. We come to know the Truth through the signs in the world and in our own selves. We discover It in ourselves and return to It as the One in the many. As William C. Chittick has noted:

> Only what is known in the depths of the soul, without intermediary, is intellectual in the proper sense of the word. No one can pass such knowledge on to someone else, nor can it be found by reading and studying. It must be realized within oneself through a long process of mental training and inner purification.[19]

12. The Scales

Looking at the *čaršija* as an area lined by shops, the *mekteb*, and the *musafirhana*, the most prominent feature to the right-hand side of the trapezoidal area is the *tepa*, a space covered by a pyramidal roof resting on four pillars.

This is where the scales and weights are, putting a clear and definite emphasis on the decisive importance of fair measurement in all forms of human relationship. The world was created in harmonious proportion: the creation involved no imperfection. In this way, the world reveals its Creator as the perfect shaper and measurer, governor and judge: everything He has created is perfect in form and proportion, and we are the epitome of it all. Perfect proportion and form are both the frame and the core of our selfhood.

The world is a revelation of Unity through a countless multitude of pairs: giver-receiver, light-dark, male-female, low-high, hot-cold, soft-hard, and so forth. Coming to know the world means comparing. Comparing means measuring. Analytical reason is precisely that, comparison and measurement.

No comparison or measurement can, however, be perfect. This is so because nothing which exists in a pair is or can be a principle. Final and just measurement belongs only to Him who is neither alike nor comparable, who has no other. The principle of His creation is Intellect, in which the totality of all things comes together. The heavens and the earth and everything between them represent simultaneously the distinction and the gathering of everything that is. This is the manifestation of Intellect through difference. Nothing in existence is ever entirely without connection to Intellect. Nor can it be reduced to any other thing. Intellect ensures authenticity or connection with Unity.

We can approach God only by taking responsibility for every measurement and comparison. The more exact they are, the closer we are to Him. And *vice versa*, the further we are from exact measurement and comparison the further we are from God. This is what the *tepa* emphasizes, as the symbol of comparison and measurement as the means for bringing about justice, which is the speaking and showing of truth. The truth of creation as a whole is simply God: there is nothing that has not been created with Truth.

The presence of God as the constant other in every gathering determines human relations:

> Three men conspire not secretly together, but He is the fourth of them, neither five men, but He is the sixth of them, neither fewer than that, neither more, but He is with them, wherever they may be.[1]

According to God's word in the Book, His presence is essential to all human relations with the other or others. The above-mentioned impossibility of comparison without remainder simply means that the Truth abides with all things: there is nothing lacking or excessive in all existence. Comparison and measurement indicate the truth in everything, but these things are only signs. None of them has any meaning beyond signifying the truth of creation. The point of our interaction with the world is to discover the truth of the self. Any knowledge involved in this interaction is small, but nonetheless sufficient for love of Him whom the signs in the world and in ourselves disclose.

This is the confidence which embraces all our individuality and all human community. In understanding and bringing about our interaction with others, there are always two possibilities. Knowledge and love together are the birth of belief, our relationship as knowing and loving subjects with God as the Known and Beloved, the One, who the knower and the lover trusts. When they are present, openness, which transcends duality, allows comparison and the acknowledgment of difference and so of the remainder which raises us from one station to another on the road back.

Our being is necessarily in the world, which is simultaneously in us and outside of us: it is impossible for us to know something and for that knowledge not to be within us as knowing subjects. Nor is any form of relationship possible to anything or anyone without knowledge. But human knowledge is always small. What we know is at best testimony to what lies beyond or what we may only come to know.

The first possibility for relating to the world and other people involves us recalling God as the Governor and Judge of everything that occurs. This is why every contact we have with other people is in fact contact with God. Everything we have received, we owe to God, but we can acknowledge and return that debt only as He is revealed through the things of the world, which also means through the world as a whole, the people in it, and through people as the epitome of creation.

Once we accept that existence as a whole is God's kingdom, our self-realization becomes the acceptance of His kingdom within our own selves. God is always present and is the King of every day and all that is in them: each of our days is a Day of Debt to the King whom nothing eludes, whether in the world or in us. This is so, but nonetheless we are expected to accept this monarchy and to purge our inner core for His enthronement. We are expected to receive into our hearts nothing less than the entirety of that kingdom and that means confessing our own poverty in our hearts and souls. Absolutely poor, we can receive whatever belongs to the All-Sufficient, for He is All-Merciful.

The other way of relating to the world and other people means excluding or forgetting His presence in the world, relying on our own free will alone and our analytical assessment of what is better for us. Then we consider ourselves independent measurers and assessors and suppose that what we do is subject to no final perfect measurement or evaluation. Analytical reason does not step outside the boundaries of the quantifiable world. We can raise up analytical reason to the indisputable position of our guide only if we have excluded the other world and denied the mystery of death. We will find no answers to the question of death through analytical reason alone. Analytical reason is derived from intellect, for which the world and our own selves are simply means of self-revelation. Intellect is close to both God and the world, but analytical reason is not. Intellect is one, but its unity is revealed through the countless multitude of things of which it is both source and destination. No meaning can be found for any of these things outside of Intellect, whether in their similarities or their differences, and analytical reason can only conjecture ceaselessly at that meaning.

The original meaning of the *čaršija* is the acceptance, signification, and proclamation of order in which God is always present. Two vertical lines in the *čaršija*—the minaret and the clock tower—speak particularly of the constant presence of God and His sending down of the Revelation through His chosen Messenger. These are inseparable symbols of the connection between body and spirit or between earth and heaven. They correspond to the two sides of our debt to God as Truth. Both of these vertical lines hint at the insufficiency of temporal and spatial measurement. The reason and purpose of our presence on earth are not exhausted by the four cardinal points, north, south, east, and west, or the four seasons of the year, winter, spring, summer, and autumn.

We are an upright being, connecting earth with heaven. The verticality of our uprightness corresponds to the steps whereby our consciousness ascends towards God. This is the human debt of uprightness or of ascent through the confession that there is no self but the Self. For, the self is a countless multitude of appearances. Each of these appearances is false. Only the Self is One and Real. Each of the selves established outside the Self is a coverer, idolater, or little god, while our self is expected in its measurements, in its analytical association with Intellect, to topple or overturn all of the false selves beyond the Self, all the illusions which appear in our *čaršija* or within ourselves. Only the Self is worthy of being within the human heart. When that is the case, then the signs of the Self are to be seen in every aspect of the manifold, and its dignity is undeniable and inviolate.

The four seasons of the year are not sufficient for this act of witness, as the human being is not enclosed within time. At any given time, our orientation is towards the Eternal.

The literal meaning of minaret is "tower of fire." The balcony is there to allow a fire visible from a distance to be lit. Fire brings together light and warmth, and light corresponds to knowledge. God is light.[2] His knowledge embraces everything,[3] but we are given little of that knowledge.[4] Since we have been created in most beautiful uprightness[5] and our Creator is perfect, whenever we turn our little knowledge towards God, it is enough for us to love Him.[6] To love God and to follow the Praised[7] is the path on which God has placed us. The union of knowledge and love is faith, and we relate to God as the faithful to the Faithful.

The lover desires union with the Beloved. He desires to disappear or be consumed in the heat of his love. It is this faith, the necessary unity of love and knowledge, of which the minaret speaks as the place of fire. The union of knowledge and love in faith is shaped by the confession that there is no god but God and that the Prophet is His servant and His Messenger.[8] When the meaning of faith, represented by the fire, is expressed in speech, then it is the call of the human voice:

> God is most great. God is most great. God is most great. God is most great. I bear witness that there is no god but God. I bear witness that there is no god but God. I bear witness that the Praised is His Messenger. I bear witness that the Praised is His Messenger. Come to prayer. Come to prayer. Come to salvation. Come to salvation. God is most great. God is most great. There is no god but God.

God calls on us to bear just witness in all things:

> O believers, be you securers of justice, witnesses for God, even though it be against yourselves, or your parents and kinsmen, whether the man be rich or poor; God stands closest to either. Then follow not caprice, so as to swerve; for if you twist or turn, God is aware of the things you do.[9]

Society is made up of its members, individuals whose selves pass through unique but constantly changing configurations. Their free will pulls them in all directions. Society is the framework of tensions and conflicts involving selves more or less remote from or close to Peace. Peace is one of God's beautiful names. Fulfilling one's potential as a human being means returning to God, through all of His names. But He requires of us that we put the name of Peace in first place on our path back. Using this name as a universal greeting bears witness to this, but also to God's affirmation of being-at-peace as our relationship to Him.

Selves come to know themselves through others, whom they necessarily know insufficiently well. Justice is speaking and showing truth, and God demands justice of us. Societies become communities through the acceptance of justice as the form of relationship to oneself, others, the world, and God. The *čaršija* is a stage on which one may see how far or close people are to this requirement of justice. This is why the *čaršija* and everything in it is shaped and ordered so that we are constantly reminded of our original oath to God our Lord. The spaces where human relations take place meet, touch, and separate in the *čaršija.* Each of us is present in our original or authentic dignity, but also with our claims and debts to each other as hosts and guests. Forgetfulness of this appears under the guise of corruption and disorder and lies and false measurement. Corruption and disorder in the *čaršija* have more visible and more destructive consequences than in other places. The health of any community is visible in its *čaršija.* For this reason, there are signs everywhere in this hive of human relations calling us to bear just witness.

The place for public weights and measures is in the center of the *tepa,* under the pyramidal roof on its four stone pillars. Under this roof are the scales—the crossbeam and the weights, the pounds, the cubit, and the bowls. Everything is equally accessible to the one who is measuring and those it is being measured for. The possibility of perfect measurement is confirmed by the fifth door and the human heart, given the preference for perfection in every human heart. This preference may be seen in our desire to be happy and to live on after death.

Perfect humanity is the capstone of the world order. Every part of the *čaršija,* as a sacred unit, speaks in its own way of our search or quest for order within ourselves, society, and the world, that we may confirm through our lives that there is no disharmony in God's creation of the heavens and the earth.

> He created seven heavens one upon another. Thou seest not in the creation of the All-Merciful any imperfection. Return thy gaze; seest thou any fissure?[10]

The order in creation may be read as measure and proportion, as harmony and beauty. As beings created by God with His own hands, we are expected to act in the best way, with measure and proportion, harmoniously and holistically. The pyramidal roof over the scales and measures in the middle of the open area of the *čaršija* signifies the sky. Measure and proportion and harmony and beauty encompass everything in the sky or on earth. They have been sent down to reveal the Creator, while heaven and earth and everything in between are intrinsic to our being, as combinations of body and soul and everything between them. The capstone at the height of the roof signifies the Praised as the first revelation of divine creation: he is the perfect man through whom God gave the world the ability to praise.

Conditions in the human home reflect conditions within the conscious selves of the host and his fellows. As it is at home, so it is in the *čaršija.* And conditions in the world are reflected in the microcosm of the *čaršija.* But the world shown in the *čaršija* is inseparable from the self-image within the self. The *čaršija* at the center of the world is reflected in the *čaršija* of the self.

13. The House

The bottom of the valley symbolizes the extremity to which we came by the loss of our original and perfect position, our descent, imposed upon us by God as a consequence of our willful insult against the Holy. This descent took place within the human self: the valley in the external world is an image of the lowest depth within our own selves and that which tempts to evil. But even there, at this low point, in the lowest depth, God and His mercy are with us.

Life after the fall offers two possibilities—the first, original and perfect, than which nothing higher or more beautiful has ever existed, and the second, to which we have come and from which only hell can be worse or lower. Just as the first condition should have been preserved, so the second must be left behind or abandoned, as we make our way back up to the highest level and return to what we once had, but lost by violating what was forbidden. This upward path leads up from the self at the lowest level, or that in us which tempts to evil, all the way to the self on the most beautiful height, or that in us which satisfies and is satisfied in Peace. There can be no return without enlightenment of the depth, without a renewal of humility in front of God or consciousness of the seven heavens through which we must rise, past all the traces and all the signs in the world and in ourselves, to the highest height, to our original authenticity, to the mighty nature of the Praised,[1] who was sent as a mercy to all the world.[2]

It was not possible for us to attain or aspire to anything higher than this authentic and most beautiful uprightness of being. Had we accepted the inviolate nature of the center, we could have lived and remained in that state of being what we knew and knowing what we were. But it was possible for us to lose it, and we did. Once we reached the bottom of the valley, there were three possibilities facing us. One was to rise again to our original perfection and cleave to the most beautiful example. The second was to fall even lower, through the seven earths to the depth of hell.[3] The third was to live on the cusp between ascent towards the most beautiful height and descent to the depth of hell: to be in error on the surface of the earth, between the two turns—towards the self in Peace and the self which tempts to evil, between the garden and hell properly understood.

Enlightenment of the depth means seeing the valley clearly, as a sign of our new turn towards God out of the condition we reached when we lost our original station. Its symbol is the House in the holy valley of Mecca, which signifies our humiliation at the lowest depth, from which we are turned by the "received word" towards the most beautiful height. The human is necessarily split between two extremes—the lowest depth and the highest height. The lowest extreme does not terminate in nothingness, not even if we descend past that low point of the valley into the depths of hell, because God's mercy comprehends all: both paradise and hell.

It is with purpose that God's creation of everything allocated fullness of being to us, but it is to be reached by an unknown path beset with risks and dangers. At the lowest depth, the darkness of our ignorance urges us on to descend even lower. But our higher self intervenes, calling us to ascend, for our darkness is never absolute: even in the darkness, light is always to hand, just as below the light, the darkness is never absolute. This pairing stimulates us to turn and make our way towards Peace, which lies beyond that polarity. The human self finds satisfaction only in the fullness of Peace. That is our final abode:

> People of the Book, now there is come to you Our Messenger, making clear to you many things you have been concealing of the Book, and effacing many things. There has come to you from God light, and a Book Manifest whereby God guides whosoever follows His good pleasure in the ways of peace, and brings them forth from the shadows into the light by His leave: and He guides them to an upright path.[4]

Travelling on those roads of Peace is being-at-peace as the relationship between ourselves, as recipients of Peace, and God, as the giver of Peace. On this road, we pass all the stations in order to arrive at the House of Peace: "Theirs is the abode of peace with their Lord, and He is their Protector for that they were doing."[5] We are called to this House of Peace: "And God summons to the Abode of Peace, and He guides whomsoever He will to an upright path."[6] Jesus, the son of Mary, ascends to this house, in order to show the path from the lowest depth to most beautiful sublimity.[7]

The inviolate tree in the center of paradise bears witness to God as the perfect Creator, while the House in the valley of Mecca, as the simplest form of building, announces our obligation to regain the condition we have lost through effort. It is a symbol of the human heart. We are called to consciousness of the fact that we are at the bottom of the valley and that we can arise out of it to the hilltop, that we are on earth but can pass through the heavenly gates.

This affirmation of being at the lowest depth and turning to ascend towards the height involves us in our entirety. This is why all the roads along the hillsides, between the gardens and the courtyard, from every corner of the house, lead towards the *čaršija*, its mosque, and the *mihrab* as the gate to the house of return. Our descent retains the memory of the height, our former condition and the eternal possibility of regaining it, which is nothing other than that perfection in which the countless multitude of things share at all moments one and the same center.

Our consciousness of being in the depth shapes our connection with the Inviolate Place of Annihilation,[8] while our consciousness of the possibility of return and of ascent to the height shapes our connection with the Further Place of Annihilation. There are thus two symbols on earth, one in the valley and one on the mount, which speak of the split within ourselves—one corresponds to our connection to the earth, while the other to our orientation towards heaven. Such is the case with the human self—our lower side pulls towards the darkness and action within it, while our authentic nature, the self which rebukes, turns, and pulls towards the House of Peace, is our higher moment.

The center of the garden is the tree. Throughout their expanses, the trees bear witness to the inseparability of the horizon and the human self, of the horizontal and the upright. The center of the valley is the house. The units of the town are houses and the relations between them. The tree in the center of the garden and the house in the center of the valley are inextricably linked: what was the tree on the height has become the house in the depth. We are expected through our attempt at return to transform the house into the tree and the tree into the house.

One will know the place of annihilation, the place of prostration, by the confession that there is no god but God. Our guide on this path from appearance to the Real is the Praised. For if we love the Real, we will follow the Praised, and God loves all those who follow him who He sent down as a mercy to the world. The Praised is in the house: he represents our essential potential, and so the world axis, and our turning, and ascent. None are closer to God than him, and so no ascent is possible without him: he is the City of Knowledge, but also its focal point. The Prophet says: "I am the City of Knowledge and Ali is the gate; therefore whoever wants knowledge should learn it from Ali."[9] It is important to recognize in this word the Praised, the perfect man chosen by God as His Messenger, and Ali the exalted, he who has adhered to the Praised as the most beautiful example and risen to the greatest closeness to him, becoming the gateway to the city which announces the mighty nature of the Praised as the gift of mercy to the world.

The city towards which the Praised calls is on the mount. Nothing can hide it, for nothing is complete without the presence of the Praised in whatever is built. Only with him can the city be transformed into the garden. And we can understand why the self is clearly directed to prayer in human speech in the book of Psalms, sent down by God to all of us through the prophet David:

> Open to me the gates of righteousness: I will go into them, and I will praise the Lord! This gate of the Lord, into which the righteous shall enter! I will praise thee: for thou hast heard me, and art become my salvation. The stone which the builders refused is become the headstone of the corner. This is the Lord's doing; it is marvelous in our eyes![10]

The house and the city have been planned by proper builders to whom two things appear in everything they do—their under-realized selves and the realized Self of their Lord. Given their absolute poverty, for they cannot have anything which they have not received from their Lord, even their skills and their works announce His Self. And insofar as they see their own selves reflected in their skills and works, to that extent they hate the "headstone" or "the last" and "missing brick." That "headstone" or "missing brick" is the Praised as the finest moment of humanity. Those who know and accept their own poverty will follow him as the proof of their love of God. In their poverty they know that their death is nothing in the face of God as the Living. All the prophets together were insufficient, without praise as the relationship between humanity and God. The Praised is our highest possibility. Without him there is no perfection. That is why all the prophets, all 124,000 of them,[11] experienced the Praised in preexistence[12] as their own seal.[13] And the Praised says of this:

> Both the Apostles and I are like a person who has built and completed a house and made it whole but for one brick. People entered and wondered at it, saying: "If only there had been a brick." The Messenger of God—may Peace be with him!—said: "I am that place of the missing brick and I have come as the seal of the Apostles."[14]

The Praised is the condition of the completion and perfection of both of the houses of humanity, the one in this world and the one in the other. But the grave is a sign of both houses. Every sign on our path back is encircled by graves and graveyards. The graveyards which surround the entire Stolac *čaršija* are called *harems* by their inheritors, a word which recalls the inviolate nature of the human condition even at the lowest depth of earthly presence, even when one enters the grave.

Death and dream, it is worth mentioning once again, are given an entirely different meaning in the holy traditions than is usual for beings closed within just one of the levels. In sleep, we exist on a higher level than when awake. But, with death we cross over to an even higher one. There is no thing and no time that is beyond the reach of God's mercy, which is always stronger than His wrath. This is a rule which He imposed upon Himself : "My mercy takes precedence over My wrath."[15]

Denial of the other world, as higher than the world of sensory perception, entails denial of death. In the absence of another world, death ceases to be the passage into that world and so the turn towards a renewal of life and the resurrection. This is why the vulnerability of the grave is such an important factor in all denial of the matter-spirit and this-other world distinctions, which also means the debt towards our Lord which can be neither denied nor delayed, for it is in every small and every little thing we do. By denying death as the transition towards life, we deny both finally and fully the just judgment for each particle of good and evil done in this world.[16]

Travelling from the house and courtyard along the streets and paths towards the *čaršija* and its mosque recalls for us the full range from the lowest depth to the most sublime height or from the self, which through self-reproach realizes its own absolute poverty, to the house of the Self. This journey downwards and the recognition of the inviolate nature of the depth is brought together in the great symbol of the house in the holy valley of tears, to which we are called as we become conscious of the return to the most beautiful sublimity:

> And when We settled for Abraham the place of the House: "Thou shall not associate with Me anything. And do thou purify My House for those that shall go about it and those that stand, for those that bow and prostrate themselves; and proclaim among men the Pilgrimage, and they shall come unto thee on foot and upon every lean beast, they shall come from every deep ravine that they may witness things profitable to them and mention God's Name on days well-known over such beasts of the flocks as He has provided them: So eat thereof, and feed the wretched poor."[17]

Even though the valley towards which we are constantly journeying, in confirmation of our condition, and the place from which we began our return to perfection is in front of us at every moment, it reveals its meaning in our consciousness of ascent. There is no place anywhere between the depth and the height which is worthy of our authentic creaturehood, that the traveler might take it as his goal, so that it were not merely a station on the road back to God. Wherever we find ourselves, the Face of God is in front of us always.[18] Everything fades except that Face.[19] We are always face-to-face with God. But there is no face except the Face. Our journey back is from the Face towards It, and we realize ourselves in the moment of union, when we see and hear ourselves with God's sight and hearing.

None of the traces in the world or within ourselves have or can have any value aside from Him who left them. It is this that the uprights of the minaret and the clock tower point to. Both are symbols of our return towards the most beautiful sublimity and warnings that the flat horizons of the earth represent a constant temptation to our greed, diverting us from the possibility that we travel towards the Inviolate Mosque and from it onwards to the Further Mosque.[20] Regarding this, God said:

> Gross rivalry diverts you, even till you visit the tombs. No indeed; but soon you shall know. Again, no indeed; but soon you shall know. No indeed; did you know with the knowledge of certainty, you shall surely see hell. Again, you shall surely see it with the eye of certainty then you shall be questioned that day concerning true bliss.[21]

As one passes down Uzinovići street, from Vrsnik in the south, towards the center of the *čaršija*, one arrives exactly in front of the gates of the Old Harem. There, at those gates, the road splits, left and right. The gates lead in to the old graveyard; that path leads straight towards the mosque's *mihrab* from the other side. Above the graves and the tombstones there are cypress trees and the occasional wild almond tree or hackberry: the winter blossom of the almond announces the beauty and scent that comes during the dead time of winter, comes, but passes quickly; the hackberry with its tiny and niggardly fruit warns of the meanness and insufficiency of this world, as well as of the blessedness and fullness of the other; and above them all are the steadfast cypresses, symbols of forbidden fruit which inform our discovery of purpose in our turn towards the House of Peace.

The traveler must turn left or right, so that by taking a new direction he may enter the *čaršija*, and through it the mosque. On entering, he turns towards the peak of Vrsnik, and through this turn towards the south or the House in the holy valley of Mecca he becomes conscious of both of the ways that one can leave the material world—the first which is brought about by death and the other in life through the *mihrab*. But both lead to the House of Peace.

There are two ways of travelling in one and the same direction, from the edge towards the center or the house in the holy valley. One is through the *harem* gates, which involves turning one's back on the peak of Vrsnik, the mount which symbolizes our ascent, as well as the human heart, whose general symbol is the house in the valley. The second is to face towards the *mihrab*, the peak of Vrsnik, and the house. These two ways involve two different approaches to life and death. They confront us with the question of the house as the ultimate goal of all journeying. No house on that path or journey has any meaning other than as an *aide-memoire* that God is the sanctuary of all.

14. Doors and Windows

Some of the heirs to the Stolac *čaršija* say that 99 doors and windows could be counted on the stores and the houses, the mosque, the *mekteb*, and the other ancillary buildings in the courtyard, which together made up the *čaršija* proper. They still say that those who knew the *čaršija* well were able to pair each one of the windows or doors with one of God's beautiful names.[1]

Situating a sacred center requires knowledge of all the most beautiful names. It should not be approached without coming to know and realizing the most beautiful names: they are like steps on the ladder by which one ascends towards the Holy. The holy names were scattered across the horizons, but they were also gathered within the human self before we came into existence. All the names constitute His Unity. Unity is replete with love that it be known as revealed through all the names. These names dispersed when we came into the world, so that the path of our self-realization is the translation of everything within the reach of our sensory perception into the concept or thought of that which is absent, but marked by the present. In this way, we ascend towards that which binds all the most beautiful names to the one, single, and ineffable Name.

The Hour is fullness revealed by time and space through their own measures, from earth to the furthest heavens, from each individual particle to all of existence.

The clock tower announces that the heavens and the earth are pregnant with the Hour,[2] while the upright of the minaret, recalling the relationship between earth and heaven, and the five calls made from it, admonish us that our exit lies at the ultimate boundary of our journey—through the heavenly gates of which all the signs in the world and ourselves speak.[3] These gates abide within every symbol in the world or the human self. There is nothing on earth or in the heavens, no matter how great or small, nor in any other thing that does not celebrate with praise our great Lord. He created everything with Truth and the meaning of everything lies in revealing that Truth to us on our path to self-realization, to be a window or a door that opens onto the Truth.

The fact that we are faced with the world as a whole, as well as with each individual sign in it, has meaning only if it is "In the Name of God the All-Merciful, the Ever-Merciful."[4] Addressing the world and the things of the world and ourselves and all that is within us in this way is to confess that the Name is inscribed in every one of the countless multitude of signs. Our consciousness of this requires that we admit the other aspect of that "In the Name of God the All-Merciful, the Ever-Merciful." And that other side is to say before all: "Praise belongs to God!" In this way, all things are encapsulated within this human relation, so that they are simultaneously both the doors and windows of the world from which we came and of the world to which we return.

The Stolac *čaršija* has not met with understanding in the modern period.[5] The reason is quite understandable: the *čaršija* as a whole represents the unity of holy doctrine and the sacred arts gathered and revealed through individuals who understand themselves as created on the infinite road of return and approximation to the Creator. The modern individual has inverted this image, so as to appear at the apex of the entire development from nothing or some approximation of it to human reason as the greatest achievement in all existence.

Activities take place in the *čaršija* on the basis of the most various forms of knowledge and skill. They range from the simplest weaving of baskets and fabrics to the most complicated art of writing and illustrating the holy books. No matter how simple or complicated an art or skill, and regardless of what purpose it serves, there does not exist one which fails to include some association with the Holy. The things we do have no purpose, unless we discover in and through them the truth that is in every particle of dust to the same degree as it is in the totality of the heavens. The goal is to discover Unity in the greatest possible simplicity. This is why the recitation of the Revelation and the writing of it down are entrusted to the steadfast ear, throat, eye, and hand. In them, Breath is in the breath, Speech is in speech, Sight is in sight, Hearing is in hearing. All additional means are subordinate to human perfection, which alone, in its best and most sublime moment, serves as the servant of God, absolutely poor, but fit to receive nothing less than our Lord.

Just as the quill, needle, chisel, clay, leather, parchment, yarn, shuttle, awl, gold, silver, wood, and stone, and whatsoever else is to be found in the world are subjected to our arts and devices, so we too are at our best subjected to the Creator as the Most Beautiful. It is in relation to God as the Beautiful that we form our nature, so that we receive within ourselves or discover our original beauty. We relate as beautiful to God the Beautiful through beauty.

It is only to the neophyte that the sacred arts may appear simple, sometimes perhaps simplistic. They derive from experience of being in the world, in which everything has been created with truth, and consequently for truth: it is expected of us that everything we do, from the slaughter of livestock to the digging of graves and the creation of grave mounds, be done in the most beautiful possible way so as to maintain beauty as a way of relating to the Most Beautiful. Precisely this is our inevitable and constant being before God, who is always with us.

God is always present; it is we who are in a constant danger of being absent. Similarly, God is always infinitely close to us, but we are always infinitely remote from Him. Our actions, whether in silence, speech, or gesture, are beautiful and good to the extent that we are conscious of the presence of God in them as the Beautiful and Good. Without such consciousness, all our acts, whether in silence, speech, or gesture, are in vain, no matter how they may seem to us. Once we cease to approach everything "In the Name of God the All-Merciful, the Ever-Merciful!", concluding with "Praise belongs to God!", they cease to connect us to God, and if they do not connect us with Him, then they connect us with something else. But there is no god but Him.

Only in this context can we understand the inviolate harmony that exists between the stone and wood, vegetation and water, which enter into all areas of the *čaršija.* Their presence in the courtyards and the gardens, and on the hills which surround the city, speaks of everything which is concentrated in the *čaršija* to bear witness to the human mode of being, the world, and God.

When we lost paradise, its contents did not disappear, the beauty of its waters and springs and paths and trees. They merely became dispersed, occluded, and difficult to approach: wherever they are to be found in the world or in ourselves, there too are obstacles and dangers. Our coming together and returning to our original perfection means bringing together the signs in the world and in ourselves so that we see the truth of creation within everything. This truth of creation connects everything that has been scattered. This is why everything we do must involve knowledge, and behavior, and virtue, which were sent down from the truth and with it, that we might pass over and conquer the obstacles and dangers and find the truth of creation in all that is.

Every thing in the world or in ourselves is a sign. The decisive question for us relates to our approach to the sign, for what we find in the world or in the self mediates or expresses that which is real, which is the only thing that can be found. So long as we find anything there other than the Real, the truth is concealed. If we accept that the sign is part of this concealment, then dealing with it is a means of discovering or passing beyond that which covers. Our consciousness that such passage is possible orients us towards the higher or the signified. This is why one may say for any sign in the world or the self that it is a window from inside out or from outside in;

every sign may be understood as a door through which one ascends from one level to a higher or descends from a higher to a lower level.[6]

Our existence in the city, following existence in the garden, cannot be comprehended except as a descent from the higher to the lower. Doctrine, virtue, and ritual, to which the city serves as stage and frame, are a constant reminder of return from the lower to the higher, from the city to the garden. This is why, insofar as they lack connection with the signs and their two sides, the inside and the outside, windows and doors, whether given or something that we continuously build, can neither be seen nor walked through. Their purpose is to open a stage on our journey back, our discovery of ourselves as indigent recipients to whom God gives Himself.

But, every other thing, from the tiniest to the greatest in the world or in us, partakes, in line with this, of the nature of both door and window. So it is with all human acts: God created us and whatever it is we do.[7] But the windows and the doors are ordered from the lowest towards the highest, and from the little towards the great. The earth, with its wide windows and doors, is turned or open towards the heavens. A ladder leads from it to the heavenly infinite: from above, water and the Word descend, but they too return towards heaven. All the passages from the surface of the earth towards its interior are narrow. However hard we try to hide within the earth, she prevents it. Only our grave is there, and even in it we wait for resurrection. We enter it that we might rise again and leave it. So too it is with our bodily relationship towards heaven: the only passage is the spirit, and that requires guidance which includes doctrine, ritual, and virtue. People are scattered, but we come together only with Him who brings together. For, God says to the Praised, the most beautiful example and a mercy to the worlds, of his presence amongst the scattered people:

> And if their turning away is distressful for thee, why, if thou canst seek out a hole in the earth, or a ladder in heaven, to bring them some sign—but had God willed, He would have gathered them to the guidance; so be not thou one of the ignorant.[8]

Neither window nor door exists for us, if we enter or exit on the road without God's guidance. The Praised is the guide on that road, because God leads him. The world lies in front of us. It is spread around us in all directions. If we desire it as a stage for discovering what we do not know and acquiring what we do not have, then the self and the world as a whole are at war. In all our attempts to find fault with the world and justify a war against it, that we may fix it, we return to ourselves both tired and confused: the impact of that warfare and fixing is always the spread of corruption.

If one takes the world as a gift or book sent down by the Creator to serve as a mirror for the self, clear of any distortion, then the world as a whole appears in the guise of the garden or city. Every tree bears witness to the inviolate center, while every window opens onto the goal towards which we journey. What we see in the world and in the self, through the windows of the signs and the doors of the heavens, is the essence of our hearts which comprehend immeasurably more than the heavens and the earth.

When we say that the total process of return includes knowledge, the path, and virtue, we are indicating our orientation towards Unity from whatever condition we happen to be in. God comprehends everything through His knowledge, and there is nothing, no matter how large or small, that is beyond His knowledge. Every process by which we come to know involves a relationship between us as knowing subjects and God as the Known. When this is our orientation, then our knowledge comes from God and is revealed doctrine. Whatever we do will then be connection or sacrifice—connection as affirmation that we have nothing we have not received and sacrifice as division of what has been received in order to confess our absolute poverty. Thus we will bear witness to God in everything we know and turn towards Him in everything we do; and our every state of being will be an affirmation of poverty and the passing on of what we have received to others. Thus shall we come to know and confess God as the Giver.

The openness of the valley, and consequently of the *čaršija*, towards heaven, all the doors and all the windows, announce that no human action is entirely meaningless, any more than any divine act is without point: "He created the heavens and the earth in Truth."[9]

This is why we are expected to realize ourselves by always acting in such a way that we find both windows and doors through which to look and ascend to a higher level within the self. Nothing, literally nothing, has meaning without these windows and doors. Through them we connect with the Praised and follow him in our love towards God. Nothing we do is beyond doctrine, ritual, and virtue.

This is even the case with the drinking of coffee. If served properly, coffee is always prepared for the individual, although normally drunk in company. The overall presentation is made on a circular tray (*tabla*),[10] with a glass filled with water, an empty porcelain cup (*findžan*),[11] and a vessel with a handle in which the coffee has been prepared (*džezva*).[12] The *tabla* signifies the totality of existence. It is circular, drawing attention to the center. The very same center may serve countless circles: all of which are distributed between the center proper and absolute infinity. Moreover, the *tabla* is yellow and shiny, pointing out that things are signs through which the unity of Intellect or of the Enlightenment that comes from God as the Light is filtered and revealed. The glass of water refers to the purity of existence in which life is revealed. It corresponds to the authentic and original purity of the human soul. The world as a whole is an image of the human soul, while the *findžan* is a reminder of that relationship,[13] and the *džezva* signifies all human action which serves to darken or conceal the unity and purity of the created world and of the human being within it.

There are three signs placed in front of us on the *tabla*, as the symbol of all existence, perfect, given to us that it might reveal the perfect Lord. The first is the water as a symbol of that which God gave to us through His prophets, as Jesus the son of Mary says: "But whosoever drinketh of the waters that I shall give him shall never thirst; but the water that I shall give him shall be in him a well of water springing up into everlasting life."[14] The second is the *findžan* as the sign of our original purity in the perfection of creation, a symbol of the perfect world as image of the Perfect itself. The third is the *džezva*, which means fire-brand; it signifies the faith we put in our own will over and against God's, in our love for a world without God. Such an attitude towards the self in the world is concealment or darkening, ignoring what is most obvious in the world and in the self. "The likeness of them is as the likeness of a man who kindled a fire, and when it lit all about him God took away their light, and left them in darkness unseeing."[15]

The act of drinking starts with the water, so that the mouth and throat are washed to begin with and prepared for the coffee. Then the coffee is poured from the vessel with a handle using the right hand to fill the porcelain cup, whose pure whiteness is transformed into a dark disc edged by a thin white circle.[16]

According to this doctrine, the circular tray signifies the Well-Preserved Tablet[17] or the Mother of the Book;[18] everything that is in existence has its prototype on that Tablet; this is what gives perfect sense or meaning to everything in the world and the self. The water corresponds to the treasure house of life which is raised up in its relationship with Spirit, while the vessel with coffee corresponds to the brand as the symbol of enlightenment and understanding, which are subject to the Will. Once we desist from bearing witness that there is no will except the Will, our right hand, or the power that has been given to us, takes over the government of the brand or the lamp, so that we may become its bearer and order the world as disorderly. Then we take our own selves for independent and sufficient for the governance of both ourselves and the world. This endeavor gives rise to darkness and evil, which is action in ignorance, which is in turn the sense of sufficiency when it comes to guiding oneself towards the best goal.

Evil enters the world through us: we darken our own selves through action based on the conviction that there are no obstacles to our will and that there is nothing inviolate or whose consumption is forbidden. This is the source of corruption and disorder in the world.

Return to purity is the turn from everything towards the Truth, admitting poverty in relation to God. All the worlds, the earth and the heavens, and everything between them were created perfect. But human beings possess will, which relates us to our perfect Creator. Our attempts to rearrange or fix the world on the basis of our enlightenment and understanding, as that which we govern with our powers (symbolized by the torch in our hand), results in our authentic and original and pure self, our pure and open heart (signified by the cup), being filled with the darkness of ignorance. Violence is any action not based on knowledge. All knowledge is little. Its confirmation is in the self, in the deepest recesses of our humanity. When we are convinced that this knowledge is in our hearts, we may be expected to love that we know this. But we may not love anything ugly or evil. Only God is worthy of our love. When we love God, we come to know His creation and the reasons for loving that which has been created as the Revelation of the Creator.

Thus, ignorance and violence come into the world through our own selves, acting as doors and windows. Were we to return to our original authentic perfection, we would confine the darkness of ignorance and violence within ourselves, that is, subject them to the annihilation of our will, and that is the meaning of the drinking of coffee.[19] Through it, we turn from ourselves towards the Self, from the sign towards the Signified, from god towards God.

Through the recognition of sinfulness and transgression, which are the inevitable consequences of the will of the self beyond the Will of the Self, we return towards our authentic and original poverty, or find ourselves already within it, and approach the gate of our Lord as a beggar. We knock on the door and beg Him that he give us something of the knowledge of the Self, of the mysteries and of lordly things.[20] For, God has called on us to be "Masters in that you know the Book, and in that you study."[21]

15. The Labyrinth

Many writers on perennial philosophy see gold as a symbol of the purity of the original and authentic human self as enlightened and uncorrupted. Each individual is born with this original purity.[1] In all its pairs (matter and spirit, earth and heaven, male and female), the order of the world announces the Unity behind all our experience of both external and internal worlds.

In the world, we experience our own darkness and the consequent lack of clarity of things in the world and in the self. This is because we fell from the station where our inner purity was reflected in the external order of the heavens and the earth. But, there is no loss we cannot recover, no suffering from which we cannot learn. It is our purpose to learn the meaning of things in the world and of that which they announce, namely the Unity that is always both present and absent.

Our search for what was lost and for liberation from suffering drives us from one place to another and causes us to turn from side to side. But, no location or turning leaves us bereft of self: the world constantly extends from us, always gathering again within us. Our self is revealed to us as a center: source and destination. It contains the cause both of being lost and of suffering. Does it also contain the finding of what was lost and the resolution of suffering?

The world is a labyrinth. In it, we seek the center or the peak which brings together the manifold, towards which and from which all roads lead. Within the realm of the manifold, which is always present to us, we seek Unity, albeit partially and falsely, that it might satisfy us and we might thereby have everything. This is a need common to us all. Each of us yearns for what has been lost. None finds peace in our volitions. We search for Peace that we might be at peace. This is why the seeker or traveler after the hidden center or peak also searches on behalf of others and recognizes their paths. So long as there is a single seeker in the world who suffers, no one enjoys absolute discovery or liberation. The seeker and the climber may suffer pain and evil, but they always requite it with good: they pray that good may be to everything that is in existence.

The more the traveler is turned towards what he seeks and the further along he is on the path towards the center, the more he celebrates what he seeks: separation from the sought object becomes increasingly difficult, the closer it is. He celebrates his desire increasingly and yearns for it increasingly; he grieves and cries for it more frequently. Separation from the longed-for center towards which all entrances and roads in the labyrinth of the world lead transfers to the inner core of the seeker: when he has found the center and become one with it, when he has razed and erased his own self, and so all the little gods other than God, who says "I am," then all the roads and all the walls become like a stream of light from that center, like rainbow colors filtered from one and the same arc.

The city has become a labyrinth in which we search for the sacred center of the lost paradise, the original non-opposition of the two wills, ours and God's. The "city" is the place of culture and self-cultivation, just as the "garden" is of agriculture.[2] Everything that we have inherited and established in the city should serve our return to the garden, to the most beautiful height, and so facilitate that our original human nature, symbolized by gold, overcome through its luster and purity the darkness and foulness that has obscured the self in the depth. This is coming to really be through repentance and turning to God, so that He is satisfied with us and we are satisfied in Him. Harmonizing the two wills, by bearing witness that there is no will except the Will, we return from the darkness to the Light, from dispersion to Unity, from fractiousness to Peace. The entire city is a labyrinth in which we search for the sacred center, the inviolate tree commemorated by the Inviolate Place of Annihilation marked by the House.

This sacred quest for the Sacred is expressed by the apples atop the minaret. At the top of the tower of fire, they remind us of the story of being in paradise and how we insulted the center. They warn us that it is only by accepting the inviolable nature of the center that we may discover and disclose our own inviolable core, so that Intellect, Spirit, and Light may take up residence within the human heart.

When our quest leads us to our goal, which is the Sacred, the city will be restored to its original nature as the garden with the sacred or inviolate tree. The city will become the City. Everything in it will bear witness to the garden of the most beautiful height on which and because of which we were created. Then will dawn the day in the world and in us when God's promise will be made real: "Even he who gives his wealth to purify himself and confers no favor on any man for recompense, only seeking the Face of his Lord the Most High; and he shall surely be satisfied."[3] This satisfaction lies in bringing to light and becoming aware of everything in justice: "And the earth shall shine with the light of its Lord, and the Book shall be set in place, and the Prophets and witnesses shall be brought, and justly the issue be decided between them, and they not wronged."[4]

Locating the Book in its proper place means that every sign or symbol will be restored to its original meaning. Everything in the world or ourselves will clearly reveal the Truth. The Book is the collection of all the signs in the world and in us, for there is nothing that is not mentioned in it: "And not so much as the weight of an ant in earth or heaven escapes from thy Lord, neither is aught smaller than that, or greater, but in a Manifest Book."[5]

The place sought is marked by the mosque: its red carpets with vines signify the garden for which we seek and which we may find by following the Praised. The designs on the carpet take the form of the vine whose branches embrace the center, creating a square to symbolize our presence on earth and our attempt to receive here what God has sent down from heaven. The center is the original or uncreated nature of humankind, which the shadows of the world have darkened, but whose light nothing can quench. That center is the divine I: everything announces it, but in such a way that it is always both inside and outside, first and last. However near we come to the center of everything in existence, we can never deny how peripheral everything is. And conversely, no matter how far we stray from the center, the periphery speaks of nothing but the Unity that inheres in and beyond everything.

Love of God, which is the meaning of the red color of the carpet, is the desire to unite with the Beloved. This union, or approach to the Beloved, wherever it may take place, does so through the Praised. Love of God means following the Praised, for there is no return to God without His Apostle.

By following the Messenger we bear witness to our love of God and we earn God's love of us. The rose red of the mosque carpets, as an image of paradise, speak of this love. The entire town, as an obscure image of the lost garden, is turned towards the mosque as its center. All 19 paths on the hillsides, all the roads through the valley and the passes, all the alleys and footpaths, all the ways we take from our homes and our courtyard, from our gardens and our vineyards, through door or window, across threshold and bridge, all lead to the *čaršija*, which is the focus of the labyrinth; the closer one is to it, the greater the temptation. Looking for its hidden center, the inviolate sanctity in the multiplicity of its forms, the traveler searches for him or herself: he enters the state he yearns for as for a lost treasure.

We find ourselves always between the depth and the most beautiful height, and the process of self-realization involves admitting the fact of the depth and our responsibility for it, as well as realizing that our ascent towards our highest moment comes about through the mercy of God. This admission involves the understanding that the center is both holy and inviolate, and everything is in perfect order within it. Everything in the world points to the garden as the image of the center: the perfection of the circle is made clear in everything. Every permitted tree recalls the inviolate center and gives constantly that which could have been our legitimate desire. We could not travel anywhere, did the inviolable nature of the center not guarantee our safety: it protected us on that most beautiful height. In the garden, none of the paths were mysterious: we were always at the peak, so that the upright path appeared to us as the Unity of knowledge and being.

When we fell, we lost the clarity of the center of the garden: the inviolate tree was replaced by the inviolate house. The world was divided into its six dimensions. Each of these dimensions involves a direction, but there is an infinite multitude of other directions between them. The inviolate house reduces the clarity of the circle, which was visible everywhere within the garden, to the square, as the earthly image of perfection. We are expected to discover it in our actions, which are indivisible from our rituals and the knowledge God sent down to us through the chosen prophets. But action has no meaning, unless it serves our discovery of the light of our authentic core. Such action is always virtue, whether in the form of humility or generosity.

We are expected to produce or realize actual perfection from this earthly image of perfection. This is the meaning of each of our rituals, which are focused on the House as the center, as we turn towards it and journey towards it and make the seven circuits around it. That is the house in the valley. It is the fundamental symbol of the city as labyrinth in which we search for the center. If we look at our wider surroundings from any point within the Stolac *čaršija*, we may recognize a number of levels. First is the square on the surface of the earth, marked out by the buildings. At the edges of this square the vertical lines of the pillars and walls, with their doors and windows, rise up. Then, the slopes of the roofs, which draw an irregular frame within the valley, above which arise the minaret and the clock tower, and various trees. And finally, the hilltops which describe the final boundary of the valley at which heaven and earth "touch."

All of the paths by which one descends into the valley or rises out of it, all 19, lead to the center which gathers their differences. But the longer we are in the labyrinth and the closer we are to its center, the more obscure and the less attainable the goal of the journey appears. But this does not mean that the complex space of passages and doors, windows and chimneys, courtyards and fences, flowers and tombstones, does not have a center from which it extends and towards which it leads. The purpose of everything that is there or that might be done there is simply our discovery of ourselves in the world and that harmony and beauty are to be found in everything. To journey is to seek hidden gold, which is simply the light that lies hidden at the heart of our original nature.[6]

On approach, the number of walls and turnings, voices and differences, challenges and threats is constantly increasing. It is only in this concentration that we see the differences of the world from which we come. The *čaršija* brings together traders who are links to the whole world through what they buy and sell.

> They bring them from distant and far-flung areas, by land, sea, plain, or mountain, from where people cannot reach and do not dare to go, for they are peaceful and there is no fear of revolt from them, and they are quiet with no fear of treason. Look after their affairs before yourself or wherever they may be in your areas. Know along with this that most of them are very narrow-minded and awfully miserly. They hoard goods for profiteering and fix high prices of the merchandise. This is the source of harm to the people and a blot on the officers in charge. Stop people from hoarding because the Prophet of God has prohibited it. The sale should be smooth, with correct weights and prices, not harmful to either party, the seller or the purchaser.[7]

Travelling overland and trade do involve being amongst countless differences, whose purpose is the finding of God as Other, through whom the traveler discovers the truth of everything that is in existence, so that he passes through forms to the Unity which is in everything and with everything.

If the *mihrab*, or "battlefield," is a symbol of the center towards which all roads of the city-labyrinth lead, overcoming obstacles and temptations is a war in which we may find what we have lost and come to know the world and our own selves as the revelation of God.

When we are in front of the *mihrab*, the vaulted niche in the wall, it is as though we face the entire world: the self and the world in their full disparity which may be resolved by bearing witness that He has no other. All action—whether movement or skill or act of imagination or feeling—takes place on that battlefield and is subject to the outcome of the war. If the self retains any thing of its own, it will be defeated. But if it acts entirely in accordance with the will of the Self, nothing will remain of duality: the self and the world will be as two mirrors in which the One is clearly seen.

Bearing witness to Unity and the Praised as Its perfect revelation is the meaning and point of all action, and, when actions do not partake of that witness, they increase our dissatisfaction, unrest, fear, greed, and envy. Then we are unable to find any windows or any doors in any thing. All the signs have become like doors and windows which have been bricked up. They have ceased to be signs, and action becomes the only purpose. We seek and develop the arts of deconstructing the world, by material means in a material world, with a self reduced to the material, seeking access to the material, for beyond it and other than it there is nothing.

The *čaršija* calls us to center ourselves on Unity and to bear witness to it as a sanctuary whose entrance is within the self. This active witness involves the entirety of the self, transforming it into nothing, absolute poverty. Thus, the individual becomes the place of annihilation and a beggar: he encompasses the totality of existence and accepts it in its entirety as a gift, and all are called to this act of witness, just as all are called to attain salvation. This is the knowledge which unites the knowing subject with what he or she knows, with the Eternal Principle or God.

Only thus is it possible to explain the meaning of the cross inscribed on the circle as the symbol of the *čaršija.* The circle signifies the perfection of the world as the revelation of Unity. We find ourselves in the perfect world as though in a circle, so that wherever we are, our purpose is to realize and come to know ourselves as the center at which the cardinal points cross. And, our heart is that center. As such, it is the house of God. Opening up our hearts to the praise of God, the Lord of the worlds, the All-Merciful, the Ever-Merciful, the King of the Day of Debt, we become both guest and host in the world, in the full meaning of both terms.

16. The Valley and the Mount

The Stolac *čaršija* is a focus of meaning, due to its situation at the bottom of the valley between hills, which is to be interpreted on the basis of two principles that form part of every sacred tradition. The first is the principle of the confession of Unity. The other is the confession of perfection as our reason and purpose.

According to the first principle, we are all constantly involved in distinguishing truth from lies. The confession that there is no god but God relates to the most evident of the things placed squarely before us. There is no knowledge that is clearer than this. Nonetheless, knowledge is always a relationship between the knower and the known. The confession that there is no god but God is due to our being in duality.

Nowhere can we escape being in duality, nor is there any measurement which can overcome difference or the fact that everything was originally created with truth. Nothing in the world can be reduced to something else, no matter how similar. This aspect of our being is focused in our confession that there is no god but God. And precisely this confession, which is independent of place, time, or language, and which partakes of our deepest nature, clearly sets forth our path.

According to the second principle, we must ascend towards or flee our highest state, which involves knowledge of the path or the seeking of what is known. In sacred doctrine and sacred art, which inform the *čaršija*, we are guaranteed the existence of a most beautiful example and a higher possibility of the self. We may cleave to this example and this higher possibility. When we follow this higher possibility, which is the Messenger, we are on the path back to God.

This most beautiful example is both within and outside us: there is no sign in the self or in the world which does not announce him. We are never cut off from reception and so from ascent towards the Beautiful. This possibility contains and focuses the confession that the Praised is God's Messenger and one of us. He brings together in the self knowledge of our potential, but always as turned towards Peace. He is the first amongst the people of peace, always, both before and after.

Relating to the Praised and his teaching at every level of the self means we enjoy an inexhaustible opportunity to rise towards our authentic and ultimate potential. We were created in most beautiful uprightness, on the most beautiful height, so that our body, which God formed with His own hands, received His Spirit, that it might contain within itself knowledge of all of His names.

But we came down from that most beautiful height to the lowest depth.[1] And that is what the human mode of being is, being sent down to the lowest depth but with experience of the upward path that leads from that extreme condition of humility to the most beautiful height. Ascending on this upward path requires that we bear witness that the Praised is the most beautiful example and the highest condition of the self. The sign of the Praised is his presence at the bottom of the valley of existence, the place of tears for the lost paradise, where the Inviolate Place of Annihilation is.

God carried the Praised from that low place, from the Inviolate Place of Annihilation, to the Further Place of Annihilation:

> Glory be to Him, who carried His servant by night from the Holy Mosque to the Further Mosque the precincts of which We have blessed, that We might show him some of Our signs.[2]

Ascent from one to another level of the self is our way of finding and bearing witness to the Praised. On this path, we are never sufficient to ourselves. None of our conditions on this path is without shadow, and our goal is the Light and exit from the shadow before It. This is why the Praised is like a lamp to us, which constantly burns in front and above us, within the limits of the world and within our own selves. On this path, we are always both host and stranger, host and guest. We are host because we have received into ourselves God's Spirit and all His most beautiful names and confidence. We are stranger, because there is no sanctuary for us in existence so long as we remain separated from our Beloved. And we are guest, because everything we have on our road back we have received from the Host who has made a gift of His revelation to Himself through the existence of everything.

We have a claim on every other individual, insofar as they are hosts. This claim is a consequence of our obligation or debt that we offer ourselves as host to all others as guests. In this way, we fulfill the command of the Praised that we recognize the claim of everything that has a claim on us.[3] This is possible only if we accept in our hearts that there is a God who says: "My earth and My heaven comprehend Me not, but the heart of My believing servant does comprehend Me."[4] Such a heart makes us host to everything God shows us in the world or in our own selves—to everything, but always with greater responsibility towards the weak and the greatest responsibility towards the weakest. Thus, our being host reveals our meaning for others who are thirsty or hungry, sick or persecuted, weak and helpless, deaf and dumb. The limit point of this responsibility is our relationship with the dead. This responsibility is greater to the extent that the dead are unknown to us, strange, and remote.

Everything we have we owe to God, which means that God has a claim on everything we have and do. God gave existence to everything in the world. As Creator and Governor, he has a claim on everything, from the smallest atom to the totality of existence. We have a debt towards everything in existence, because we owe a debt to God, and consequently everything in existence has a claim on us:

> Salman the Persian said: "Your Lord has a claim on you, your soul has a claim on you, and your family has a claim on you; so you should recognize the claims of all those who have a claim against you." The Prophet said: "Salman has spoken the truth."[5]

Should anyone deny the claim of the world and of the things in the world, and so deny his debts towards them, he has turned a deaf ear towards God. Only by recognizing and returning our debts to God do we realize our own claim or right to be entirely happy, through final return to God the All-Merciful.

All things are created with Truth. That is their right. Admitting the truth in the creation of everything means admitting the right or claim all things have upon each individual. We are the bearers of confidence, offered to us by God which we accepted willingly:

> We offered confidence to the heavens and the earth and the mountains, but they refused to carry it and were afraid of it; and man carried it. Surely he is sinful, very foolish.[6]

This confidence, as the relationship between God and humankind, was offered by God. We could have refused it, but did not. By accepting the offer that our relationship with God as the Faithful be one of confidence, we marked ourselves as faithful. By doing that we ensured our little knowledge is always sufficient for the love of God: human knowledge of God and love of God are brought together in faith as our relationship with God the Faithful.

The possibility that we may express ourselves through violence is indistinguishable from our being ignorant. All action based on little knowledge involves the possibility of violence, and we never have more than a little knowledge. We cannot be redeemed from this situation without love: only with love of God, who embraces all with His knowledge, can we establish a relationship with Him as the Faithful. Only love of God the All-Merciful can render an individual of little knowledge merciful. But do we not thirst after mercy?!

So long as we were in the garden and loved God through His revelation in everything, our debt to everything was equal to our claim. The exception was the inviolate or sacred center, given body in a single tree. We had a debt that the tree be inviolate to us and, when we violated it, everything in the world had a claim on us, and we a debt to everything. This was when we were sent down or fell to the lowest depth, to the bottom of the valley. And at that depth and in that low place, we understood the height of the hill on which we had been, but which we had lost by transgressing our debt towards the inviolate tree and the sacred center as a treasure of infinite value.

There was light in our hearts, but the violation of the inviolate darkened and hid it. Everything became remote to us: the sky fled from us, and the fruits that had been within reach of our hand no longer were. Our point of view became inverted. Before the fall, we had looked upon the world from above, so that all seven heavens had been within our sight. After the fall, we looked at the world from below. The seven heavens appeared to us as a single heaven. And we yearned to return, that heaven might be closer to us and multiply.

And we cried, in the low place of the valley, as the ultimate point of our descent. Our sojourn at the bottom of the valley revealed to us the perfection of the lost garden at the peak of existence. Our tears bore witness to God's mercy, which had been visible to us in the garden and approachable in all things. And Mercy was sent down to this lowest human level, to the very bottom of the valley, through these tears: through our remorse, the lowest level became the valley of tears. Ascent started from these tears and their signs, and the prophets of all the peoples and all tongues have borne witness to this possibility. God says of them:

> These are they whom God has blessed among the prophets of the seed of Adam, and of those We bore with Noah, and of the seed of Abraham and Israel, and of those We guided and chose. When the signs of the All-Merciful were recited to them, they fell down prostrate, weeping.[7]

When the traveler in the *čaršija* mosque, at its *mihrab*, turns towards the house in the valley of tears, he faces the path which crosses the graveyard and rises up towards Vrsnik Peak. And when he prostrates himself in worship, which is in principle always an expression of our consciousness of the signs of the All-Merciful and our connection with them through tears, the dry and infertile valley which he remembers in his repentance is transformed into a spring, whose tears connect us to the lost and green garden. These tears swell out into the city, transforming it into the garden, and from that same spring a flood spreads into the city that is purification and grace.

At a place called Zabrđe, which is beyond Vrsnik Peak, to its left, and so also in the direction of the House, there is a well, and around it *stećci* or tombstones. The people of Stolac valley and around come together in this place each year on the day of Elijah, which is also the day of Ali.[8]

Every 40 years, a flood flows from those wells on Zabrđe towards Stolac valley, down the meadows and gardens, directly towards the *čaršija*. By this flood from Zabrđe, which is at once a mercy and a punishment, people are warned and called to purification. For Ali is the door of the gates of knowledge gathered and revealed through the Praised. We may therefore say that the flood comes from the gates of the Praised as the city of knowledge. In his powerful nature, the valley is connected with the mount, and the city with the garden. Following him as the servant of God and God's Messenger, Ali, the son of Husayn, prayed:

With Thee lies the remedy of my illness,
    the cure for my burning thirst,
    the coolness of my ardor,
    the removal of my distress.
Be my intimate in my loneliness,
    the releaser of my stumble,
    the forgiver of my slip,
    the accepter of my repentance,
    the responder to my supplication,
    the patron of preserving me from sin,
    the one who frees me from my neediness!
Cut me not off from Thee
    and keep me not far from Thee!
O my bliss and my garden!
    O my this world and my hereafter!
    O Most Merciful of the merciful![9]

In the valley, we have land from which we may grow things and on which to live and the sky above us. Nothing is so significant a connection between our earthly depth and the heavenly height as the mountains. Their peaks are a sign of return, but the heavens, the earth, and the mountains have no will except the Will: they are entirely at peace and entirely what they know. We have a will which directs us towards the peaks of the mountains as places of ascent. But they are only symbols of our return to God. Neither the mountaintops nor all the heavens are the location of our residence. They are signs on the way. Of those who would ask about the mountains from the bottom of the valley, God told the Praised:

> They will question thee concerning the mountains. Say: "My Lord will scatter them as ashes; then He will leave them a level hollow wherein thou wilt see no crookedness neither any curving."[10]

All our coming down and going up will be determined in relation to that leveling. Only thus will there be a just judgment on our acceptance and bearing of this confidence.

Although valleys are presented in the outside world to us as low places and hills as high places, the final solution of our ascent lies not with them. The ascent is within the self. Only when our knowledge brings about the confession that there is no self except the Self, do we attain the condition of having been raised up, of which God says to us:

> And as for the night, keep vigil a part of it, as a work of supererogation for thee; it may be that thy Lord will raise thee up to a laudable station.[11]

The leveling of the earth and the raising of the self to a laudable station signify the self-becoming of the Praised as the Messenger:

> The most excellent, balanced, and correct of mirrors is Muhammad's mirror, so God's self-disclosure within it is more perfect than any other self-disclosure that there may be.[12]

17. Earth and Heaven

What does it mean to be human?

This question cannot be answered without asking at least another four questions. The first is: what is being-at-peace? The second is: what is faith? The third is: what is acting well and beautifully? And the fourth is: what is the Hour?

Answering these four questions is the way we learn about and realize ourselves as indebted to everything that is through our debt to God the Creator. That debt exists at every moment of existence. To seize that moment or the Hour means to realize our humanity[1] and to take our place at the center of existence, so as to bear witness to the Unity of being. The heavens and the earth are always pregnant with or replete with the Hour,[2] but the non-existent past and future constantly conceal it. All of existence and everything that entails exist within the Hour. Self-becoming through the confession of Unity means discovering the fullness of the Hour and so exiting delusion based on nostalgia for the past and expectations of the future, for human delusion is darkness and ignorance. It cannot be removed without passage through things, and such passage cannot be realized without help that transcends human will.

Our perspectives on the world are perspectives from it, from the earth, which provides us a stable place in relation to all the changes happening around us. We are thus the central thing in all existence. All our views or images of the earth, heavens, and what lies between them are from this central position, which, viewed externally, appears as an absolute depth, the low point of all existence, from which one may rise, but to which one may also descend.

If we wish to know the world and God, we must first know ourselves. Everything we know is cut to the cloth of our self, so that if we exclude the question of the self in knowing the world, we ignore and exclude the relationship between the knowing subject and the known. Then what we know appears independent of us and of our condition. Such an approach towards the known insists on establishing limits within which knowledge has validity: What is known must be measurable. This is the reduction of existence within limits which deny and exclude both eternity and infinity. This world is closed, and one consequence of it is that we too are closed. All levels beyond the limits we have imposed upon ourselves are ignored or denied.

The openness of humanity towards infinity and eternity is precisely the key question for the perennial philosophy.

Both sun and moon, like everything else in the heavens, circle around us. We do not circle around them. Other images, like that of the sun at the center and us circling around it, involve a translocation of our position that may be clearly viewed from outside. This does not put in doubt our central position in the totality of existence. It merely reshapes our continuous experience by imposing on it an image that is opposed to what is clearly evident.

Our centrality presents itself immediately as being in the world: it reflects our continuous experience, so that the world appears as a shadow or the revelation of one and the same principle. The *čaršija* or the cross in the circle is a symbol of our being split between two possibilities—becoming centered and realizing the self within the heart or embracing and making oneself equal to human perfection. The world as a whole reveals human perfection. The human heart focuses it. In principle, the heart or authentic human nature brings together the entirety of the world and so human perfection too.

Accordingly, being in the *čaršija* confirms our connection to the earth: in and through this connection, we understand the Hour as the entirety of existence, in which our self and everything in the world around us are One. Our centrality ensures that from the fullness of its location at the center of the world the self receives and maintains balance, as all possible directions meet within it and start from it. If that centrality is displaced somewhere outside of us, as is the case with the modern image of the world, with the sun in the middle and the world separate from humanity and turned into a means for our action, then the balance becomes impossible; regardless of how appropriate the image may be to the facts, it is contrary to our immediate experience.

By simply looking, we never see a round earth or the sun around which that earth travels. For us, the earth is as we see it—straight as far as we can see, with the sun coming up from the furthest horizon in the east, rising in the arc of its journey, and descending along it towards the furthest horizon in the west, where it sets. Consequently, the sun has a central place in everything external to us: from the earth to the furthest boundary of the seven heavens. It is a symbol of the revelation and of that which we receive directly in our self and by which our interior is lit up.

The moon is also a symbol of this reception and being enlightened. The coupling of the sun and the moon in the outside world corresponds to the coupling of revelation and interpretation. As signs in the world, both sun and moon have correlates in the human self. The sun is the sign of the

Intellect in the human heart, while the moon is that of analytical reason or our ability to analyze the things in the world and within ourselves, the things which are brought together within Intellect.

God's Throne comprehends both the heavens and the earth,[3] but the earth is at the lower level. From this lower level, we may turn in any direction. There is a direction for every star in the sky and a ray which connects each viewer with it. Each one of us is the center for the sky, which is behind everything visible:

> There is no creature that crawls, but He takes it by the forelock. Surely my Lord is on an upright path.[4]

What relates every living creature on earth with God as the Governor is the link between the lowest and the highest, being on that upright path by which we ascend from the depths towards the Highest. The people on earth are governed from His Throne:

> Surely your Lord is God, who created the heavens and the earth in six days, then sat Himself upon the Throne, directing the affair. Intercessor there is none, save after His leave. That then is God, your Lord; so serve Him.[5]

Everything that is in the heavens or on the earth is subject to this government from the Throne: "None is there in the heavens and earth but he comes to the All-Merciful as a servant."[6] The totality of existence and everything in it is poor in relation to God the All-Sufficient, as it owes its reality to God. The gift of will allows us to revolt, however. Our revolt against God is a revolt against our own selves and the truth of our being. Only lies or the denial of the most evident thing which we can know—the truth that there is no god but God—may justify it.

Everything in the heavens and on earth gathers within us. For us, self-realization involves coming to know everything. This is return to God and the approach to His knowledge:

> And thou shalt see the angels encircling about the Throne proclaiming the praise of their Lord; and justly the issue shall be decided between them; and it shall be said, "Praise belongs to God, the Lord of all being."[7]

As the angels constantly circle the Throne, their relationship with God is glorifying by praise. He reveals Himself through praise, for He is the All-

Praised, so that praise is both in Him and with Him. This is why His first self-revelation is as the All-Praised. The angels bear witness that He is the All-Praised through the Praised who reveals Him. But everything which is lower than them in all the seven heavens and on earth also receives the same praise, so that it is a revelation of the Praised, as the first recipient of praise, but also as the one who passes it on to all of existence.

Praise is the relationship of God as the All-Praised who contains everything within Himself and by Himself and everything which, as a recipient of that praise, reveals Him. The fullness of this reception is the totality of existence. Each individual thing, including all the angels, receives only part of the totality of praise. Nothing may bring it all together except the epitome of existence which is human perfection, and that human perfection is the Praised as the recipient of the totality of God's praise. He is, accordingly, at both the beginning and the end: this is the first revelation of God's being First and the last revelation of God being Last. This is the innermost revelation of God being Inner and the outermost revelation of God being Outer.

Regarding this position of the Praised, as the supreme purpose of God's creation, the Council of God and the angels says the following:

> And when thy Lord said to the angels, "I am setting in the earth a viceroy." They said, "What, wilt Thou set therein one who will do corruption there, and shed blood, while we proclaim Thy praise and call Thee holy?" He said, "Assuredly I know that you know not."[8]

This conversation between the Lord on His Throne and the angels circling around Him and glorifying Him about the viceroy on earth, in the lowest depth, below all seven heavens and the Throne above them, indicates an intention which transcends angelic closeness and of which they know not, which is such that it requires of them that they genuflect before its realization through the creation of humankind on earth, given life by the breathing in of God's spirit.[9] As such, with our knowledge of all the names, we bring together everything that is on earth, in the heavens, and between them: we are praised in our purpose. This is the meaning of our precedence over the angels even in our humble station on earth. This is the meaning of the ascent of the Praised from the lowest depth to the highest height, from the Inviolate Place of Annihilation to the Further Place of Annihilation, from the low point of the valley to the high point of the mount, from the earth to the highest heaven.

The Praised says: "I came to know everything in the heavens and the earth."[10] As such, the Praised is the reason and goal of creation. He is the highest human moment: "The Prophet is nearer to the believers than their selves."[11] Whatever our condition, he is the shining lamp and the best example; he is the city of knowledge in which each of us realizes our self. All the prophets bear witness of him:

> And when God took compact with the Prophets: "That I have given you of Book and Wisdom; then there shall come to you a Messenger confirming what is with you—you shall believe in him and you shall help him; do you agree?" He said. "And do you take My load on you on that condition?" They said, "We do agree." God said, "Bear witness so, and I shall be with you among the witnesses."[12]

All of God's prophets spoke for their peoples, at different times and in different tongues, regarding this authentic and original witness of the Praised. This discourse could take on any number of forms, but its essence remained one and the same—the praise of God as the connection of everything in existence with Him. The Praised, as the gathering of all praising, is the best example of this connection with God as the All-Praised. The *čaršija* is a symbol of this coming together in the center and comprehending all of existence. This is the Praised as the Messenger and he abides in us as our highest expression.[13]

The Praised, who said that he had come to know everything, loves what he knows and knows what he loves. His love of God ensures that nothing which he has come to know is sufficient. But with all the degrees of this knowledge, he knows the reasons for humility and generosity in the signs in the world and in the self, which makes of the world a path towards God for him. Because he is above the angels in his potential to know and because he wants nothing but God, the Praised always represents for us a higher possibility of love of God. By following the Praised we attain the divine requital of love.

One may say of the city of Stolac that it presents an image of the human soul. According to this image, the final limits or boundaries of the human self are the hillsides which surround the valley on all sides. Roads lead towards the center of the valley through narrows and along the hillsides; to that same center also come the waters of the river and the mountain streams.

Everything comes together towards the center or the meeting point of the four quarters of the earth. The uneven hilltops touch the sky which covers the entire valley as though it were a vault. The relationship between the valley and the sky corresponds to the relationship between the human body and the Spirit, between which lie all the conditions of the human self, from the lowest to the most sublime. Watchers guard over all the passages towards the valley or towards the center of the human self: they are concerned with all who come, whether friend or enemy, whether stranger or known. They are all there to help us return to God or to turn us from that purpose, and only the conscious and aware, who have surrendered themselves to the mercy and grace of their Lord, can differentiate the one from the other; and only they, in love for that which they know, can find the paths by which we may rise in virtue, humility, and generosity. And every day at dawn, when the birds glorify their Lord with praise and when the hills on the eastern side are gilded by the sun as it begins to rise, and at the end of the day, when the sky reddens in the west, on the hills and over the narrows through which the river flows into the distance, we repeat in our self our desire to find there our transcendence of all seven heavens and that in our day there be no king other than God, repeating the words which God revealed to us as the Opening:

> In the name of God the All-Merciful, the Ever-Merciful,
> Praise belongs to God, the Lord of all Being,
> The All-Merciful, the Ever-Merciful,
> The King of the Day of Debt.

And then, just as in every moment, our recollection is turned towards the center at which the quarters of the earth meet. And the news comes from all quarters of the earth of all the prophets contained in the response to God's call:

> Say: "We believe in God, and that which has been sent down on us and sent down on Abraham and Ishmael, Isaac and Jacob, and the Tribes, and in that which was given to Moses and Jesus, and the Prophets, of their Lord; we make no division between any of them, and to Him we surrender."[14]

18. The Tree

In the divine discourses sent down to Moses and to the Praised in the Torah and the Quran, the condition of the depth to which we came following the loss of the garden, which God had set for us as our original residence, is explained. The core of the self shone with the divine Spirit breathed into the human frame. In the garden, as the original condition, both the horizon and the self were lit up: there was nothing unknown and nothing contrary to human will. Knowledge comprehended everything and there was nothing imperfect within our view.

The violation of sacredness, which is violence or action against the will of God, brought about a darkening, for violence is nothing other than action without knowledge. Then action raises itself above knowledge, and we overturn clarity in its shadow. In such conditions, it seems to us that our will is a sufficient guide in itself. This is manifested as greed: it seems to us that we know even though we do not. Only after experiencing the consequences that come with following such an unbridled will do we learn to know our own inability to be established at the center instead of the Center. This is what the story of paradise tells us: there all the trees were at our disposal and to be eaten of, and only one was inviolate and not to be eaten of.

God made of the garden our original home. Everything in it, including ourselves, bore witness to the Creator, but in such a way that everything was for us. All the external world of that garden was also in the clarity of the human interior:

> And We said, "Adam, dwell thou, and thy wife, in the garden, and eat thereof easefully where you desire; but draw not nigh this tree, lest you be evildoers."[1]

All the expanses of the garden had the inviolate tree at their center, in absolute harmony, and this was also the case in the human self: all the forces were in balance, so that the outer and inner appeared as two sides of the same. Wherever one turned and for whatever one reached, our desire was God's desire: everything we did pleased God, and we were pleased with what God had given us.[2] In this way, everything was in its place and accorded its right.

So it was, so long as we acknowledged the sacredness of the inviolate tree which God had singled out from the countless multitude. Our desire to take nothing from that tree was the same as God's desire. Our knowledge of the tree was only as one in the countless multitude of vegetation in paradise; we knew it as similar and different, as shown and separated, as discovered and concealed. It was accessible, but as such forbidden, inviolate, and sacred. The sacredness of the tree determined the meaning of every other thing in paradise and in ourselves. This sacred and inviolate thing in the middle of the world bore witness to that which is sacred and inviolate in the center of our own being. Through it, both sides of existence, the world and human beings, were clearly linked and clearly separated in the confession that there is no god but God. Our self was illuminated both from within and without, absolutely pure and open to receive everything that was in the world.

The relationship between God as the Creator and us as creatures is established as confidence. God offered this relationship to us, and we accepted it. God invested His knowledge and His mercy, which is all-embracing, in this relationship. And we accepted this offer with knowledge that is always little. And if the offer that a given tree not be eaten of should seem incomprehensible, it is part of the covenant of confidence. By accepting that the fruits of this tree not be eaten, we confirmed the meaning of our covenant with God, which opened up the possibility for ourselves that we might ascend and bring about union with the Beloved. However small our knowledge, it is always sufficient for us to love the Known.

At the moment when we changed our desire to have nothing from the inviolate tree into a non-desire, or into a desire to have, our will was no longer God's, and the two wills collided, and access disappeared to the expansive garden on the most beautiful height. We arrived at the waste of the lowest depth, in the darkness of our will without a sacred center or the garden of the inviolate tree. We reached the bottom of the valley, and there wept bitterly, turning to God and admitting our sins to Him. The low place in the valley became the place of our descent into darkness, but also the place of saving remorse.

In the darkness of our new condition, God showed us the Inviolate Place of Annihilation in sign of the inviolate tree. Road and guidance were set out for us to reach the lost garden, but requiring ceaseless journeying and effort, order and goal. The sacred center did not cease to be. It simply became concealed in the labyrinth of the world and the darkened self. God calls on us to follow His guidance and to pull back the veils over the signs in the world and the self and not to be of that party which covers the signs in the world and in their own selves with their own ignorance, and not to fall even lower thereby. For, falling is action out of ignorance which appears to us as knowledge—violence against the self and greed, in which one follows one's own passions.

Sin and the insult against God's command regarding the fruit of the one tree in the garden that was not to be eaten were the causes of the darkening of the light that is our essence. The balance between the human self and the totality of existence has been overturned. We may complain against our new condition, but it is we who have done true violence against ourselves. This is not what is expected of us, however. Turning from the unreal to the Real, seeking for what is lost, and returning from strange lands to the residence of Peace, these bring meaning and knowledge and ritual and virtue in the new condition. We know what we have lost, and we hope to find it again, but this can be ensured only by relationship to God as the Truth of all existence, whereby we serve God as our Master.

We are at the lowest depth, but that condition is not exhausted by any state of ours. And God's mercy is with us. We may approach this mercy and open up ourselves to it, but only if we admit our own poverty and the richness of God. We may, however, also move away from it and descend even lower, and both eventualities are linked to our voluntary relationship to the truth. Dependent on this relationship, people are divided into those who descend lower, without even noticing it, and those who consciously struggle with the effort of their ascent on the steep path:

> Of those We created are a nation who guide by the truth, and by it act with justice. And those who cry lies to Our signs, We will draw them on little by little whence they know not.[3]

This distinction is our earthly doom. We are split between the earthly depth and the heavenly height, which is shown in us by the limitations of the body and the concealment of the Spirit. We are torn between two minds—one which calls to us from the lower self and tempts us to act in ignorance and another which hails us from the self in Peace and calls us to bear witness that there is no self but the Self. We are always between these two extremes: our self is never free of doubt and recrimination given the possibility of this choice.

Resolving this duality presupposes that we become conscious of the effort required to exit. This effort is the fiercest battle, in which everything human is involved—all our property, all our self.[4] The goal is for us to fulfill our authentic potential and return to the garden, in which the outer and the inner were one.

One may speak of the human beings within the garden as a duality which reveals and testifies to Unity. The garden in which God placed us has its clear image within the self. The couple was united in consciousness of the sacred, whose presence was always and everywhere indicated by the inviolate tree. When we turned our will against God's, the dam broke: we and the world parted company, and we no longer clearly saw ourselves while looking at the world, nor the world while looking at ourselves:

> Two gardens, one on the right and one on the left: "Eat of your Lord's provisions, and give thanks to Him: a good land, and a Lord All-Forgiving." But they turned away; so We loosed on them the Flood of Arim, and We gave them, in exchange for their two gardens, two gardens bearing bitter produce and tamarisk bushes, and here and there a few lote-trees.[5]

The sparse vegetation on the rocky and steep sides of the Stolac hills reminds us that we human beings live in a valley with "two gardens bearing bitter produce." The small flocks of goats which graze there, the blossom of the wild almond trees at the end of the winter, and the sage blossom in the spring bear witness to divine mercy, which He has sent down into the depth:

> It is He who sends down to you out of heaven water of which you have to drink, and of which trees, for you to pasture your herds, and thereby He brings forth for you crops, and olives, and palms, and vines, and all manner of fruit. Surely in that is a sign for a people who reflect.[6]

But, wherever there are trees from which we may eat, there too are thorns and trees from which nothing may be taken: cypresses and hackberries, oak and haw, hornbeam and cornel-cherry, ash and dog rose. Beneath them are scented and healing herbs, but also stinking and poisonous ones, gentle flowers, but also thorns and weeds. All this points to our loss, in which we search for profit, of the confusion which we attempt to transform into justice, judging and distinguishing everything which is in the world or in our own self.

The steep and rocky hillsides are oriented towards the center of the *čaršija*. The meager vegetation on the hilltops is replaced by the garden floors with their crops and fruit: pomegranate and olives, figs and almonds, cherries and mulberries, and the flowers in the courtyards—roses and jasmine, Turkish carnations and hyacinths, geraniums and basil. There are practically no fruit trees in the *čaršija* itself or in the graveyards. Here it is mostly male and female cypresses, hackberries and wild figs, with the occasional rosebush or box hedge, wild vine, or gentle winter flower.

They say that once in the center of the *čaršija* there were two very old trees, an elm in front of the gates of the mosque courtyard and a male cypress to the right in the courtyard. During a violent disturbance, when much of the town was devastated in an earthquake, these two trees disappeared. Both before and after, the only trees in the *čaršija* were cypresses. Their meaning is clear: the city is the place of "two gardens bearing bitter produce," and we are expected to choose the less bitter and thus steadily ascend towards blessedness. The Prophet tells us that the blessed tree in the garden was called the "tree of bliss" because there was none like it on earth.[7] No tree is equal to it on earth, but every tree makes reference to it: the fruit of any earthly tree is bitter in comparison to the sweetness of the fruit of that tree. We are called not to accept any fruit except the fruit of that tree.

Therefore, the male and female cypresses mark out any earthly condition as a battlefield on which bitterness cannot be overcome until we re-enter the garden. The cypresses, as signs within the horizons of the world, remind us of the meaning of our constant turn from the many towards the One, from the lower to the higher, from dark to light, from matter to Spirit. They remind us of the bitterness and poison involved in accepting signs in place of the Signified.

The 19 columns in the *čaršija* mosque and the 19 trees painted on the sofa walls, to the left and the right of the gates which lead into the mosque interior, signify through their multiplicity the unity of the garden around the Sacred. The obscurity of these images, their meanness, and their division into dryness close to fire and freshness close to life refer to the road back, with its many sides and many byroads, to Unity which is the goal of the upright path:

> And that this is My path, upright; so do you follow it, and follow not divers paths lest they scatter you from His path. That then He has charged you with; haply you will be conscious.[8]

Turning towards God means recognizing the depth of our position. Believing in the return to the garden means fighting with all one has and with all one's self to rise up out of the depth and the shadow to the height and the light. This road begins in the depth, in the city as a place of the two gardens with bitter produce, and each one of those trees recalls the Praised, to whom the travelers swear in their search for a way out of the city into the garden:

> God was well pleased with the believers when they were swearing fealty to thee under the tree, and He knew what was in their hearts.[9]

The oath to the Praised under the tree has its image in Mary's giving birth to Jesus under the palm tree.[10] This revelation is not in disagreement with the tradition that Jesus was born in a stable, within a cave. Palm tree and cave, as two symbols, are two sides of one and the same descent and reception of the Spirit: the *mihrab* is a sign of the palm tree and the cave, and it is not to be wondered at that the Lady Mary is present in all Bosnian *mihrab*s, where the following holy text is also practically a matter of course:

> Whenever Zachariah went in to her in the Sanctuary, he found her provisioned. "Mary," he said, "how comes this to thee?" "From God," she said. "Truly God provisions whomsoever He will without reckoning."[11]

The leaf on top of the minaret and the five apples below it refer to the end of human searching in the city: the return of everything to its place and the confession that everything is created with Truth. With this confession, we may exit duality which is in conflict for duality which announces Unity and Peace.

It is precisely this self-realization that is the vision of the tree as the Word, namely that which God sent down to the heart of His Messenger.[12] Only with this Word, which is the essence of all creation and of everything in it, can we attain that self-realization in which there are fruits in all seasons:

> A good word is as a good tree—its roots are firm, and its branches are in heaven; it gives its produce every season by the leave of its Lord.[13]

The world is like a tree. God's traces are revealed through it overall. But they are also gathered in us. "If [the Perfect] Man were to leave the cosmos," says Ibn al-Arabi, "the cosmos would die."[14] The human being is different from all other beings in the world. Only it is an entire disclosure of God. What the fruit is to the tree, we are to the world. Our attempt at self-discovery cannot be satisfied by anything less than the realization of all the names through which God discloses Himself. This is why human love, or the desire to unification with what one has come to know, is our approach to each individual thing and to existence as a whole:

> None but God is loved in the existent things. It is He who is manifest within every beloved to the eye of every lover—and there is nothing in the existent realm that is not a lover.[15]

But the relationship of the lover towards the beloved exists only for the lover's happiness and satisfaction. Insofar as the world is concentrated in him, the lover participates in both dispersion and gathering as the disclosure of the Lover.

19. Oblivion and Recollection

Evliya Çelebi, who passed through Stolac in 1664, makes no mention in his "Book of Travels" or *Seyahatname* of the clock tower. On the basis of this, Hifzija Hasandedić concluded that it must have been built after that year. This assumption is not, however, in agreement with the Stolac tradition that the clock tower was raised 40 years after the *čaršija* mosque was completed, which would suggest 1559.

The truth about the building of the Stolac tower does not depend on any individual human feeling or any sort of record. It is such as it is. Oblivion and recollection are conditions of the human self. No veil within us can destroy the uncreated and uncreateable essence of the self. Recollection always remains a possibility. It is the location of our redemption from the depths and the darkness.

There are many reasons why Evliya Çelebi might not have included the Stolac clock tower in his recollection and record, as well as other details which gave the town its look at that time. Any record is simply a shadow of what was seen. Only God knows what Çelebi saw and forgot, but he did see and record the type of clothing which the people of Stolac wore then, during the second half of the seventeenth century, and how they spoke:

> The people wear fur lined caps and white turbans. They speak Bosnian. But they are true warriors, great friends to strangers, and people of their word.[1]

As to the white turbans on the heads of the old people of Stolac, their gravestones bear witness through the centuries. The word "turban" has in its root a verbal form linked to "dust and earth." It seems to us that the authority of consciousness and knowledge and the feeling of life are comprehensible without death, but it is not so. Life cannot be understood without death. Both our now and our death are entirely certain. If we want to understand our present hour, then it behooves us to accept the reality of death. Our now entails the certainty of life, absolute and undeniable clarity. But, death too is real, absolute, and undeniable. It is clear that these two realities—the living and the mortal now—are two images of one and the same thing. In this image, life predominates, because the world is overall the will of the Living whom death does not comprehend.

The turban, which Çelebi saw on the heads of the people of Stolac in his day and which is today to be seen on the tombstones of the dead, is our crown as God's regent and vicar on earth: until death, we are responsible for this earth of ours, both that which is given to us as a body and that which comprises our existential environment. Around our heads is bound the totality of matter, beyond which is the Spirit. Symbolically, it gathers together the totality of the worlds, but with death this wrapping action ceases, and the turban is unwound into a garment to clothe the corpse on its journey to the grave. The sign of the turban on the grave is a confirmation that business is ended but that the reckoning awaits: the hour of life and the hour of death are shown to be two sides of one and the same act of being.

In the records of the Stolac court for 27 February 1769, the clock tower is mentioned. The record reads as follows:

> Emin-aga Jašarbegović to the *mutevelija* (endowment trust [*waqf*] guardian): the bequeathed sum of money in cash is 50 kuruş. It is entered, according to the statement of the *mutevelija*, that, at the time of the bequest, condition was made for any increase on this amount to be used for repairs and maintenance of the clock tower. With the knowledge of the *mutevelija*, the heirs of the individual named Emin-aga reduced the first amount of 100 kuruş in half. Reduced in half. The 20th of Sheval, [11]82.[2]

This citizen of Stolac left part of his property for the maintenance of the clock tower. The history of Stolac is replete with such bequests. People have left land and houses, mills and money. Everything it is possible for us to own, we have received from God. Returning what we have received is confirmation that we bear witness that there is no god but God. It may have seemed to Emin-aga that the clock tower had a claim upon him, as an omen of the Hour, given that forgetfulness of the Hour is the source of all the confusion in the world. Is not this what is meant by the well-known conversation between the angel Gabriel, who appeared in the likeness of an unknown man, and the Praised:

> Then the man said, "Tell me about the Hour." The Prophet replied, "About that he who is questioned knows no more than the questioner." The man said, "Then tell me about its marks." He said, "The slave girl will give birth to her mistress, and you will see the barefoot, the naked, the destitute, and the shepherds vying with each other in building."[3]

There are many ways to read the record of that conversation. The Hour is the fullness of existence: it is always one and the same, but it may come to be in countless ways. He who knows the Hour encompasses all in his knowledge, and no one does that but God.

The inversions cited—"the slave girl will give birth to her mistress," "the shepherds vying with each other in building"—refer to our arrival at the final limit of corruption of the perfect order in creation. We can never leave our position of poverty and servitude. When we have completely realized our nature as impoverished, we have reached the height of our ability to receive. Then we have become the slave girl. No matter how much we may deny our highest potential, we cannot be the Master. The more we wish it, the more our desire deforms us. Being a shepherd signifies preservation of our original nature, which is confirmed by the earth and the heavens and everything between. There is nothing lacking in all of existence, so that all building should act to confirm perfection. Where this is not the case, we have ceased to be guardians and become corrupters of perfect order. The Real fades within the twilight of the self, and we see building as self-affirmation, even when it is really closing-off of the self and destructive of the material world.

Given that corruption is only possible within narrow limits in existence as a whole, the Hour, as the Real, will play a decisive role in that impossibility: people will see clearly what has been veiled.

The fact that Çelebi did not mention the clock tower or the fortress in Stolac may be understood if one reads his account carefully. At that time, the town and the surrounding area had been attacked, burned, and pillaged by brigand bands. Nonetheless, from his plain account it is clear that Çelebi was arrested by its beauty:

> (This place) is surrounded on all four sides by rock. It is a beautiful small town; it has a major mosque, three small mosques, a small *hammam*, an inn, 10 shops and around 280 stone-roofed houses, with gardens, vineyards, and their own waters.[4]

Without consciousness of the Hour, our turn from the apparent to the real is not possible. If the people of whom the old traveler speaks were conscious of this turn from ignorance towards knowledge, they would have required a clock tower as a sign to be seen above the roofs of their town, whose ticking might be heard in the blindness of the night.

The clock tower was destroyed on the eve of the Second World War, at a time when the criminal project of the destruction of Bosnian cultural heritage took on political form as the Cvetković-Maček pact for the division of the country between Serbia and Croatia. This project was informed by the inherited Christian view of Muslims as fundamentally and dangerously different: in spite of their views on peace and freedom, Muslims were construed as a hindrance and a threat. In the ideologies of the nineteenth century, they were represented as a hindrance to nation building, as that which needed to be excised. Muslims were shown as an obstacle to everything which the ideological picture considered the golden past of the people. Their humiliation, persecution, and murder were presented in advance as a necessary condition for the liberation of the people. All achievements in this endeavor were presented as inverted: the humiliated, persecuted, and killed were themselves guilty of the humiliation, persecution, and killing of those who committed the acts. Thus, the victim became the killer, and the killer the victim. This is the basis for the narrative of the liberation of the nation.

In this way, recollection of events involving people and what they had built was presented in an absolutely inverted fashion. What had been raised that it might be visible and admonish us that it was our purpose to walk humbly on the earth[5] and that we might come to know and affirm that we had been created in most beautiful uprightness,[6] faded from the sight of its owners. The expectation was that by the next generation it would all be forgotten. The clock tower fell silent and then was toppled.

It did not take much time to pass after its destruction—compared to the total lifespan of the *čaršija*—before knowledge of the clock tower was the preserve of very few of the people of Stolac. The place from which one once raised oneself up no longer meant anything. In this way, people began to forget themselves. And oblivion of oneself is oblivion of God, and *vice versa*—to be oblivious of God is to be oblivious of oneself.

The leveling of the entire Stolac *čaršija* in 1993 may be considered a continuation and culmination of the same criminal endeavor which had lasted so long. The destruction of the entire *čaršija* was then achieved. They did not spare the *musafirhana*, the shops, or the *kiraethana*, or the *mekteb*, or the mosque, or anything about it. Nor is that all. The people to whom it all belonged were called upon and expected to admit their guilt for the fact that the *čaršija* had ever even existed. Any memory was to be reinforced by a feeling of guilt. And so memory became worse than oblivion. This crime contributed to the ignorance of the inheritors and the defenders of the Stolac *čaršija* as built heritage of the greatest value both for them and for the world. This is ignorance which conceals both the reason and the purpose of our being in the world at all. Everything in the *čaršija* had made reference to that reason and that purpose: everything had had its image in the self.

The Commission for the Preservation of National Monuments of the State of Bosnia and Herzegovina declared in 2003 the *čaršija* mosque and the *čaršija* in Stolac national monuments of Bosnia and Herzegovina.[7] This decision meant recognition that basic human rights could not be restored in the town without a healthy state and social order, but also without the right to restore destroyed heritage. In this one might do well to recognize that perennial thought of Jesus' words: "Man shall not live by bread alone, but by every word that proceedeth out of the mouth of God."[8]

This is why the restoration of the *čaršija* mosque and *čaršija* in Stolac was a way of opposing crime and advocating human dignity and civic trust. Human dignity finds itself always between denial and affirmation. The inversion of order threatens it, when the beautiful and the good are presented as ugly and evil, and the ugly and evil as beautiful and good.

The destroyers of the Stolac *čaršija* tried to force this inversion of the order of the world on its heirs. A crime was committed against these people of Stolac, but the criminal continues to try to present it as the fault of the victims. It is assumed that these victims are unable to recognize what their rights are and what their debt and that they will crumble under that impossibility, just as their *čaršija* disappeared.

But that is not the case. So long as human beings exist, there is hope that they may discover and find their sublime potential through ascent from their condition, whatever it may be, towards the Most Beautiful.

The *čaršija* is a theater for the concentrated multiplicity of human relations. Our potential does not seem to be tested anywhere so much as in the *čaršija*, from the lowest depth all the way to the most beautiful uprightness. Here we reveal ourselves in all our weaknesses and in our virtues. Only through such testing can we discover and reinforce humility and generosity, clemency and justice. In this theater of life, we are searchers after our own higher possibilities. And it is right for us to know that the heavenly axis of our journey on the upright path has two ends—persistence and restraint. Persistence relates to recollection of God, while restraint tamps down the passions which threaten and disable our ascent from the darkness towards the light.

In every act of our approach to ourselves, to other people, and to the world as a whole, our consciousness of the certainty of the judgment when a reckoning will be made is tested:

> And We shall set up the just balances for the Resurrection Day, so that not one soul shall be wronged anything; even if it be the weight of one grain of mustard-seed We shall produce it, and sufficient are We for reckoners.[9]

Relations with other people are decisive for the self-realization of any self. These relations contain both fatal dangers and saving decisiveness. Insisting on the recollection of God and on resisting our passions, we act well and beautifully in all circumstances. All our friendships will reflect this insistence on recollection and opposition to the passions. No one and nothing will have any significance for us beyond their connection to God as the Truth and the Friend.

Distortion and destruction of the self is the cause of distortion and destruction of the *čaršija*:

> You have only taken to yourselves idols, apart from God, as a mark of mutual love between you in the present life; then upon the Day of Resurrection you will deny one another.[10]

But people do live with distorted and destroyed self-understanding. This is clear from their confusion and the ruins of their *čaršija*. If exit from this condition is sought in the doctrine of our debt to God as Truth, then the desired change in this condition is contained in the call:

> Remember the name of thy Lord, and devote thyself unto Him very devoutly. Lord of the east and the west; there is no God but He; so take Him for a Friend.[11]

> Surely God bids to justice and good-doing and giving to kinsmen; and He forbids indecency, dishonor, and insolence, admonishing you, so that haply you will remember.[12]

Recollection is our return from oblivion and negligence to the confession that there is no god but God, and this knowledge is contained in three books—the world, humanity, and the revelation. This is so since always and forever. We come from it and we return to it. Returning is also the discovery of our original nature which makes possible our knowledge of all the names. Only we comprehend all the names of God. As such, we are the greatest name of God. From the moment we came to realize this name, we have been followers of the Praised. This confirms our love of God, and guarantees that God will love us, if we love Him and follow the Praised.

In all of creation, the capacity to know all of God's names is given only to us. Only we were made after the form of the names which encompass everything, God's names, which include both His fullness and His infinity, His essence and His attributes, His incomparability and His similarity,

His transcendence and His presence. Only the human form describes the meaning of God's reality which encompasses everything.

The city is the image of the garden, the garden is the image of Adam, and Adam is God's image. All of God's names are brought together in Adam. But these names have been scattered in the garden. To this scattering across the garden there corresponds the gathering within Adam. The *čaršija* is the focus of the city. Through it we renew our image of the garden and so of ourselves as the focus of all the names. Ibn Arabi said to us: "You are the clearest and most magnificent denotation of God, for you have it in you to glorify Him through yourself. . . . You are His greatest name."[13]

Afterword

Given the modern project of disenchanting the world, most people today will be astonished by any claim that Stolac and its *čaršija* represent "a city of the Spirit" or "a sacred city."[1] Such astonishment can only be understood if we consider the people who have inherited and built the town over the centuries and how they viewed it. This disenchantment or desanctification of the world, which has taken place principally in people, has rendered many cultures unintelligible and as such surplus to requirements. Their heirs have rejected and destroyed them out of their own ignorance.

The entire Stolac valley (with its *čaršija*, mosque, and *mihrab*, which signify our role as foci of the world), has been progressively destroyed through the twentieth century. This process of destruction has reflected the condition of those humans to whom this sacred architecture and all its contents were entrusted as their most valuable inheritance. The framework of this distortion of the human self and the consequent destruction of their cultural heritage has been the three modern ideologies—nationalism, communism, and fundamentalism. Although differing and mutually opposed, they share one and the same essence. The destruction of the Stolac valley through the long twentieth century is proof of this.

If one is to understand any culture—that is to say, grow into its meaning—one must have love for it. Love is the attraction of what loves for what is loved. This attraction does not allow the lover to be satisfied until he becomes what he loves or comes to know it in its entirety, and so becomes what he knows and knows what he is. Something may be loved only if it reveals itself to its lover through beauty, which bears witness to value independent of time, place, and the forms in which it appears. Every true culture contains and reveals one and the same value, as its material, imaginal, and spiritual content, without which we cannot reach self-realization. These contents are not the purpose of our love. They are simply the constant self-disclosure of Him who it is ours to love in everything and all people, but who may never be reduced to what exists or to the finite.

Every true culture is the harmony of two wills, the human and the divine. Both in what we do and where we do it, we reveal ourselves as beings of conscience, will, and power in the world which has been given to us and into which we have been "sent down" as into the center. At every moment and in every place, we are that center—both as an individual and as the epitome of all existence since always and forever.

The architectural integrity of the Stolac *čaršija*, with the mosque at its center, is framed, when the valley is viewed from a distance, by graveyards to the west, south, and east.[2] The *čaršija* and its mosque are the low point of the valley. All the hillsides come together at this flat point of the valley, as do the paths between them. The slopes let themselves down more or less steeply from the hilltops, transforming into the gentle inclines of garden and courtyard, alleyway and street, as they approach the bottom of the valley.

They say that there are 19 paths on the hillsides, which surround the Stolac valley. It is by them that one descends into the valley or rises up from it. There is the same number of pillars on the *čaršija* mosque. This number signifies the holy name of the Single One. By it we are called to bear witness amongst the multitude of things in the world and the eternal flux that everything comes from Unity and returns to it. This confession is brought to the fore in our descent and return: we were created on the most beautiful height, in the garden of paradise, with universal plenty as the gift of God. The inviolate center of the garden was marked by the tree which God, the Creator and Ruler of the garden, showed to us as the focus of everything which He had revealed through the creation of the heavens and the earth. We violated this center and lost our original purity and our most beautiful uprightness, of which we are reminded by the hilltops and the sublimity of the clouds within the horizons of this world and by Intellect, Spirit, and Light within our own selves, concentrated in the Praised as the most beautiful example.

The insult to the center of paradise brought about the Fall or descent from the most beautiful height to the lowest depth. In this way, we came to the lowest depth, but we preserved in ourselves the recollection of our sublime origin. In our most profound central core, we remember the beauty of our original creation and yearn for it, and try to find it in the world and beyond it, in ourselves and beyond that too. This return is the key question for humanity, as the essential element of all knowledge and all skills and arts, all ways, and all virtue. It is contained in God's words:

> Thereafter Adam received certain words from his Lord and He turned towards him; truly He turns, and is Ever-Merciful. We said, "Get you down out of it, all together; yet there shall come to you guidance from Me, and whosoever follows My guidance, no fear shall be on them, neither shall they sorrow. As for the unbelievers who cry lies to Our signs, those shall be the inhabitants of the fire, therein dwelling forever."[3]

And now we are here—the low point of our soul in darkness, its peak entirely illuminated, with the earth and our grave on it, and God's throne entirely illuminated. Now we are here, at the low point of the valley, at whose center is the battlefield on which we attempt to overcome everything that would prevent us from returning to the most beautiful height. Facing us, at the other end of the valley, is the peak with its mosque. All roads lead to that mosque; each one of them beginning and ending in Unity. Everything around, all the hills and the passages, determine and limit the soul, which wants to return to its Lord in peace. Participation in this return, finding ourselves in whatever is, is the happiness of discovering the unending and always new divine self-revelation in the creation of everything from each moment to the next. This is the knowledge of all the names.

There are signs for us in the world and in our own selves which announce God to us through His most beautiful names. These names are like doors and windows presented to us in everything and on every side.

So it is with the human soul. It includes many windows and doors on all sides. The soul's desire to return to God finds satisfaction in Him and satisfies Him. The soul is split by this between the lowest depth and the most beautiful height. This line of distinction is the path of uprightness and the direction which leads us to find Peace. The Self realizes itself in the world as the stage on which there is neither too much nor too little for us to find ourselves as pure images of our Lord. This is the reason why there are signs throughout the Stolac valley, its *čaršija*, and the mosque at its center that each and every human being is the center and the witness of the Unity of the world, originally established and constantly maintained, and of the Only Creator. Our centrality means that we can always find this vertical line of the self from the depth towards the height, whatever the condition of our self.

God is both our Creator and the Creator of what we do.[4] Moreover, God's creation is perfect; there is nothing lacking in it:

> Thou seest not in the creation of the All-Merciful any imperfection. Return thy gaze; seest thou any fissure? Then return thy gaze again, and again, and thy gaze comes back to thee dazzled, aweary.[5]

Our relationship with God is one of confidence, based on our free will. Whenever our will is not in harmony with God's, then it appears as a factor of opposition to the Will which has given purpose to both the world and to us. This means that the contrary human will causes disorder and violence. The perfection of creation becomes darkened and concealed in our understanding of the world and ourselves. The world is no longer revealed in the perfection of the Creator, and the disorder and uncouthness of the external horizons will reflect the condition of our own self. It will be darkened, under the rule of ignorance, with no orientation to free it. Any action under such conditions will be violence towards the world and the self, the consequences of which are suffering and destruction, and the spreading of corruption and ugliness. We were created in most beautiful uprightness and for it, in perfection and for it. The question of coming to know the goal and of realizing the self within it as perfection is a human one. Whatsoever we know or do lacks point, if it does not contribute to finding and discovering our perfection, in which and for which we were created.

The most beautiful uprightness in which we were created reveals the union of the external and internal: whatsoever is in the world corresponds to whatsoever is in the self. Recognizing the inviolable center brings about balance in the soul. Insult to the external center leads us to the low point of existence. The lost garden must be found in the city as its image. But this image is nothing other than the turn towards the Highest and recognition of the Praised as the City of Knowledge. This is so, because the Praised has the most sublime nature.[6]

This most sublime and most mighty nature is a possibility for each of us. This is the case, and cannot be otherwise. The human self has the Spirit of God at its center. This is why human nature may be realized only in that center and in relation to it. Assisting that nature to recognize itself and find its balance in relation to the four sides of the world, so that it sees itself as the self-revelation of Intellect through the heart, leads it towards equilibrium and beyond.

But the recognition of our debt to existence as a whole is not our goal. The debt is only a relationship with what is loved, and we can learn to know what we love; so long as we are separated from the object of our knowledge, we cannot repay our debts, which means we cannot become one with the Beloved. On this path, no individual thing can stand in for the whole, but they all speak of it.

The totality of existence is minute in comparison to the Seat, which is only a sign of God as the King of all existence. His kingdom is in the human self. He is not contained by the heavens and the earth. He is contained by the heart of the faithful servant—the one who loves Him, but is not satisfied with any knowledge yet attained. He is faithful, because he loves what he knows and knows what he loves. He is a servant, because he gives himself over fully to the Beloved. He wishes for no property other than Him.

In perennial wisdom, as the essential and decisive content of all sacred traditions, the secret of happiness and of the path of return to perfection must be discovered within the human self, given our position in the world, and not in the external world. This is the meaning of God's command to the Praised: "Say: 'O my Lord, increase me in knowledge!'"[7]

The inheritors of the Stolac *čaršija* preserved a tradition of Veli Dede. It is said that he received the confession of the Praised, who they called the Paraclete, from his grandfathers. He reinforced this news of the Praised through his travels in the world and his association with the friends of God. In the center of Stolac, he worshipped with his friends and passed on to them the glorious news of the Praised. They say that he spoke of the damnation of the entire world and everything in it, and so of the entire Stolac valley and everything in it, the damnation which comes about when recollection fades within of God as the King of the world and of human beings. It is not difficult to recognize in this the passing on of the message of the Praised to all those who conceal their separation from God as the source and purpose of all praise.

We realize ourselves in knowledge. This is the clear message of the confession that there is no god but God. The totality of existence refers to this confession, everything that is in the heavens and on the earth and between them. This knowledge does not depend on anything in time. There is no prophet who did not bear witness to it. But, we are beings of oblivion and neglect. What is most obvious in existence escapes us into oblivion and neglect. The prophets remind us of it. In this way, what was most obvious and independent of history becomes present in history: its presence is possible only through the discovery of our original nature. This pure original nature is the perfect example of the Praised, in whom and with whom we find ourselves. In finding ourselves, we find God.

The world is damned and everything in it, except recollection. But everything in the world exists for recollection. All the signs in the world and in ourselves are there because of Him whom they signify. Everything in the heavens and on earth and between them has been created with truth.[8] Nothing in creation escapes being with truth: "Our Lord is He who gave everything its creation, then guided it."[9] This creaturehood of all things is their disclosure of the truth.

Our task is to recognize the truth in everything in the heavens, on earth, and between them. This is the claim everything has on us: "Your self has a right against you, your Lord has a right against you, your guest has a right against you, and your wife has a right against you. So give to everyone who possesses a right his right."[10]

Everything has a claim on us, given that that claim or truth of creation is our debt to God through creaturehood and guidance. This is why everything in existence, once its claim has been admitted, is a source of human blessedness. What, without recognition of the truth of its creaturehood, is corrupted and damned, in recollection and in knowledge appears blessed.

Given that the world contains a countless multitude of things, and each of them has a claim on us, we may say that we have a countless multitude of debts: each thing has a claim against us, and that means we have a debt towards it. Certainly, our first and greater debt is towards God: we owe Him our creation and our guidance. Recognizing and meeting our debts towards everything in the heavens, on the earth, and between them is impossible, unless each debt is put in its place, the first in the first place and so on—in which we are led by the Praised:

> Say: "If your fathers, your sons, your brothers, your wives, your clan, your possessions that you have gained, commerce you fear may slacken, dwellings you love—if these are dearer to you than God and His Messenger, and to struggle in His way, then wait till God brings His command; God guides not the people of the ungodly."[11]

God's first claim on people, or their first debt to the Lord, is to serve Him and to associate nothing with Him; and our first claim on the Lord, or His first debt towards us, is not to punish us but to give us the garden as our reward for meeting His claim.[12]

When we live so that we meet the claims of God, we can do so only by meeting the claims of everything that has been created. Consequently, everything reveals itself with truth. All the signs in the world are reflected within ourselves. Afterwards, in the other world, all the signs in our self will be mirrored in the horizons of the external world.

Images of the *Čaršija*

1. "Turn thy face towards the Holy Mosque; and wherever you are, turn your faces towards it!"
2. The mosque in the valley faces Mecca
3. The *musafirhana* or guesthouse
4. Justice as exact measure
5. Being open and closed towards the mosque
6. The gateway links two worlds
7. At the bottom of the valley, over water
8. The Book as the third revelation of God
9. The house of learning
10. The minaret—the tower of love and knowledge
11. The tower of the hour
12. The horizontal and the vertical
13. The mortuary bathhouse
14. The view from the southern entry
15. The view from the western entry
16. The view from the eastern entry
17. The view from the northern entry
18. The book as our bond to the world
19. The human being and the world: focus and dispersion

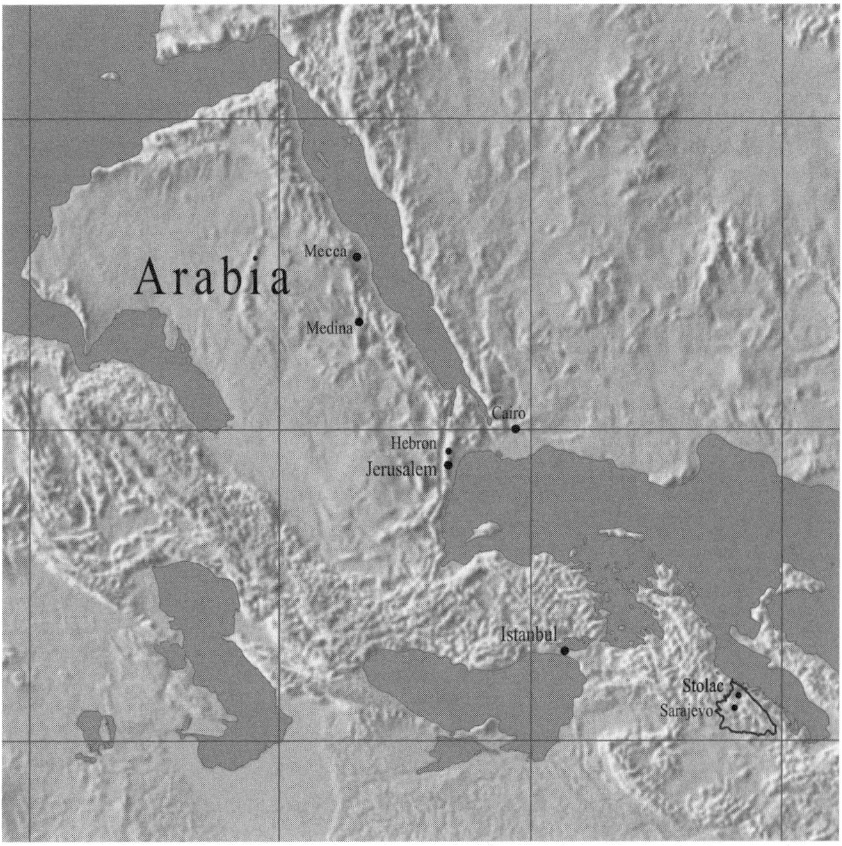

1. "Turn thy face towards the Holy Mosque; and wherever you are, turn your faces towards it!"[1]

We are on earth as part of the cycle of fall and return. This began with the covenant we made with God before existence, which will bear fruit on the Day of Judgment. The key symbols of our fall and rise are the two mosques, in the valley and on the mount. Of the mosque in the valley God says: "The first House established for the people was that at Mecca, a place holy and a guidance to all beings."[2] By his command establishing the House, God enabled any place on earth to become a "place of worship." With the confession that there is no god but God and that the Praised is His Messenger, every place houses our connection to God through His Messenger. It is precisely through this link that we confess our connection to God as the center of all existence.

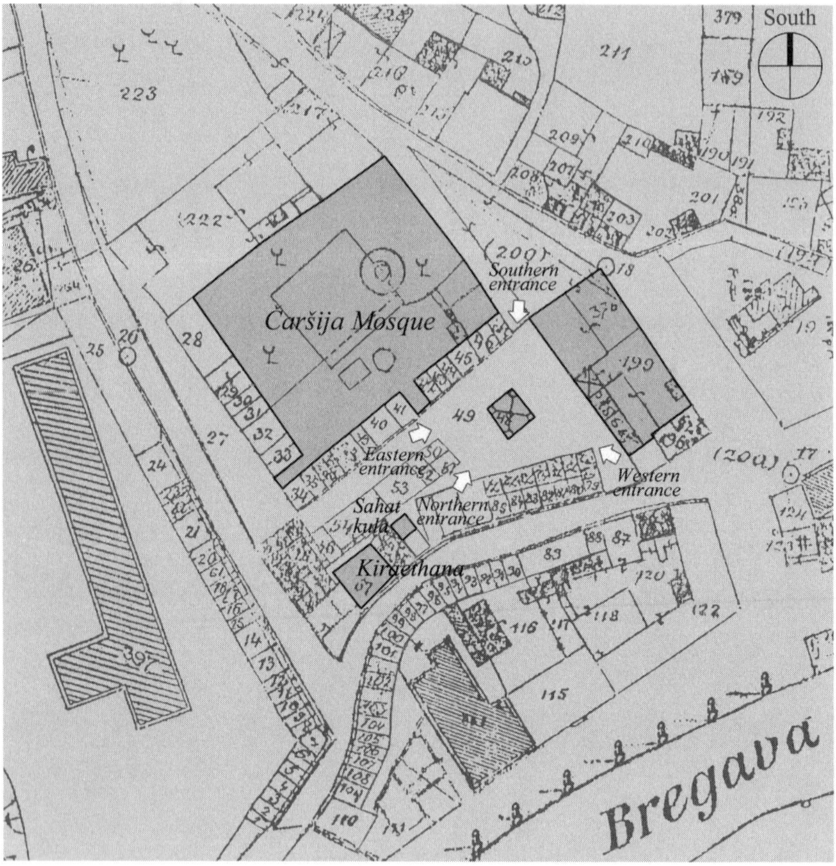

2. The mosque in the valley faces Mecca

The Stolac *čaršija* took its form from the mosque at its center. This is why it is the Čaršija Mosque and the *čaršija* was the mosque's. The *čaršija* drew its origin from the mosque and returned to it, according to the principle: "Surely we belong to God, and to Him we return!"[3]

3. The *musafirhana* or guesthouse

Mary's son, Jesus, prayed: "O God, our Lord, send down to us a Table out of heaven that shall be for us a banquet, the first and last of us, and a sign from Thee. And provide for us; Thou art the best of providers."[4]

This prayer expresses our desire to experience the world as consecrated, to receive it and its contents as a banquet sent down by God at which we are all guests. The Stolac *musafirhana* was open to east and west, to welcome guests coming to and from the *čaršija*, expressing the openness of human nature. This meaning of the *musafirhana*, its welcoming and accommodating of guests, is what justified its size and prominence from all sides. It was made in the form of a great *stećak* or Bosnian tombstone to signify the relationship between life and death. To realize this relationship, however, we must first recognize the claims of all things, in the following order: our own claim, our Lord's claim, and the guest's claim.

4. Justice as exact measure

At the heart of the *čaršija*, in front of the mosque, there was a covered area with weights and scales. Justice is showing and speaking truth, and the path of the just is allegiance to the truth. The four pillars under the roof referred to the four principles (the hour, the debt, resurrection, and judgment), while the fact that the space was open on all four sides told of how we are all called to measure justly and to check all measurement. The order of the world reflects God's justice, and we are called upon to admit and realize it through trust or confidence in God. There was a pyramidal roof atop the four pillars of the square base. This represented the connection between the earth and heaven. The four pillars have many meanings—the four books sent down (the Torah, the Psalms, the Gospels, and the Quran), the four degrees or levels of self-realization (the *sharia* [the exoteric way], the *tariqa* [the esoteric way], the *haqiqa* [realization], and the *marifa* [gnosis]), and the four rivers of paradise (water, milk, wine, and honey).

5. Being open and closed towards the mosque

There were 14 shops in front of the mosque courtyard. They were divided by the entrance into the courtyard. The *mekteb* was on the right-hand side. None of these shops had an entry into the mosque courtyard. To enter the mosque, one had to leave the place of commerce. As the place in which books are written and read, the *mekteb* was open both towards the *čaršija* and the mosque.

6. The gateway links two worlds

The gateway into the mosque courtyard separated or split the shops. It was the link between the two parts of the *čaršija*—the one comprising the mosque complex and the other its extension into the marketplace. Thus, the gateway was a sign of the indivisibility of our existence on the earth's surface from our relationship with heaven.

7. At the bottom of the valley, over water

The Stolac *čaršija* brought together all four sides of the world in the valley, at its bottom, in the center. Everything in the valley was shaped as a confession of the levels of existence and our desire to rise up out of them. The minarets and the clock tower signify our turn from the depth towards the height. Whatever one saw in the *čaršija*, as an external expression of humanity, had its mirror image within. If this connection between the human nadir and the original height is to be made, existence must be recognized as a stage on which we appear and from which we will exit. We must first turn to the surface of the earth and then towards the height: this is the sublimity in humility. Once facing the *mihrab*, the gate beyond the world, our path lay "over water." The river flows from the left down across the plain. Making one's way towards the mosque, one passes over water and realizes oneself through purification. On this path "over water," images of purification multiply: the river, the channel in front of the shops, the fountain in the mosque courtyard, the cisterns, and the removal of shoes.

8. The Book as the third revelation of God

God reveals himself through His creation of the world and humanity and by His sending down of the Book through His prophets. What is dispersed through the world is gathered together in us. God's revelation is His word sent down in human language through the prophets, who passed on what they received to their people. In this way, we are all recipients and bearers of the Book. That the *mekteb* links the interior of the mosque with the external world signifies the origin of the Book and that it comprehends everything to be found in people or the world.

9. The house of learning

The *kiraethana* is in the further corner of the *čaršija*. It is the house of learning where all knowledge, regardless of its origin, is accorded its proper dignity, following His command: "Recite: In the Name of thy Lord who created, created Man of a blood clot. Recite: And thy Lord is the Most Generous, who taught by the Pen, taught man that he knew not."[5]

10. The minaret—the tower of love and knowledge

The literal meaning of minaret is "the place of fire." It is the raised place on which fires are lit to be a light visible from all sides. Two signs or symbols are raised above the horizontal surfaces of the town—light and warmth. The light corresponds to knowledge and the fire to love. Knowledge and love together are faith. When these are knowledge and love of God and for Him, it becomes possible for us to live justly in the world, as this means that God is for us always First and Last, Inner and Outer. The minaret reveals this and is a constant reminder of it.

11. The tower of the hour

We have no excuse for flight from the self towards either past or future. We are always already within the hour, which is nigh. Our virtues and justice can be realized only within the hour. That is why it is decisive, as symbolized by the "tower of the hour," its visibility, and its audibility. As the shops, like the rest of the elements of the *čaršija* complex, were set on the ground, they could serve our self-realization only thanks to their connection to the minaret and the clock tower. The only way for us to realize ourselves is in most beautiful uprightness, whose inseparable elements are the "debt of uprightness," "the path of uprightness," and "the day of uprightness," particularly in relation to God, who is on the "path of uprightness."

12. The horizontal and the vertical

The entire Stolac valley, its surrounding hills, and the river running through it come together in the Čaršija Mosque and its *mihrab*. The relationship of coming-to-be-at-home within the world on the basis of building, both within the valley and on the hillsides, can only be understood with reference to the fullness of our purpose, namely complete return to God and building His most beautiful names within our own selves. The whole and its elements are revealed in all their meaning only once we have found our place within the earth and the heavens and all that lies between them, as a traveler returning to God. The details of the Stolac *čaršija*, as the city, have meaning for the doctrine that integrates metaphysics, cosmology, anthropology, and psychology within the framework of perennial philosophy. With this doctrine, we can render ourselves capable of receiving, so that the city can be revealed as garden, and the garden as city.

13. The mortuary bathhouse

That earthly life is inseparable from heavenly vistas is the revealed meaning of human life: we have come from God and we return to Him. After all our earthly wanderings, with all our service and our fault, we return to God, abandoning ourselves to His mercy. The path of the dead lay through the bathhouse. They were brought to it from the *čaršija* and then carried off through the mosque courtyard to the grave, in the faith that our house is in God: "Theirs is the abode of peace with their Lord."[6]

Given that the dead are entirely powerless, their rights to be bathed, dressed, and escorted, as well as our concern for their will and burial, are sacred and inviolate.

14. The view from the southern entry

The *čaršija* was a complex fabric, its horizontal, vertical, and sloped lines determined by the materials used in its construction—the stone with its passive coldness, the wood with its patient warmth, the iron with its urgent cold. The regularity inside this fabric was hidden, but present nonetheless in every look and touch. The harmony from which we come and to which we leave at death was sought and could be found in everything that went to make up the *čaršija* complex. The four cardinal directions determined the *čaršija.* The key one was from and towards the south, which in Stolac effectively means from and towards Mecca. The southern entry into the *čaršija* area lay between the *mekteb* and the *musafirhana.*

15. The view from the western entry

The entry from the west was between the shops bordering the *čaršija* area from the north and the *musafirhana.* This approach, like all the others, was governed by the verticals of the clock tower, the minaret, and the pillars and roof of the weighing and measuring area. The main orientation of all movement, however, was towards the mosque gate and, beyond it, the *mihrab.*

16. The view from the eastern entry

The approach from the east lay between the row of shops in front of the mosque and the building that housed the bakery and the smithy. It gave the clearest view of the *mekteb*, the *musafirhana*, the pillars and roof over the scales, and the shops. Turning towards any part of the *čaršija* area from that side, however, revealed the mosque gateway as the determining boundary of the *čaršija* as a whole.

17. The view from the northern entry

The northern entry or exit from the *čaršija* area had shops to one side of it and the *kiraethana* and clock tower to the other. Coming from this side, one was directly facing the mosque gateway, so that all the other elements appeared as either to left or right of the path towards the main focus of everything one saw on entering the area. The intricate network of streets and alleys in the valley and on the hillsides disclosed itself, due to the geometry of the *čaršija*, through the constant hide and seek of meaningful elements, from the tip of the minaret to the very lines in the pavement.

18. The Book as our bond to the world

The *mekteb* connected the inner area of the mosque with the *čaršija* complex. One entered from the mosque courtyard, but the windows opened onto the *musafirhana* and the shops. The children and their teacher would climb up into the *mekteb* to gather around, listening, reading, and writing the Book sent down by God through the Holy Spirit into the heart of the Praised, so that we might have assistance in our ascent from darkness towards the light. This insight into the Book through listening, talking, writing, and reading acts as both warning and guide in all the doings of the *čaršija*. The sending down of the Book and the obligation to do whatever we do in the most beautiful way are both central to all our doings with the world and each other.

19. The human being and the world in focus and dispersion

The entrance to the Stolac *musafirhana* was flanked by shops, four to either side. There are four wooden pillars to both the left and right of the entry into the Čaršija Mosque. These groups of four shops and of four pillars, and the various other forms derived from that number, signify the earth on which we have been given to serve our vicariate. To the extent that we do so well and beautifully, the heavenly order shines on earth through us, albeit in different ways at different times and places. This is one meaning of the eight signs on the *musafirhana*, each one on a square from the center of which a different geometrical shape is drawn out. The center corresponds to us as vicars on earth, but also to the Spirit God breathed into us; the developed geometric shape corresponds to the perfect revelation of the perfect center.

Post Scriptum: My Ruins

Hear my prayer, O Lord, and give ear unto my cry; hold not Thy peace at my tears: for I am a stranger with Thee, and a sojourner, as all my fathers were.

Psalm, 39:12

Say: "Journey in the land, then behold how was the end of them that cried lies."

Quran, 6:11

And his body did embarke
On its voyauge thorough the dark
But a voyce did falle below
And ring forth thorough the stillnesse

Did ring forth thorough the stillnesse

A voyce which forever flyeth
Which up to heaven hyeth

Yea which for ever flyeth

Dizdar, "The Rightwise"

1.

In 1993, I dreamt the destruction of the *čaršija* mosque. I saw its walls laid low and heavy forklifts loading its substance onto great trucks to be dumped as rubbish in some crevice or other. I do not remember a worse dream. Over the years, images of the destruction of my *čaršija* and its mosque have continued to surface in my dreams.

I was in besieged Sarajevo when I had my dream and what it showed me was actually happening in Stolac, though I received news of it only later. No account or testimony I have since received has overlaid the images from my dream. Everything in my recollection of that dream has remained clear, and no doubt always will, down to the last detail.

In my childhood, the view down our street was dominated by the minaret of the *čaršija* mosque. It is the center of everything I hold to be mine. Nothing in the world has replaced its centrality. I have always compared any other center I have since come across to this one, as higher or lower in some detail. Whenever I have been in some far-off city in the outside world, it has brought me some new insight into my own *čaršija* and mosque.

When I first returned to Stolac, some six or seven years after the destruction, there was nothing there, where the center had been. I saw this as confirmation of the accounts and images which had reached me from all sides. My world appeared to have changed utterly: I existed, but bereft of a tangible *čaršija*. Where the *čaršija* mosque and everything around it had been, a void now yawned. My own sense-of-self was threatened by this absence of everything that had, since my very first presence in the world, filled that space, now a void, bereft of material form.

After this Sarajevo dream and my first visit to the *čaršija*, of which not even a wall remained, during a certain time of planning and striving to restore the *čaršija* mosque, I saw the entire valley in all its detail once again, in a dream that went like this:

> Watching and listening high above the valley.
> A voice comes from the direction of the north star.
> The view is to the southwest and downwards.
> There is nothing except that view and the voice, which are clear:
> They meet in a self without a body.
> Both the view and voice are pure and light.
> In the peacefulness of the view, the voice is shaped into speech:
> "After learning all he could,
> He no longer wrote of anything,
> Except what you now see."
> The view encompassed the entire valley:
> The hillsides and the gardens and the houses,
> And the roads and the fruit trees and the waters,
> And the low point of the valley and the *čaršija*,
> And the tallest cypress growing at its middle,
> Slender, blue-green, its tip rounded.
> It had grown up from the center of the valley,
> In the place of the mosque.
> That male cypress served the entire view
> As center and axis and revelation.
> Around the cypress was a flock of white doves:
> White on the blue green background of the cypress,

And more beyond, above the valley;
The endurance of the cypress,
And the white vision of doves:
The union of peace and movement,
The show of darkness in light.

2.

Mary bore the Praised a son, Ibrahim. The night the boy was born, the Angel Gabriel came to the Prophet and addressed him as never before: "O father of Ibrahim!" And the next morning at the mosque, after dawn prayer, the Prophet told his Companions: "I have named him by the name of my father, Ibrahim [viz. the Prophet Abraham]."[1]

What joy the mother and father took in the child! This son of the prophet Muhammad and of Mary, his wife born out of Egypt, began to walk and speak. But, he fell sick. His father was with him in his last moments. When his son breathed his last, the Prophet took him to his bosom, and his tears flowed. His companion, Abd ar-Rahman ibn Awf, was with him and, seeing the Prophet cry, said, "O Messenger of God, this is what thou hast forbidden. When the people-of-peace see thee weeping, they too will weep." The Prophet continued to weep and when he could find his voice he said, "Not this do I forbid. These are the promptings of tenderness and mercy, and he that is not merciful, unto him shall no mercy be shown. O Ibrahim, if it were not that the promise of reunion is sure, and that this is a path which all must tread, and that the last of us shall overtake the first, verily we should grieve for thee with a yet greater sorrow. Yet are we stricken indeed with sorrow for thee, O Ibrahim. The eye weepeth, and the heart grieveth, nor say we aught that would offend the Lord."[2]

When Ibrahim had been buried, the Prophet ordered the grave mound with his own hands. Then he said, "When one of you doeth aught, let him do it to perfection."

Of his work on the mound, he said, "No harm it doth nor good, but it giveth relief unto the soul of the afflicted."[3]

So did the Praised, of whom God says that he is of a mighty nature, a shining lamp, the most beautiful example, a mercy unto the worlds, and the seal of the prophets. He spoke to the dead, he carried out the ritual of preparation and of burial, and he ordered the grave mound with his own hands. He did this in front of people who bore witness that he is the servant of God and God's Messenger. In front of them he visited the graves of his loved ones and with them he prayed.

3.

Only God knows how many times I have cried. One of these tears has been repeated many times, always in silence.

Outside the courtyard gates of my native house, there is an alley that runs perpendicular to the major road from the center through the valley towards the peak that dominates the town, Mount Vrsnik. The road continues to Dubrovnik, past Ljubinje, Kotezo, Popovo, and Trebinje. This road, after dropping gently towards the center, splits in front of the gates of the old graveyard, which the Muslims of the town refer to by the Arabic word *harem*, which means a forbidden place, a sacred precinct. The iron gates of the *harem* stand between two great pillars, flanked by high walls, and behind them cypresses and tombstones. The cypresses are mainly female, with only a few of the spear shaped ones we call male. There are also a few of the winter blossoming wild almond trees. Their blossom comes and goes quickly, reminding us of the shortness of our life on earth. There are barren fig trees and hackberries, bare when the almond trees flower. Their infertility and niggardliness, and that of the cypresses, reminds us of the meanness of this world compared to the one both living and dead are headed for, the world in which real fruit awaits, of which the fruit on earth is mere intimation, a promise of the reward the blessed will receive for their patience and for requiting evil with good.

A hundred meters further on towards the center, after a break filled by houses belonging to a noble Stolac family, the Šarići, the *čaršija* mosque complex begins.

Turning right at the gates into the old *harem*, the graveyard wall is to one's left, the Čelić and Mehmedbašić houses to one's right, all the way to the New Mekteb.[4] Beyond the New Mekteb and behind the row of shops lining the street, all the way to the sloping vineyards on the hill, lies the Great Harem.[5]

Turning left at the Old Harem gates, to one's left are the courtyard walls and gates of houses belonging to the Čohodarević, Opijač, and Šarić families. The street splits again at the *musafirhana*. To the right is the entry into the *čaršija* proper, to the left the Šabić house and the Ratkovina *harem*, with the *muselimat* in front of one, on the way to the Bregava River.

Or rather that is how it was. The Old Harem and the Great Harem were both destroyed between 1949 and 1960 by the Communist authorities.[6] I retain fuzzy images in my memory of this violence against the powerless dead and the cowed living. Through my childhood, bones of the dead and fragments of smashed gravestones surfaced, some of the latter bearing carvings and inscriptions.

It was only later, when their graves were already under a playground for children, that I found out that my own ancestors, going back to before my great-grandfather Mehmed-aga, had been buried in those graveyards.[7] Both they and I called those places *harems*, which is to say "sacred, forbidden, and inviolate." Their actual fate, of course, was the opposite of what their name meant and announced.

The more I have thought about the destiny of these *harems*, the more I have experienced silent tears. They, my dead ancestors, lacked descendants to defend their sacred claim to inviolability. Their descendants seem not to have known that it was their duty to do so. Had they known what could they have done?

4.

The secondary school was being built on the lot of the Great Harem and, like everyone else, my mother had to join in the work there, while Aiša, my late uncle Azim's daughter, would carry me to the building site. And my mother would nurse me.

At that time, as for every other child during the first period of life in this world, crying was my only recourse. My infantile helplessness and my crying burst upon the world as an irresistible force: no one can listen to the crying of a child and remain indifferent. I used this crying in my native house to instruct Aiša to pick me up and carry me to my mother, at work on building the school over the ruins of the Great Harem. Had Aiša not done it, someone else who heard my crying would have. My grandfather Derviš certainly would have, with his nearly 90 years, all spent in his native city.[8]

This infantile crying was connected, it seems to me today, with the helplessness of my dead against the violence of the living: there was no one to honor their claim to peace in the graveyard, no one powerful enough to acknowledge their claim on us in their helplessness. No other obligation outweighs protecting the dead, who have an absolute claim to inviolability. It was their right, because they were known to the living and were now powerless, even to weep. Does not precisely this absolute helplessness bind irrevocably all the living?

I experienced the destruction of these *harems* as a *fait accompli.* I was alive, but helpless. My elders—my grandfather Derviš and my father Zulfo? My father's brothers—Džemal, Mustafa, Mehmed, and Remzija? Or their sons, Alija and Ahmed? My brothers, Azim and Mirsad? Where were they? How did they experience and view it?

My grandfather Derviš was almost 90 years of age. All his children were communists, building a new world, whose masters had no mercy for anyone on their path and wanted nothing to do with mosques and graveyards.

My father and his brothers and their sons were part of this building a new world. My brothers were just young boys. My mother told me how my grandfather would come home bitter and melancholy. He would squeeze out an angry word or two. If he said anything in the *čaršija* itself, it was without weight. For the builders of the new order, his was just the voice of an honest old man out of joint with the new time.

Did my grandfather cry then?

He saw them destroy the graves of his mother Hasnija, née Muftić, and of some 100 relatives, including his grandfather and grandmother and his beloved teacher Ibrahim Hromić, through whom he was connected in a spiritual chain going back to the hand of the Praised, who received the allegiance of his companions under the tree. His character was formed by his mother's stories of the world and of ancestors and of the reason for human existence and for confidence in return to the Creator, which gives an inner peace that both finds satisfaction in and satisfies Him to whom we return. From early childhood on, he would go to the Great Harem with his father and his father's brothers to visit the departed, who spoke to them of the world split into visible and invisible. He would look at the roses and vines, lilies and hyacinths, violets and heather around his mother's headstone and those of his close relatives. He would strip the shoots of ivy from the stone walls and the headstones, protecting their cold passivity from encroaching concealment.

He escorted his own dear ones there and participated in their burial. His kin had taught him to remember the denizens of the graves to God through the Opening, that part of the revelation which opens the Recitation. And he taught his own offspring to do the same, because the grave is like a door between two sides of one and the same world, this lower, visible side and the higher, hidden one. And, as it is with the world, so it is with us. We have two sides, a visible and an invisible. Realizing our humanity means opening ourselves towards that other, higher, purer side and bearing witness that this pair, the visible and the invisible, are a revelation of the Truth which is always one.

5.

At the end of the nineteenth century, the Stolac *čaršija* was a crystalline whole, each facet connected to all the others. No change in heaven lacked reflection in these earthly facets. Each change in heaven found its response in the whole. The characters of its inhabitants were in such harmony with the whole as to be coextensive, albeit in a constant and fluid quest after that always-and-everywhere intimated Unity.

The form of the *čaršija* derives from understanding our place in existence as a whole. A single and unchanging essence is revealed to the world, split between the visible and invisible. The visible side includes the heavens and the earth and everything between them. Everything dispersed within the visible and invisible worlds, as revelation of Unity, is focused within us. Consequently, the world and we are two sides of one and the same revelation of the Creator. When we build, we bear witness to Unity within the manifold of existence, an image which began to be undermined both from without and within during the nineteenth century.

The destruction of the *čaršija* lasted from the end of the nineteenth to the end of the twentieth century. People viewed the *čaršija* from various perspectives as a messy remnant of a previous time. Parts were destroyed in ways presented as "repairs," "progress," and "development." Individuals were sought out and supported who might demonstrate, whether directly or indirectly, in thought, word, or deed, that this was not a sacred heritage to be preserved inviolate and that the only contribution it could make to the building of the new world was as material to be extracted by the destruction and crumbling of whatever had been built before. They were expected to affirm their fitness for the new age by readiness to deny and destroy. Their humanity could no longer afford to recognize anything as forbidden to profane action or any form of irreducible openness towards Eternity. Everything could be denied, except the authorities established by the revolutionary movement.

This culminated after 1948, when the destruction of the Old and the Great Harems began. Behind the movement lay the ideology encapsulated in the slogan "Death to fascism, freedom to the people!" The apparatus encompassed everything from the chief officers of state to the municipal secretary. There was nothing left capable of standing against this ideological movement, directed by the national leadership through its various organs.[9]

The perpetrators of the act of destruction itself were sought amongst the children of the dead. They were required to confirm their "progressiveness," which cut them off, in full consciousness and willingly, from any beginning other than that contained within the ideological picture of the world. With a burning desire to prove themselves, they toppled and shattered their ancestors' headstones.

This violence against the graves was interpreted as a precondition for liberation from poverty and injustice. The vulnerability of the dead in their graves had to be demonstrated, while any sense of responsibility towards them was simply proof of insufficient distance from the past, which was to be despised. Faith in God and another world was, according to them, a folly of the ignorant. The desecrators were promised liberation from their second-class position as guilty, helpless, and contemptible in comparison to the builders of the new order. They hoped through this denial of their own selves to ensure their rights to survive and be happy, the requirement for which was that they join the builders of the New World.

Looking today for answers regarding the condition of the individual and of society that caused and provided a context for this destruction, one finds it in Communism as the name for the overall structure, including the leadership, the ideology, the apparatus, and the perpetrators. This destruction was, however, largely directed against Muslim heritage. Communism provided a framework within which the action of territorial nationalisms was facilitated. For all these nationalisms, whether Serb, Croat, Albanian, or whatever, Muslims served as fundamentally other and, as such, a hindrance to attaining the goals incorporated and set out in the ideological image of the world as it unfolded towards the end of history. The modernity of communism and nationalism had at its disposal any number of reasons for despising and eradicating the sacred forms of Muslim heritage. These forms were ancient, while the participants in the various revolutionary movements had introduced a new beginning and a ceaseless production of "the new" to the heart of existence.

6.

In considering the development of the Bosnian sense of self over the longer term, as we must if we wish to draw any conclusions about it, we must first point out that it was formed through immersion in the prophetic tradition and confession that we and the world are essentially open towards our transcendental principle. This inheritance, whether in its Christian or Muslim form, is manifest as an integral image of humanity as it relates to the world and to God. In this image, knowledge is our relationship as knowers with God as the Known. The Known reveals Himself in three ways, through the world, through us, and through the Word He sent down to His chosen prophets.

Such knowledge is always a relationship with God. Nothing attained through such knowledge can ever be final. This is why all knowledge is both sufficient and insufficient for our self-realization. So long as we are oriented towards God, whose knowledge embraces everything, then no sign within the world or in our own selves can usurp the goal towards which we make constant progress. This sign is always a window towards the Signified, and whenever we desire to take this sign in exclusion of the Signified, it closes and darkens. Our self-realization takes place, accordingly, within Intellect, which connects us with the One through the entire manifold of being, as both source and destination of all existence. Unity is the essence of humanity, which contains knowledge of all the names and limitless potential to approach the Signified.

Given that we ourselves enter existence, it is our essence that tells us to turn towards it as our goal. What we can desire as our point of orientation can never be just a finite thing or even all of them together.

Intellect is Light which stores up treasure in itself and unites complete knowledge, but Intellect exists independently of us. We, however, depend on Intellect. We may relate to it through instrumental reason as its reflection and through direct experience. One should stress that instrumental reason is limited to one level of existence, namely the spatial and temporal, and that the qualities of phenomena are accessible to it only through the traces they leave behind, but that it can never comprehend them through the process of measurement. Love, beauty, fear, and hope cannot be determined by analytical or instrumental reason, which is imprisoned in the world of matter and movement. Analytical reason knows the countless multitude of things of the quantifiable world. Intellect, however, can do without any of them, but none of those things in existence have any meaning in the absence of Intellect. Just as concentric circles reveal the same single center, so all the things of the world or in us reveal one and the same Intellect.

Only direct experience can orient analytical reason towards Intellect as its highest principle. In any such orientation, a relationship is established between the human being, as the epitome of all creation and the image of God, and God. This relationship opens us to return through the manifold to Unity and to find in every sign in the world or in ourselves witness of God, who embraces all with His knowledge.

In the period since the Renaissance, western humanity has turned from this openness to Intellect, as its highest moment, towards analytical and instrumental reason, as the supposed culmination of our ascent from dead and mindless matter, from mud and blind force, equating our knowledge with being. Analytical knowledge does not transcend the world of the manifold. When being is reduced to analytical knowledge, it becomes imprisoned within the quantifiable world. Then the world appears independent of the self: its being and knowledge of it are one, and he who knows the world seems to be its master. According to this picture of the world and human beings, the quantifiable sciences become the only indisputable source of knowledge. Prophecy and direct experience are excluded as sources of knowledge both for any such science and for the philosophy that is its fellow traveler.

7.

As modern western worldviews advanced in Bosnia, the holistic traditional vision of the world, humanity, and God has fragmented. The Christian side of this division received support from the influence of the enlightenment and modern ideologies, which, in spite of their anti-Christian elements, retained many of the forms of that culture that grew up within the framework of Christianity. The Muslim heritage, however, was simply read as "outdated," "foreign," and "incompatible."

As this fragmentation gathered strength, Muslims were called upon to join the currents of modernity and, consequently, to distance themselves from their own heritage. Readiness to do so became the primary way of showing their allegiance to the promise of modernity. During the twentieth century, none of the educated people of Stolac, insofar as one can judge from their written works, showed the slightest consciousness of either their own rich cultural heritage or the dimensions of the suffering their own people had undergone.[10] What they considered knowledge was firmly placed within the rational view of the world as quantifiable and finite. They did not believe in any source of knowledge not firmly grounded in experience in that world. They considered intellectual knowledge, which entered the world at its beginning, to be literally meaningless.

One possible exception was the poet Mehmedalija Mak Dizdar. All true poetry derives from the poet's connection to something that transcends the individual and analytical reason. Insight into the suffering of the Bosnian people was somehow sent down or given to him. And it seems to have been articulated nowhere so clearly as in his *Stone Sleeper.*

The abandonment and even the denial of their traditional heritage in favor of an expression of Muslim openness to western culture appear as a general phenomenon in weak Muslim colonies facing powerful western colonizers,[11] as well as in the face of instrumental reason and its uses to manage people, the world, and the qualities derived from Intellect. This dominant rationalist picture of the world and the views of humanity, society, and the world based on it informed modern ideology and its familiar expressions in the West (Conservatism, Liberalism, and Socialism, for example), which have in their different ways penetrated the consciousness of Muslims throughout the world, whether they accept or reject them. This penetration of the Muslim world has taken place a century or two later than the process amongst western Christians.

The period of modernity in the west was a period of weakness and the decline of political institutions and states in nearly all the areas of the world whose inhabitants are considered Muslims, whether by themselves or others. This feeling of powerlessness provokes a reaction or opposition which is essentially a form of imitation of the more powerful party. This produces a "schizophrenic culture." There is an ideological rejection of the content of western modernity, which is nevertheless *de facto* adopted by the various forms of Islamic reformism. The Islamic content becomes little more than the dogmatic and emotional expression of this sense of powerlessness and trauma, while the core intellectual teachings of our origin and purpose are ever more rapidly fading from the minds and hearts of modernized Muslims.

The "defense" of these forms of Muslim identity generally lacks any capacity for or indeed faith in patient exposition. It takes place in closed circles of people of like mind with an unrelenting sense of grievance against the other and the different. Most people in such societies, whether individually or as groups, effectively put their faith in the study of modern sciences and skills—medicine and engineering, technology and international law, etc. As William C. Chittick has pointed out:

> Given that modern schooling is rooted in topics and modes of thought that are not harmonious with traditional Islamic learning, it is profoundly difficult for any thinking and practicing Muslim to harmonize the domain of thought in theory with the realm of faith and practice. One cannot study for many years and then be untouched by what one has studied. There is no escape from picking up mental habits from the material to which one devotes one's life. It is most likely, and almost, but not quite, inevitable for modern thinkers with religious faith to have compartmentalized minds. One compartment of the mind will encompass the professional, rational domain, and the other the domain of personal piety and practice. More generally, this is the case with most people who grew up in a traditional ambience and were then educated in the modern style.[12]

This cultural schizophrenia reached its peak for Bosnian Muslims during the most violent period of Communist dogmatism, which acted in a symbiotic relationship with fundamentalist reformism. The significance of traditional institutions escaped both Communists and Muslim reformers, and their response to the abolition of the *mekteb*, which took place immediately after the Communists took power, generally took the following form: "It was therefore a perfectly rational and understandable decision on the part of our national authorities, in 1946, to forbid children of school-going age, that is from 7 to 15 years of age, to be called to the *mekteb*."[13] The precise forms taken by this cultural schizophrenia and the resulting mental outlook of Muslims have received little attention as phenomena.[14]

Given that the modern worldview developed against the backcloth of Christianity, so that while it excluded Christian intellectuality it preserves the cultural forms of that world, it has had a doubly destructive impact on Muslim heritage: both Muslim intellectuality and all its cultural forms are considered foreign and incompatible with the modern secularized worldview.

The so-called reformist movements amongst Muslims during the nineteenth and twentieth centuries are essentially just attempts to reconcile these two incompatible points of view. The core elements of the Muslim intellectual heritage have suffered within them too, even though the external forms continue to be presented as "Muslim." It is the same essential content of secularism dressed in apparently Muslim garb. This has simply deepened the confusion. It has been used to justify the denial of the authentic original dignity of the individual. This original dignity, guaranteed by God, is what makes it difficult to bend people to political projects and violence.

This conflict between the traditional forms and the modern worldview is evident in the moralizing and fundamentalist confusion which spreads fear and destruction. These are the occasions of secularizing and fundamentalist infatuation amongst Muslims.

The closed view of the world, which excludes consciousness of the invisible, covers over and darkens intellectual knowledge as the decisive content of the Muslim philosophical tradition. The confession that there is only one God, who is both within and without, near and far, becomes simply a form that disguises the violence of the host of gods who have become central to the lives of individuals and nations. Nearly all the forms of traditional culture have been subjected to destruction, as a result of their incompatibility with modern ideologies. We have set ourselves up in opposition to the world we are attempting to dominate, and instrumental reason is our weapon in this battle. As Wei-Ming has put it:

> Since the value of the human is not anthropocentric, the assertion that man is the measure of all things is not humanistic enough.

> To fully express our humanity we must engage in a dialogue with heaven because human nature, as conferred by heaven, realizes itself not by departing from its source but by returning to it. Humanity, so conceived, is the public property of the cosmos, not the private possession of the anthropological world, and is as much the defining characteristic of our being as the self-conscious manifestation of heaven. Humanity is heaven's form of self-disclosure, self-expression, and self-realization. If we fail to live up to our humanity, we fail cosmologically in our mission as co-Creator of heaven and earth and morally in our duty as fellow participants in the great cosmic transformation.[15]

The connection between knowledge of the cosmos and knowledge of the self lies at the heart of every revealed intellectuality. When these two sides of one and the same existence are separated, then the destruction of the world of traditional heritage becomes inevitable, as does the destruction of nature as the temple to which we were sent down and from and through which we are to return to our Principle. This is the reason why anti-Islamism, anti-Christianity, and anti-Judaism are integral elements of the finite or closed sense of self.

8.

Nearly all forms of European nationalism incorporate anti-Islamism[16] and anti-Judaism. There are at least two reasons for this. The first is that nationalism decisively rejects God as the transcendent Truth for every individual and every group. It is not possible from the perspective of a given nation to say: "Our God and your God are one and the same." From this perspective, only "our God" is the real one and he cannot be shared, not even with a related people. The God of the nation is within, and as such is the only real one, and as Muslims and Jews differ, in principle, insofar as they refuse to accept the reduction of God to any form of idol, they inevitably represent a foreign body within the nation as a whole.

Muslims who view the world of things from the pseudo-Islamic position, which has lost the openness of the world and the human being to its one and only principle, create for themselves reified anti-Christian and anti-Judaic images, but these positions are really just a projection of their own relationship to themselves. For this approach, the suffering of the nation, as it is presented by the national leaders, is always greater than any that has ever existed. It reaches all the way to "our God," and is not to be compared to any other suffering.

The second reason is that no national group can be formed without the designation of its other. That other is the enemy, if close, or friend, if remote. For, those who are close but different represent a constant challenge to the idea of the whole or group and the uninterrupted existence of the nation. That is why this other must be presented as the concentration and incarnation of everything that acts to prevent the people becoming a conscious nation. This close other is dishonest, crafty, unclean, cruel, ugly, and underhand, while the distant other may be presented as a confirmation of everything felt and experienced in the endeavor to create the future which the elite promises the people.

In the projects to create an image of and so establish the Serb and Croat nations, the Muslims have systematically been presented as those others responsible for the suffering and loss incurred by Serbs and Croats through large stretches of their history. They are the historical incarnation of everything ugly and dangerous; they are Saracens, Tatars, Turks, cruel Agars, who have through history threatened and defiled everything beautiful and good, and they are all the more dangerous when they cannot be recognized immediately as such.

Communism inherited the general European reduction of the world picture to positivist science as the only real form of knowledge. It could not exclude from itself the essential content of the other ideologies. It could not, because all the ideologies of modernity share the same core or essence, namely the anthropomorphic image of the world whereby human beings emerged from matter, rather than having been sent down into it, that they might arise out of it again.

The twentieth century saw Muslims attempting to come to terms with the widening gap between the ideological movements and their desire to retain their particularity and so preserve something of their heritage. Unfortunately, none of their approaches to bringing this about has proved all that successful. Their tradition as a whole is under attack by the ideological movements. The purpose of the sacred in the conduct of life, education, architecture, and dress has faded from their views on the human being, the world, and God. All this has been thrown out, sometimes violently, sometimes lightly—the house and the courtyard, the furniture and the way of dressing, books and customs,[17] and the way of relating to other people and the world as a whole.

9.

This approach to the Muslim as other and attempts to destroy their culture received a new historical framework in 1948. In order to buttress his position in his conflict with Stalin, Tito, the leader of Yugoslavia, persecuted the Serb communists, whose feelings for Russia were very strong—given both their loyalty to Russian communism and their old affections as a result of the Serbian connection with Russia. To avoid the possibility of conflict with the Serb people as a whole, in 1948, Tito opened the doors for Serb nationalists to express their feelings regarding Muslims. The Serb nationalists had, in any case, when it came to the Russians of the day, a well developed sense of grievance against the Communists and Stalin, because they had destroyed the Imperial heritage which had formed the basis for the long-standing Serbian love affair with Russia.

It was therefore in 1948 that the most savage destruction began of the Muslim contribution to the Bosnian union of differences. This was a resumption of the project which had been so important an element of the old crusading assaults on Bosnia, from the north and the west, as well as of the "Serbian revolution" at the beginning of the nineteenth century. They had considered it part of their religious and national obligation to "clean the land" of the "Turks." This project referred to Muslims and anything that belonged to them, taking the following pattern: Slaughter a third, expel a third, and convert a third. There was a simple denial that the Muslim population had enjoyed any form of unbroken presence in these areas, as individuals who had, along with their acceptance of the confession of the Praised, continued to bear witness to Jesus and his mother, and so preserved the full burden of their ancient heritage in the lands of their ancestors.

There is another particularly important factor in this destructive project which must be noted. None of the Muslims to whom these graveyards belonged could deny their sense of self, shaped as it had been by the language and heritage of their forefathers, which brought together in witness of the Praised the full burden of belief from the beginning of the world until their own time. But there was a justification for the ideological project to destroy the graveyards and it came from the holy places of Mecca and Medina. There, the graves of all those who had seen the Praised and whom he had seen had been destroyed, and this had happened during the period when the views and positions of the fathers of the individuals responsible for destroying Stolac had been formed. The justification for this lay in the ideology which presented itself as the heir and guardian of sacred tradition.[18]

Is not this destruction of Muslim graveyards, carried out in turn by the European Christian Nationalists, European Communists, Saudi fundamentalists, and Turkish secularists, clear evidence of the nature of ideology? That the essential content is one and the same, regardless of what material has been used in constructing this picture of the world—science, culture, religion, the nation, or something else? Which of them has not made display and gloried in its power over the weak and the dead?

When God is excluded from the center of existence—and that means from the human heart—then a host of gods is established which engage in ceaseless conflict for primacy and predominance. Ideology is the attempt to establish an order to determine which god is the greatest to whom the others will be subordinate. These gods have various names—science, progress, the government of the people, the dictatorship of the proletariat, the State, the Just Society, and so on. Such projects cannot accept the God of all, who is entirely incomparable and entirely alike, extremely far and immediately near, the God revealed by both the visible and the invisible aspects of the world, of humanity, and of the books sent down to His prophets. This is unacceptable because it allows every individual to be open to the infinite and the eternal. Such openness prevents one from being confined within a closed world of the type posited by the forms of science that believe only in what can be measured. In itself, our being can never be reduced to mere quantity or equated with the soulless material order which is all that rational science allows.

For the "scientific" view of the world to be proven, human openness towards God as the absolute which embraces both the visible and invisible world must be done away with. Death and the world beyond the boundary of the finite must be denied. Those who cannot accept this denial cannot accept a government or authority which proclaims a revolution in the world order on the basis of scientistic promises.

10.

There is no more decisive measure of human dignity than how we approach the dead. This is to be felt any time we experience the death of someone close to us. It is an aspect of being human that we cannot escape the distress we experience at the death of a father or mother, the death of children. The simple fact of moving from life to death empowers the dead to impose on those affected by the event: the dead must be provided the right to protection of the helpless corpse and burial.

Is not this the meaning of the archetypal conflict between two brothers, the two sons of Adam?

Their lives involved irreconcilable understandings of the I-you-He relationship. When one of them appeared dead before the other, that other was unable to bear the impact of his own helplessness. To the killer, the victim appeared a source of that inviolate claim the dead enjoy and the sacred debt the living have towards the dead who lie in front of them as helpless corpses. We possess no derived knowledge in the educated parts of our minds, which treat everything in terms of pairs, to help us meet this undeniable debt of the living towards the dead. We need such knowledge and that is why our soul seeks desperately for it in its deepest recesses. That this knowledge is hidden from us is a sign of how far removed we are from our original purity, when we were given knowledge of all the names. The soul that has not realized itself and languishes in ignorance cannot bear this lack of answers when faced with the helpless, dead body of its brother. This is the meaning of the story of Adam's two sons.

> Then his soul prompted him to slay his brother, and he slew him, and became one of the losers. Then God sent forth a raven, scratching into the earth, to show him how he might conceal the miserable body of his brother. He said, "Woe is me! Am I unable to be as this raven, and so conceal my brother's miserable body?" And he became one of the remorseful.[19]

Gazing upon the miserable bodies of the dead, the living see and understand their own misery. The connection between the living and the dead is the only way we may gain insight into our real condition. Humanity cannot be realized without dealing with the question of death. The relationship of the living self with the thou-hood of the dead requires a Third Party that death never embraces. Only thus can the miserable body of the dead and the misery of the living be transformed into the two things we all yearn for—eternal life and happiness.

This we all know. Our dead have an inviolate claim against their living, but even more sacred than this is the claim of the unknown dead. The more ancient the grave of an ancestor, and therefore the more cut off from the emotional life of the living, the greater its claim to inviolability. Our obligation to it lies within our most profound and essential core. It is here that we should see the reason for the careful preparation of the grave and the dignified placing of the corpse within it, its closure and the marking of the grave. This confronts us with our sublime potential: the stranger and the foreigner, whose presence is indisputable, have an inviolate claim.

By recognizing the claim of the stranger, we face up to our debt towards the inviolate as such. Otherwise, we are simply a hollow tree, an empty body, whose possessor is preoccupied by external things, but whose interior has rotted entirely away.

The living walk on the earth, which means they are always with the dead. Our responsibility for our will, power, knowledge, speech, hearing, and sight affirms our relationship to earth as that from which we have been formed and which provides our grave when we are no longer alive. This relationship of the living to earth and to those who dwell within it is what determines the claim the dead have on those who will eventually join them.

> The servants of the All-Merciful are those who walk on the earth modestly and who, when the ignorant address them, say, "Peace"; who pass the night prostrate to their Lord and standing; who say, "Our Lord, turn Thou from us the chastisement of Gehenna; surely its chastisement is torment most terrible; evil it is as a lodging place and an abode"; who, when they expend, are neither prodigal nor parsimonious, but between that is a just stand; who call not upon another god with God, nor slay the soul God has forbidden except by right, neither fornicate for whosoever does that shall meet the price of sin—doubled shall be the chastisement for him on the Resurrection Day, and he shall dwell therein humbled, save him who repents, and believes, and does righteous work—those, God will change their evil deeds into good deeds, for God is ever All-Forgiving, All-Compassionate; and whosoever repents, and does righteousness, he truly turns to God in repentance. And those who bear not false witness and, when they pass by idle talk, pass by with dignity; who, when they are reminded of the signs of their Lord, fall not down thereat deaf and blind; who say, "Our Lord, give us refreshment of our wives and seed, and make us a model to the conscious." Those shall be recompensed with the highest heaven, for that they endure patiently, and they shall receive therein a greeting and—"Peace!" Therein they shall dwell forever; fair is it as a lodging-place and an abode.[20]

11.

It is not the dead who benefit from the preparation and tending of the grave; it is a need of the living, as the Prophet showed by his most beautiful example.

No one is without wealth. Existence itself is wealth. But whatever we have, we have received. None of it is originally ours. Not even our acts and actions are our own. For God has told us that He created both us and what we do.[21]

As something we have received, wealth determines each one of us, and so the possibility of giving. We are always in a position to give. And we are expected to, as by doing so we confirm the debt we owe for what we have received: there is no sacred tradition which does not consider the recognition of human poverty in relation to God and the gifting of wealth to others to be key aspects of virtue. Sacred tradition over all comprises doctrine, ritual, and virtue, which may also be expressed as intellectuality, the way, and virtue. Doctrine-intellectuality and ritual-the way can only be affirmed through virtue.

It is our duty to give of whatever we have to others. These others include those close to us, but also any who are in need—the orphan and the sick, the old and the wayfarer, the unprotected and the persecuted. The greater the need of these others, the greater the obligation to give to them.

Where, then, is the boundary of helplessness and the greatest need?

He who presents his misery and complains to others is in need, but so too is the one who suffers in silence. We have an obligation to both, but our responsibility is greater to the one who suffers in silence, to the one who may in fact be unable to receive with his own hands what is given. Our willingness to feed and care for the helpless is the measure of humanity.

And the dead are the most helpless. They cannot complain or receive, but they are not without needs. Their bodies and their graves and their wills and their legacies represent a responsibility for the living. Nothing shows human poverty like the dead. They epitomize the human condition:

> Lo, there you are; you are called upon to expend in God's way, and some of you are niggardly. Whoso is niggardly is niggardly only to his own soul. God is the All-Sufficient; you are the needy ones. If you turn away, He will substitute another people instead of you, then they will not be your likes.[22]

> O, men, you are the ones that have need of God; He is the All-Sufficient, the All-Praised.[23]

The living have received their existence and everything it comprises from the Creator. To become conscious of this, we must confess our poverty, and that absolutely: we neither have nor can have anything except what we have received. What we do have only the All-Sufficient can give us. Life and will and power and knowledge and speech and hearing and sight and whatever else goes to make up the human self come to us as the gift of the Creator as the All-Sufficient. The true meaning of this can be changed by human distortion: what we have received can be represented as our property, dependent on no one and no thing outside of our own selves, so that we take ourselves as sufficient to know the world and govern it independently. To such an understanding, questions about anything beyond the world appear foolish and unnecessary.

When we consider our existence to be our property and therefore ourselves as sufficient, we find ourselves in need of reasons to back up this opinion of ourselves, this illusion regarding the self, the world, and God. To maintain such an image, we disguise the reality of our creaturehood, and take someone or something from existence in place of the Creator. That which we have taken is presented as the principle and the measure of our image of the world.

Nothing in existence, however, escapes death. No pretensions to sufficiency can protect us against the certainty of death. In death, life reveals itself as something received, but also as something not in the possession of the one who received it or of the world itself. Nothing and no one in all existence can help us preserve life from death or restore it once it is gone. Our poverty, which we deny, is revealed by death to be the truth of our existence.

The dead exist, but are not in possession of life. They had it, but it was taken from them. No one can restore that life that was taken except Him who gave it in the first place. The dead appear to the living as an image of a station on the path which each one of us must travel but would prefer to escape.

We are absolutely poor in the face of God the Living; the absolute certainty of our death reveals our poverty, both as an attribute of humanity and as a truth of creaturehood. If our first life and death have had meaning, then we find ourselves in absolute poverty in death: the dead depend entirely on the Living as the first Giver of life, and so on Him who can give that life again. And no one else can do that. Only God is the Living in the full sense of the term. Life and death are His, but death does not comprehend Him.

12.

When an individual possessed of a distorted image of the relationship between poverty and sufficiency comes face-to-face with death as the confirmation that his understanding of the self, the world, and God is false, he may try to escape from the certainty of death into appearance and denial, into the fabrication of new lies. For such a one, the certainty of death is insupportable, so he turns on the helpless dead, against the peace of the stranger in a grave, the signs of the poverty of the dead, and attempts to destroy them. The self-evidence of the poverty of the dead and their absolute dependence on the Living as the only Giver mocks the living, who stand on the threshold of death, unable to find refuge anywhere, and who, moreover, behave as though they are in possession and not poor.

What the dead may receive from the living is protection of their bodies and graves, their wills and their legacies, none of which they can protect themselves. Their existence is the most forthright expression of poverty placed before the living. They depend for protection entirely on others, others whose existence still involves life, will, power, knowledge, speech, hearing, and sight. This is why the dignity of the dead is the measure of the dignity of the living. The dead disclose to the living the illusion of their sufficiency and the reality of their authentic, original poverty. Precisely this disclosure, this presence of the dead everywhere on earth is necessary to the living.

Everyone alive has needs that are greater in one respect or another than those of other living persons: we all have the same claim on the other as the dead; but also a claim to life, with everything that involves. The dead cannot have any debts towards the living, except through the living, but the living have a direct debt towards the dead. That God is the All-Sufficient and the All-Praised and that we are poor clearly indicate our capacity to receive everything which makes of us a creature of most beautiful righteousness: we receive praise from God as the All-Praised and thus, in our poverty, can become praised and return what we have received. In this way, we realize our discipleship to the Praised as our highest possibility, that is through our love of God and God's love of us as his followers. Each one of us, regardless of our condition, is a revelation of the Praised to a greater or lesser degree. Whatever our condition, so long as we have breath between our lips, it cannot exhaust our potential to realize knowledge of all the names and so of the divine spirit within. As beings, we are open to Perfection. The Praised is our most beautiful example, and regardless of the extent to which we realize him within our own selves, he remains that which he is—the shining lamp and the mercy unto the worlds.

For us to glimpse the reality of our life beyond the boundaries of the world, we must reach consciousness of the nature of our being in the graveyard, amongst the dead as so many images of the path back to God. Is it possible to find meaning in the great gift of life without passing through death? Can we understand the Living as the Giver if we do not accept death as a confirmation of the infinite mercy of Him who both gives and takes? Imam Ali, the son of Abu Talib, instructed people to visit the graveyards, and there to attain self-realization on the way back to God. He said:

> Put off your vanity, drop down your haughtiness and recall your grave because your Way passes over it. You will be dealt with as you deal with others, you will reap what you sow, and what you send today will meet you tomorrow. So do provide for your future and send for your day.[24]

> Know, O creatures of God, that you and all the things of this world that you have follow in the footsteps of those who were before you. They were of longer ages, had more populated houses and were of more lasting traces. Their voices have become silent, their movements have become stationary, their bodies have become rotten, their houses have become empty, and their traces have been obliterated. Their magnificent palaces and spread-out carpets were changed with stones, laid-in-blocks, and cave-like graves whose very foundation is based on ruin and whose construction has been made with soil. Their positions are contiguous, but those settled in them are like far-flung strangers. They are among the people of their area, but feel lonely. They are free from work, but still engaged (in activity). They feel no attachment with homelands nor keep contact among themselves like neighbors despite nearness of neighborhood and priority of abodes. And how can they meet each other, when decay has ground them with its chest, and stones and earth have eaten them. It is as though you too have gone where they have gone, the same sleeping place has caught you, and the same place has detained you. What will then be your position when your affairs reach their end and the graves are turned upside down (to throw out the dead)?[25]

Once the corpse is in the grave, the upright stone which marks its house, whether inscribed or not, recalls the cold passivity in which we are powerless to raise life. We may receive it, but by doing so we become absolutely indebted. The debt binds us to the one who has given to us. Returning that debt requires total self-realization, and such self-realization is not possible in the absence of being-at-peace, as our way of relating to God as Peace.

Above and beside the gravestones are flowers and trees—violets and lilies, hyacinths and orchids, roses and vines, cypresses and figs, pomegranates and hackberries, ivy and bindweed—but they all, whether they live long or short, signify the passage of time which neither the great nor the small gravestones can overcome. They are there to remind the living of our journey from Eternity and back to it.

13.

If we love God and follow the Praised as our highest possibility, then God will love us. The love between God and human beings is a mutual desire to become manifest in Unity. If we love God, we desire Him in everything and through everything, while He approaches us with His love with incomparable speed and wholeness, so that it is evident in everything that belongs to us—in life and will, in power and knowledge, in speech and hearing and sight.

Then we become aware of His presence in everything: he is the First and the Last, the Inner and the Outer. As a result, we come to accept the inviolability or sacred nature of the world, as well as the sinfulness and foolishness of any attempt to glory over it and subject it to our Lordship, instead of acting as a prudent participant and conscientious steward on behalf of its true Lord.

Viewed from this perspective of God's presence in the world, everything has a right to expect humanity to behave in a responsible fashion towards it; our purpose is to understand the things of the world as signs of God, but only that we may love and approach the Signified. Abusing, distorting, and ravaging the signs in the world produces the same effect on the human self. This is because all the signs in the world correspond to names within the self. We cannot deny the rights of the things in the world, without depriving ourselves of our own rights, because the signs in the world and in the self are there for us to come to know ourselves in the world and the world in us as aspects of the Truth.

The confession of our authentic poverty and of Divine all-sufficiency is simply an aspect of the confession that there is no god but God. This is a truth revealed by all of existence. There is nothing in the world that does not clearly show it. This self-evidence leads to another: that our humanity is determined by our ability, once within the world, to receive this revelation and, gathering it within us, to form out of it our integrated self.

This is our confession that the Praised, as the recipient of everything which reveals God as the All-Praised through the act of praise, represents our highest potential. This is because the Praised is the servant of the Creator, pure and conscious of his poverty in relation to God, the recipient who confesses what he has received, and consequently praises Him. Each of us is expected to bear witness that the Praised is the first and last possibility of the self in relation to the Self. Through such confession, we discover or experience ourselves as capable of perfection. Moreover, each revelation by God of this confession through His prophets, all of which differ in their external expression while always containing one and the same essence or content, includes or comprehends the witness of all the prophets, from the first to the last, of whom the Praised is the archetype.

These two inextricable confessions, the first of the Unity of God and the second of the apostleship of the Praised, may be sought and found in received knowledge. When that is where we discover them, they depend on the intermediaries who have handed them down. Each of us can also find them within our own selves. And when we find them there, our knowledge of them does not depend on an intermediary. On the basis of this knowledge, we realize our most profound nature, the core which contains God's lesson of all the names of His Spirit or Intellect. Everything else serves simply as a reminder of this knowledge. Only in and through this knowledge do we find the reason and purpose of our having come into the world and our going out of it.

Recognizing the claims of everyone and everything, which is what our Lord requires of us, is fairness and justice, for justice is the knowledge of the place of everything in the entirety of existence. The Creator gave each thing its place. Only by confessing the Unity of God and the apostleship of the Praised can we discover the meaning of the world and the things within it.

God is Just. Justice is our relation with God the Just, when we have realized our authentic and original knowledge of all the names. Then, we too are just. We see the things in the world and ourselves as in the place assigned to them by the Lord in His perfect creation. Our ability to be just is something we have received. It places an obligation or debt upon us, which is to be requited in everything we do by returning what has been received and confessing the claim on everything we have received. In this way, we are justified both as a recipient and giver. This is how we relate to the Just through his self-revelation in every sign in the world or the self, albeit differently each moment.

God's justice may be seen in the treatment meted out to us in accordance with our original nature. Moreover, the determination of the place of the dead, their inviolable right to peace within the grave signifies the final abode of all, the place at which all shall be happy for they have returned to the house. Neither blessing nor punishment encountered determines the nature of the place entered upon, but the character of the one who enters, and it is in accordance with this that the self will attain bliss as happiness and reward or punishment as unhappiness.

The unhappiness of the self is a consequence of its refusal to be at peace in full relationship with God and to accept its own nature. This refusal disturbs the balance of the self, a balance which reveals the perfection of our original nature. This disruption causes confidence or trust to turn to passion and closure of the self. We shall suffer the fires of hell, because we refuse to accept the confidence that binds us to God. This is manifest in attempts to tailor the world to our desires born of our passions. Ibn Arabi says of this:

> The wretched have chastisement only from themselves, for they are made to stand in the station of protest. They seek the reasons for God's acts among His servants. "Why did such and such happen?" "If such and such had been, it would have been better and more appropriate."[26]

By opposing the order of things, we debate with the Real, who endowed all things in existence with creation and guidance.[27] Everything in this creation is perfect: nothing is lacking in the order of the heavens and the earth and what lies between them.[28] Those who cannot make their peace with the order of existence and its revelation of Peace[29] have joined the band that "made a breach with God and His Messenger."[30] Such people find the peace of the dead in their graves insupportable. Their violence against the dead is due to their failure to accept being-at-peace as their one obligation to God. For the dead are clear emblems of Peace.

14.

Each one of us has always and always will be placed between two extremes—our original creation in the most beautiful uprightness of being and our having been sent down to the lowest depth. This being in-between means that we may either rise or descend further. As such we defy repetition. Each moment finds us different: we are never the same at two different points of time.

Wherever and whatever we may be, we reveal our Creator. He alone is the Gatherer who brings together all people,[31] and so gathers each one of us in a final integration. No human unity is possible in the absence of such a focus on God the Gatherer. There can be no unity or union of differences except through union with Him as the One and the Only. This takes place with Him and through Him as the Far and the Near, the Incomparable and the Alike. It is due to this that every self and each thing participates.

When things or thoughts are taken for the unifying center in the place of God, the self inevitably suffers closure, because it has taken a god in place of God. For such a self, the world appears incomplete and disordered, so that it submits the world to its attempts to perfect and order it. It cannot be otherwise. Only God has nothing above Him nor anything beyond Him. And when a god is taken in the place of God, then everything that transcends that little god must be denied. Consequently, the self is limited by this little god taken in the place of God.

To such perfecters of the world, the dead appear insupportably perfect. Their peacefulness in the grave admonishes the deformation of the self that takes itself as the measure of all existence.

The *stećci* or grave houses, upright headstones, and crosses become signs whereby the dead mock these would-be improvers of the world as powerless in the face of death. And the anger of the builders of the New World turns against them.

What is the meaning of the headstone with the turban? We are the vicars or stewards of our Lord. The turban—and it is worth noting that the root of this word means "earth"—is a sign of our vicariate, a sign that we are kings because we were made so by the King. Our kingship derives from our relationship with God as King. This kingship, however, lies in recognition of our debt towards God: that we serve Him and that we associate no other with Him. Our kingship ends at death. Everything returns to God that it may make peace with Him, with or against its will.[32]

The dead announce the possibility of voluntary return, through the peace of the grave, demonstrating that the will of the living is powerless against the will of the Living. When the closed self is confronted with this, it is provoked to action against the dead. Any such violence against the dead, however, is in reality against those who commit it. For, by it, they have denied themselves the prospect of being-at-peace in payment of their debt to the Creator.

The fact of our being king on earth in the name of the King is confirmed by death in the words of Jesus: "The kingdom of God cometh not with observation; neither shall they say, lo here! or, lo, there! For, behold, the kingdom of God is within you."[33]

We seek this kingdom, for Jesus said to us: "Ask, and it shall be given you! Seek, and ye shall find! Knock, and it shall be opened unto you!"[34]

In the alternative view, our kingdom is limited to the world, which is the stage of all that is open or possible to us. In this view, death becomes an insoluble problem, as its certainty puts in question our kingship over the world.

The kingdom of the heavens and the earth and all that lies between, as the visible side of existence, belongs to God alone. Our relationship of confidence as faithful to God the Faithful is what allows us to rule as kings in regency on earth in the name of God the King. This possibility is not unconditional, however. It is limited, as it is ended by death. Then the turban as the sign of the monarchy given to us by God is removed. What remains is for us to give account of our monarchy, which was given to us with our willful acceptance, starting with our relationship to ourselves, the world, and God on the upright path from the lowest depth to the most beautiful height.

The acceptance of God's confidence involves a relationship between two wills—ours and God's. This does not mean that our will can achieve anything other than what is God's will. We realize our highest potential only by confessing that there is no will except the Will.

15.

The human heart is a vessel. This is that it might receive what is in the heavens and on the earth and what lies between as the revelation of the All-Sufficient.

The valley is therefore an image of the human heart. When we lay waste the valley, we lay waste our heart. To lay waste a thing means to strip it of its nature as a recipient and giver of its essential creaturehood-with-truth.

Only the dead make their claim without any power. They cannot force the meeting of the debt. The living respond to the dead with full freedom of will. The sacred nature of their claim is conditioned or determined by God's revelation:

> No compulsion is there in the debt. Rectitude has become clear from error. So, whosoever disbelieves in idols and believes in God has laid hold of the most firm handle, unbreaking.[35]

By accepting the sacred nature of the debt to the powerless, we become open to the confession of Unity and realization through it: Nothing can take the place of the King in our hearts. To undermine this inner freedom from idols, violence is demanded of us against the powerless, against the dead as the most helpless of all. When the dead are attacked, then the idol or value regnant in the human heart has become the master of life, which it uses to its own ends.

The concept of liberation may be inverted: if there is nothing after death, then it should be humbled by force, denied, and mocked. Is there any little god that does not seek this?

The relationship of the living to the dead can be understood as an image of God's relationship to us. For we have no power in relation to

God, except that which He has given us. God has offered us, as indigent, His confidence, and we have accepted it. This is a covenant which God has never broken. Our acceptance of this confidence affirms the inviolable nature of the peace of the dead. Breaking that peace is a violation of the confidence we accepted from God. God's mercy, knowledge, and majesty are evident in this offer to helpless humanity, as God did not receive His mercy, knowledge, or power from any one else. We have received knowledge and mercy and power, which only makes all the more clear our obligation to enter into an inviolable covenant with the dead.

Our authentic condition is poverty, and so absolute helplessness. As such, God has given us something of sufficiency and something of power. We have what God has given us. This relationship of God as the giver and humanity as the recipient is what enables self-realization in Unity.

Witness to Unity is the underlying character of existence as a whole. And it is our underlying character. It requires nothing but what is already within our hearts, the Spirit breathed into us by God. But we were made of earth, and we bring together in ourselves all the differences of the earth and the heavens and what lies between them. As things, these differences have names, given to them by God in the word of creation.

Each human being is the gathering of the knowledge of all these names. Our self-realization is in relation to our essence as the gathering of these differences. This is our vision of the Unity in the manifold as we follow the Praised as our highest possibility. By doing so, we return to our highest but authentic and original state. We ascend from each contingent condition of the self towards Peace, in which we realize our witness that there is no self but the Self.

16.

The destruction of Stolac and its people reached its height with the destruction of the graveyards in the *čaršija*. This broke the connection between earth and heaven, body and Spirit, life and death. What took place at the end of the twentieth century was simply the toppling of a worm-eaten structure, on which had dozed the deadened selves, hollowed out like so many rotten tree trunks:

> Therefore a seal has been set on their hearts, and they do not understand. When thou seest them, their bodies please thee; but when they speak, thou listenest to their speech, and it is as they were propped-up timbers. They think every cry is against them. They are the enemy: so beware of them.[36]

Here is expressed the distinction between the inner and outer in the human self. Inside they are rotten with lies, but the exterior remains. What appears as exterior in such people corresponds to their bondage to earth and body, while they are cut off from heaven and Spirit. Such a split renders the *čaršija* impossible, as it came to be out of the inseparability of heaven and earth and body and Spirit. Its destruction is a direct consequence of this cut, without which the modern revolutionary movements are impossible to understand.

Given that the *čaršija* was subject to destruction through the entire twentieth century and by the end had been almost entirely extinguished, understanding requires insight into the situation from which this destruction began.

This condition of the architecture and the material content of the city, however, cannot be separated from the condition of the society within it. Any sustainable society rests on the spiritual condition of the majority of its members. No society can be sustained by an apparatus or force imposed from outside if they do not to some degree correspond to what its members are willing to accept. And the self never accepts anything simply because it feels forced into recognizing a debt towards someone or something other than God. The self's authentic nature lies with God, and anything other than God casts a shadow on the self. Nonetheless, the self seeks constantly for the original light of its creation and guidance.

The city and society and individuals, as they were at the end of the nineteenth century, were subject to damage and destruction through the twentieth century. In this book we have described the doctrine, ritual, and virtue, which is to say the nature, of the people of whom the *čaršija* was a reflection. The causes of destruction are to be found in certain marked changes in people caught up in "revolutionary ideologies and the movements based on them."[37]

In line with this, we may talk of a standing division of people into two groups.

The first group is that whose members have shaped their selves in accordance with their inviolate and uncreated essence, so that they are open to continuous transcendence, climbing from level to level. Their essence may be considered uncreated substance,[38] the Spirit of God breathed into them.[39] For such people, freedom is voluntary submission to the Principle. To the extent that they are devoted and submit to this Principle, the freer they are from imposing themselves on others and demanding their loyalty.

The other group are those who deny the uncreated essence, reducing their self to its external expressions, body and feeling, analytical or instrumental reason and imagination, the external world and domination over it. These are people whose hearts have been sealed or burned, cut off from openness to the Self. The very idea of freedom for such people is the subjection of everything in their environment to their image of the world; for them freedom is the ability to amass property and power and subject what is different from them to themselves.

The first group express or relate to others through confidence or trust. At no stage do they stand outside their relationship with God as the Faithful. They derive their relations with other people and the world as a whole from that. For them, God always stands with the helpless. Responsibility towards God entails responsibility towards the helpless. This is why the helpless have an inviolate and sacred claim on those more powerful than they. Lack of responsibility towards them is an act of hostility to God. No one in this group is capable of claiming that his God is not the God of all, of every other individual, society, and the world as a whole, regardless of how different those others are from him or their condition. This is why responsibility towards God and our debt towards Him entail responsibility and debt towards the other and the different.

The other group reduce confidence and trust to bargaining and rational choice. Their I-thou relationship does not include the presence of a Third. Judgment in all relations belongs to the more powerful. Relationship towards the weak does not depend on any debt or obligation on the part of the more powerful. It is their voluntary choice and right, justified by no reason other than sentiment and rational choice. Everything they do is based on the principle that subjection of the other confirms one's own independence.

17.

This division of people into two groups, those who realize themselves through a relationship with Intellect and those who admit nothing as transcending their own selves, is reflected in the two forms of knowledge—that which we have received as given to us from outside, from a teacher, and that which we find within ourselves, as there since always. If we think of the first as intellectual, then the second is simply a support. But, intellectual knowledge cannot be conditional on having been received from someone. Received knowledge is subject to illumination by intellectual knowledge. Otherwise, received knowledge could provide no guidance as to how we should realize ourselves in accordance with our highest potential.

In this lies the mystery of the human I. It cannot be unraveled without the other, who represents our "thou." The "I" can never know the other as well as his or her own self. But even that self-knowledge is little compared to the knowledge which resides with the absolute I. If the I and the thou are conscious of these limitations, then their relationship may be based on confidence, as the recognition of His constant presence as in a permanent relationship of confidence with both the I and the thou: He is always other, regardless of the I-thou relationship, which may become a multitude of we-you relationships, but He remains our highest possibility—for both the I and the thou. Whatever condition of this I or thou, they are always more or less clear images of Him.

Most people in what is referred to as the modern age or the age of Enlightenment never succeed in resolving the issue of the Third which is involved in every I-thou, I-you (pl.), we-thou, and we-you relationship. No ideology offers an adequate answer to this. That this is the case is clear from how they approach the "decayed bones" of the stranger, a perennial issue, in ignorance of which human dignity can neither be discovered nor maintained.

The issue of death is key. Two contradictory answers to it are possible. The first is that there is no life after death, and that human life or existence is limited to our period on earth. The other answer is that death is simply a transition to another different world and life there.

Neither of these answers is susceptible of proof that is decisive or comes down clearly in favor of one or the other side. The prophets were clearly and decisively in favor of the second answer. It is up to each of us to make our own judgment of the teachings they passed on to people, which many have accepted, so that each of us must decide for ourselves to believe or reject it. There has never been a time in history in which both responses have not coexisted.

The response one gives to the question, however, determines entirely the constitution of our life in this world. This difference may be seen in the following discourse on being in doubt regarding these two possibilities.

> He says, "Who shall quicken the bones when they are decayed?" Say: "He shall quicken, who originated them the first time; He knows all creation, who has made for you out of the green tree fire and lo, from it you kindle."[40]

Those who asked the Praised this question did not do so to hear his answer. They wanted to express their opposition to him as the bearer of the news of death, the resurrection, and the reckoning. They spoke against this news:

> What, does he promise you that when you are dead, and become dust and bones, you shall be brought forth? Away, away with that you were promised! There is nothing but our present life; we die, and we live, and we shall not be raised up. He is naught but a man who has forged against God a lie, and we will not believe him.[41]

Cleaving to the witness of the Praised, as the perfect example, that there is no god but God, the model disciple Ali leaves the question unresolved, thus indicating its decisive importance for openness towards the Wise. It is the most difficult question, and human salvation lies in wrestling with it:

> O people, we must all meet with that we want to flee. Death is the place life leads to. To flee it means to catch it. How many days have I spent searching for the secret to this matter, but God has allowed only that it remain hidden. Alas! It is a treasured knowledge. As for my final will, it is that of God. Do not believe in any partner to Him. And as for the Praised, do not disregard his path. Retain these two pillars and burn these two lamps.[42]

18.

It seems to us that life is real, and death the opposite. We try to confirm and protect this image of life as separate from death. In doing so, we ascribe reality to the material world and live in it. And we quite simply deny or separate the Spirit in death from matter, perception, and analytical or instrumental reason. According to Titus Burckhardt:

> For men of earlier ages matter was like an aspect of God. In the cultures that are commonly called archaic, this perspective was immediate and linked with sensory experience, for the symbol of matter was the earth. The latter represented, in its perennial reality, the passive principle of all visible things, whereas heaven represented the active and generating principle. The two principles are like the two hands of God. They are related to one another as male and female, as father and mother, and cannot be separated from one another—for in whatever the earth produces heaven is present as creative power, while the earth, for its part, gives form and body to the heavenly law. Thus the archaic way of looking at things was "sensible" and spiritual at one and the same time, for the metaphysical truth lying behind it remains independent of the simple world picture in question.[43]

For what is referred to as the *philosophia perennis*, which was common to both east and west up until the appearance of rationalism, these two principles, the active and passive, lie behind all visible phenomena, as the principal pillars of existence, determining all. In this view, matter is an expression and as such dependent on God. It is not something separate from Spirit and independent of it, but its necessary supplement. In itself, it is nothing more than the possibility of taking form, so that all things that may be perceived bear in them the seal of its active presence, the Spirit, and the Word of God. Nothing can be found in the world that has meaning outside this relationship to Intellect and Spirit. This is so because the world was created with Truth: nothing has being apart from the Truth, as its inner and external reality.

The two approaches to knowledge, that is reception or intellectuality, reach their most extreme point of difference over the issue of death, as restricting the self to received knowledge leads us to reject the confession that there is no god but God. Whatever the content of the received knowledge, it can never take the place of what is already within our own core—the Spirit of God and the knowledge of all the names. As justice is simply the confession of the Unity of God as the Unity of the Truth, revealed in the world as a whole and in the human self as the most beautiful form of existence, injustice is the concealment or denial of that which is immediate and within us. Injustice is violence against the self which commits it, as well as against all other people, the world as a whole, and God.

When we experience the death of someone close to us, we feel helpless. None of the knowledge that we have received can help us to respond to the question which now preoccupies us entirely. The experience of death harrows the self to its core. This experience is provoked by an external event, but once it has come about, it continues as an internal state which no longer depends on the external. It cannot be determined. In this state, there is no longer any clear distinction between the self that knows and that which it knows. We may say that our being has been raised to Intellect, which is its highest condition, and that there knowledge and being have come together. While news of death is perhaps the most common of all forms of news that reach us, it harrows the recipient so that none of the knowledge received or learned can prevent them from being shaken to their very core. That is how it is when the news is of the death of someone close to us.

When the Prophet says that for one who has experienced the death of someone close to approach their grave is of no assistance to the one who has died, but provides relief to the one who remains alive and in pain, he is stressing the inner nature of a condition which cannot be resolved by calling on any form of external authority to confirm knowledge received from outside.

The answer lies in Intellect, which is the most profound recess of the self. Then we turn to that recess, we turn to the house of God. Knowing it, we know God. A disaster in the external world has turned us to this knowledge, which depends not on place nor on time, nor on any other thing outside the self.

> And when you are in the ship—and the ships run with them with a fair breeze, and they rejoice in it, there comes upon them a strong wind, and waves come on and from every side, and they think they are encompassed; they call upon God, making their debt His sincerely: "If Thou deliverest us from these, surely we shall be among the thankful." Nevertheless when He has delivered them, behold, they are insolent in the earth, wrongfully. O men, your insolence is only against yourselves; the enjoyment of this present life, then unto Us you shall return, then We shall tell you what you were doing.[44]

Being on the boat is an image of being in the world. The boat is the work of human hands, but the sea and the winds of the world were made by God. The world and we are the two sides of creation, which both as a whole and in all its individual parts abides with Truth. God created both us and what we do.[45]

19.

Whenever we are inclined to see the world as independent of our own selves and subject to our will to know and rule it, which corresponds to the image of the boat sailing a fair wind towards a goal, there takes place a split in the union of human being and world. Then the self and the world appear to be two unrelated particulars. The storm on the sea and the death of someone close reveal this to be an illusion and turns us inward towards the center of the self in which the sending down of Unity into the manifold begins and towards which the manifold as a whole raises itself up.

Ignoring the debt of the living to the dead, neglecting or destroying their graves, simply represents our desire to deny our own selves, intellect, and heart, as our essence and the source of knowledge, so as to render ourselves entirely dependent on some external authority within the world. This desire may be represented by the image of the man in the boat or of the human being in the world. In either relationship, governing the boat or the world involves an elevated sense of independence and confidence in our sufficiency as a principle from which we start out as individuals.

The inviolate nature of the grave is a guarantee of the inviolate nature of the core of the human self as the house of Truth.

The destruction of the *čaršija* peaked in what was done to the dead and their graves. In nationalism as a modern ideology, "our God," the real one, is subordinated to the instrumental reason of the "enlightened nation." Affirmation of this requires an other, who has a "wrong God," so that everything that is his must be wrong and destroyed in the project to liberate the nation and arrive at the goal of incarnating "our God." In this way, human relations take on the form of anti-Islam. Generations were raised and motivated by this, as their orientation towards "freedom." Communism provided the frame for this movement and the feelings associated with it so that the living heirs of the dead in those graveyards were obliged to declare their allegiance by taking those "decayed bones" in their hands and bearing public witness that none could give life to them again.

The destruction of the graveyards of Stolac began during the period of conflict between Tito and Stalin, that is the summer of 1948 and the years that followed. This was a period of conflict between two Communist elites. For Tito and his supporters, the stakes were survival. Any waverers were judged without mercy. All those involved in this drama were required to commit: the Communist framework and the nationalist heritage that was its content presented Muslims with the choice of making the most definite declaration of submission. The destruction of their graveyards was their confession of commitment to fear, which then hovered over all.[46]

This fear, framed within ideology, spread throughout the human being and shook it to the core. People were offered the choice between survival and death. The choice of life is not simple contempt for death. Cleaving to the Giver of life should mean bearing witness that He is recognized as the Lord of life and death and that there is no expectation of happiness without Him.

But God does not place obligations on any of us that exceed our capacities.[47] It is in the deepest and most profound nature of each of us to feel pity for the dead. This pity or intellectual knowledge of death as the other side of life, of which the corpse and the grave are clear signs, cannot be destroyed without destroying our own selves at the same time. Survival and happiness are not possible unless we realize our own selves beyond the limits of this world, and so beyond the limits of death. As long as the relationship to the corpse and the grave is of benefit to the living, the inviolate and sacred nature of this relationship is a revelation of the reason why we were sent down into this world and why we are in it, and the purpose of our journey back from these material limits.

Images of the *Harems* or Graveyards

1. The *harems* within the *čaršija* complex
2. The Old Harem
3. The Great Harem
4. The *harems* as part of the cityscape
5. The Great Harem as the soothing of tensions within the *čaršija*
6. Death and life in Mary's tears
7. Gathering what has been dispersed

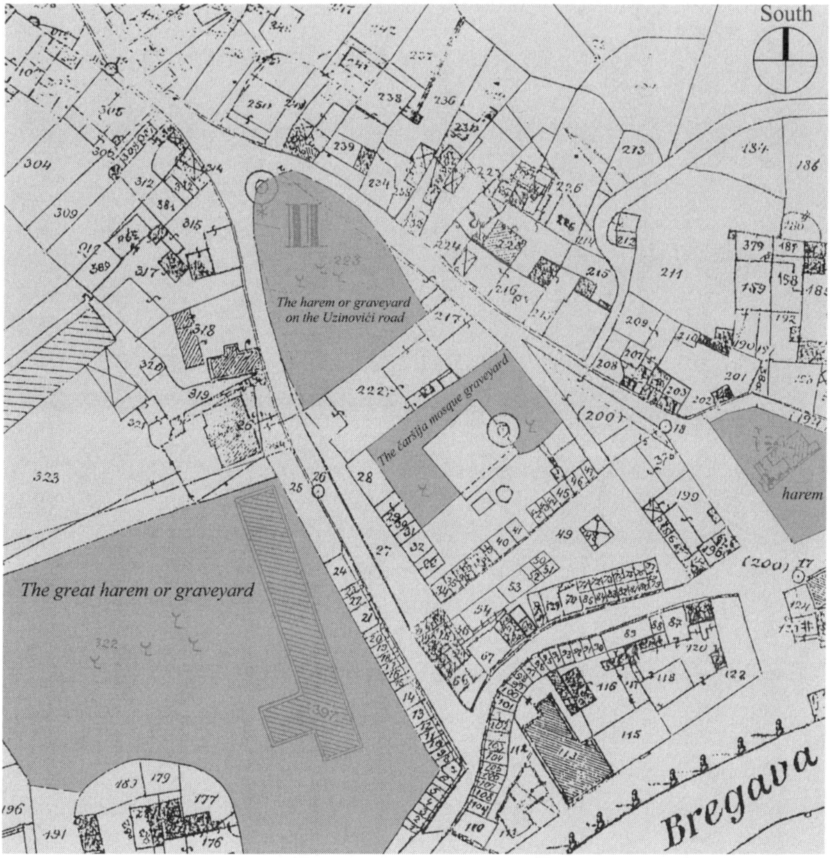

1. The *harems* within the *čaršija* complex

The *čaršija* and its contents represent the lost garden and our quest to rediscover it. The Stolac *harems* or graveyards connect garden and street, shop and house, mosque and *mekteb*. The search for the center hidden after our violation requires we renew our consciousness of return to God as a form of union and death every living being must undergo. We cannot discover any meaning to life without the presence of the inviolable dead for whom the living are responsible: defending the right of the dead to peace is a guarantee of the connection of the living with God the Living, who is Peace.

2. The Old Harem

The lines of the shops, their main courtyard doors, and their walls ending in doors facing Uzinovići indicated the direction of the *čaršija*. The resulting area was triangular. A path led far up towards Vrsnik Peak, the symbol of ascent. These pairs of doors, on the same axis, but facing different directions—one away from, the other towards Vrsnik—symbolized the relationship between death and life, matter and Spirit. The key symbol, however, was the *mihrab*, the receptive principle we search for in our desire to be happy. Each door was both entry and exit. Entering the *harem*, we turned towards death and the peace of the dead, while on leaving it, we turned towards life and motion. Entering or leaving the mosque, we are trying to return to God and attain Peace as our goal.

3. The Great Harem

The Great Harem in the foreground was bounded by shops along the roads towards the mosque and towards the bridge. The graveyard ran down the hillside towards these shops. It was the largest ordered area in the *čaršija*, dotted all over with upright and inscribed stones. Nowhere in the town could the living find more of their relatives. The peace of their graves reflected the problem of life and the impossibility of resolving it without taking into account death. The transitoriness of the hyacinths and lilies planted by those graves testified to the transitory nature of life and the need to find an answer to the question of death. The graves with box hedge and roses spoke of the permanence of love for the Living.

4. The *harems* as part of the cityscape

Responsibility for the grave, the home of the dead, brought us back from our wandering to the question of our origin, our mission in the world, and to return. Life in the town meant constantly being reminded by the reappearance of the graveyards within every line of sight. Persisting in our attempt to unravel the question of life and death, while reflecting on our sacred dead in their graves, saves us from the ignorance that can turn to fear. The Giver of life knows the meaning of death. He is the Living. If we know and love Him, we will find the answer to the question of death in our relationship with Him.

5. The Great Harem as the soothing of tensions within the *čaršija*

Its position above the *čaršija* complex, with the tall clock tower in the middle, and the number of inscribed graves made the Great Harem a book inscribed with traces of the lives of all those who had passed, for the sake of those yet to come. The dead called on all the living to read that book. This book was waiting for them, regardless of whether they accepted or rejected the call. Each one of us called by the simple fact of living has experienced the urgency of that call, the possibility that we might overcome death through knowledge.

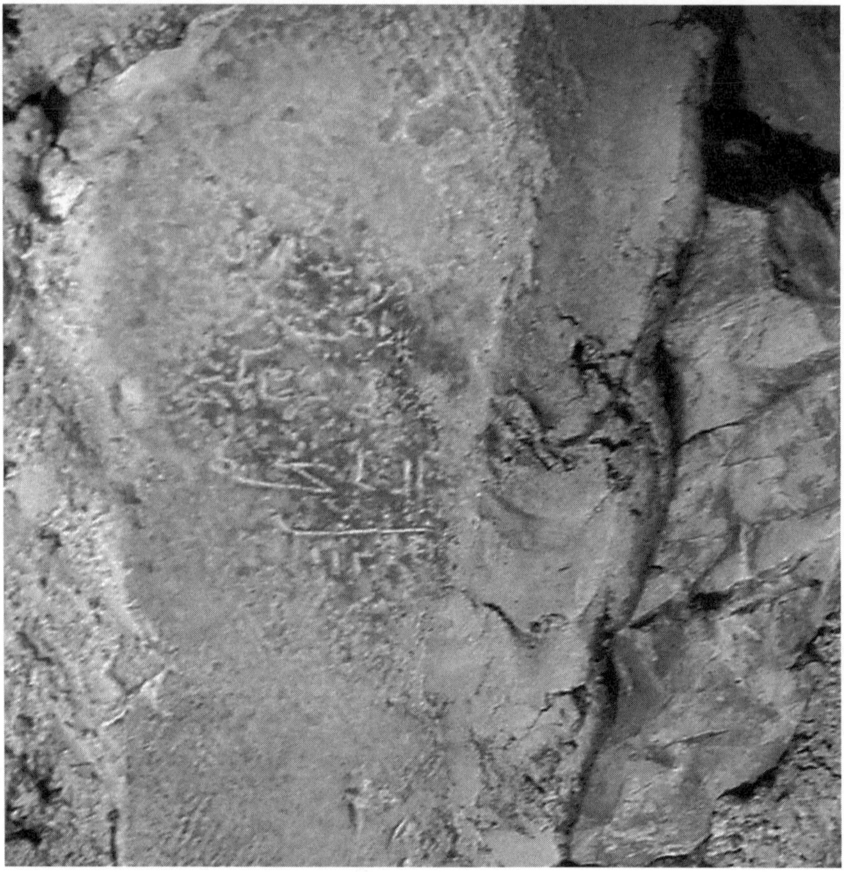

6. Death and life in Mary's tears

The destruction of all the graves and tombstones in the graveyards of the Stolac *čaršija* began in 1948. Some were shattered for use in road building; others went into the foundations and walls of the school; still others were left lying around to bear witness to the humiliation of the dead before and by their descendants. One fragment, found a half-century later in the wall of a woodshed built behind the New Mekteb sometime after 1950, preserved an inscription. It had marked the grave of one Miriam (Mary), daughter of Ibrahim (Abraham), who died in 1113 AH/1701 AD. The name of Mary was of decisive importance for the development and life of the Stolac *čaršija*, centered on the *mihrab*, a symbol of the human heart. The *mihrab* is inscribed with God's words: "Whenever Zachariah would come upon her in the *mihrab*!" This is the first part of a verse in the Recitation, which continues: "he would find her provided for. 'Mary,' he would ask,

'How comes this to you?' And she would say: 'From God; surely God provides for whom He wishes without stinting.'" Both the beginning and the meaning of this verse involve important questions for our relationship with God. The Prophet Zachariah was a servant at the Further Place of Annihilation, both heir to and one of the 124,000 prophets. He was an old man without issue. Mary and her answer from the *mihrab* reminded him of the God who had done this. God responded to Zachariah with the gift of a son, the Prophet John. Mary symbolizes our perfect ability to receive. Her reception of the Holy Spirit became manifest as the word of God, Jesus. The perfect poverty and service of the Praised also manifested as reception in his heart of the Holy Spirit, and therefore the Recitation, a Warning to the worlds. The memorials to Zachariah and to Mary, and so indirectly to John and to Jesus, in Bosnian *mihrab*s instruct us to turn to doctrine, ritual, and virtue, to what is sacred and focused in the Praised, and through him revealed to us all.

7. Gathering what was dispersed

After the Second World War, the Communists announced the New Age and the path towards a classless society. For the Bosnian Muslims, this meant their ruination would continue in the various aspects of their lives. In Stolac, the graveyards were destroyed and the tombstones shattered. Children grew up among these fragments, often ignorant that they were playing on the graves of their ancestors. Their descendents represented their humiliated ancestors as destroyers of both the living and the dead. But they remained tasked nonetheless with gathering what was dispersed as the means to self-realization and return to the self. There is no return to God without return to the self. The boy in the picture, holding a fragment of one of Stolac's thousands of Muslim gravestones, found somewhere in the ruins, is facing the question of the self and the world. Will he be receptive to this remnant of the book of existence and, through it, begin the process of bringing together the dissolute world? The fragment in his hand is inscribed: “There is no god but God; the All-Merciful . . . Ali. . .”.

Endnotes

Foreword

[1] "Seat" translates the Arabic noun *kursi* in the original. The Recitation or Quran (see note 3 below) also refers to the Arabic noun *arsh*, normally translated as "Throne." The relationship between the Throne and the Seat has been discussed at length over the centuries. God is the "Lord of the Throne" (Quran, 43:82), "the Lord of the Mighty Throne" (Quran, 9:129), "the Lord of the Noble Throne" (Quran, 23:116). Angels circle God's throne (see Quran, 39:75); at the last, eight Angels will carry the Throne of the Lord (Quran, 69:17). These Arabic and English nouns correspond to the Hebrew *kisse*, the Aramaic *karse*, and the Greek *Θρονος* and *βημα*. The throne of God is mentioned in Psalms, 113:5-6, which says that His Throne is in the heavens, while the earth serves at times as a footstool (cf. Psalms, 103:19; Matthew, 5:34-35). Our initial position was in the perfection of paradise, to which we will return. Our destiny is shaped by this perfect beginning in the garden and the suffering of pains in the earthly city. On our return, these earthly pains will be resolved into a heavenly City of Peace. God says in the Recitation: "Theirs is the Abode of Peace with their Lord, and He is their Protector for that they were doing" (6:127). And further: "And God summons to the Abode of Peace, and He guides whomsoever He will to an upright path" (10:25).

It is worth stressing that the Bosnian *krstjani* or members of the mediaeval Bosnian church were particularly attached to the Book of Revelations, in which the location of return is impressively represented as the Abode of Peace, the transformation of the city into the garden: "In the midst of the street of it, and on either side of the river, was there the tree of life, which bare twelve manner of fruits, and yielded her fruit every month: and the leaves of the tree were for the healing of the nations. And there shall be no more curse" (Revelations, 22:2-3). Life in this City of Peace is a return to the lost garden. The river of life mentioned in the quote has four streams—water, milk, wine, and honey (see Quran, 47:15 and Genesis, 2:10). This river with four streams flows at the foot of the Seat or Throne of God and the saved will participate in Life and dwell in the garden of Eternity (see John, 4:14, 7:38; Psalms, 46:5; Quran, 25:15-16). The tree of life (Genesis, 2:9) is an image of the healing of the ancient wound caused by our opposing our will to God's. The leaves refer to the ancient human instinct to cover the pudenda with leaves, marking the boundary which reveals our distinction from the world (see Quran, 7:22, 20:121) and so our immersion in duality, where we must overcome our travails by confessing that neither we nor the world are God and that only He is Real. Accursedness is overcome by return to God, through the full harmony of the two wills—ours and His (see Quran, 89:27-30). Our exile or descent from the peak or the place of original perfection towards the low point of existence and our choice there between return towards the garden or further decline are symbolized by the Rock on the mount in Jerusalem and the House in the valley at Mecca. The Kaaba symbolizes the city as our earthly effort to restore the original garden. The relationship between the Kaaba and the Rock corresponds to the relationship between earth and heaven or body and soul. Al-Azraqi reports that Ibn Abbas said of the Messenger: "The House which is in heaven is called *al-Durah*; it is built in the same way as this sacred House [the Kaaba]; if the former would fall, it would fall upon the latter" (Wüstenfeld, *Die Chroniken der Stadt Mekka*, 18, 4; cited in Wensinck, "The Ideas of the Western Semites Concerning the Navel of the Earth," 48). The house corresponds to "the inhabited house" (*al-bayt al-mamur*) mentioned in Quran 52:4. The Prophet Muhammad, whose name means "the praised," says: "This House [Kaaba] is one of 15, seven in the heavens up to the throne and seven up to the limits of the lowest earth. The highest one, which is near the throne, is the 'visited house.' Every one of these houses has a sacred territory like that of the Kaaba. If any one of them fell down, the rest would fall down, one upon the other, to the limits of the lowest earth. And every house has its heavenly or earthly worshippers, like the Kaaba" (Wüstenfeld, *Die Chroniken der Stadt Mekka*, 6, 1; cited in Wensinck, "The Ideas of the Western Semites Concerning the Navel of the Earth," 51-52). This order of 15 Kaabas, seven above and seven below the earthly one, is reflected in the oldest form of the covered part of the Further Mosque (*al-masjid al-aqsa*), which had seven naves to either side of the *mihrab* in the spacious central nave, all facing the Kaaba. For the oldest form, see Grabar, *Jerusalem.*

[2] It is usual to present God as male. There is considerable danger in this. Every determination of God places a limitation upon Him. Every limitation is a representation in terms of number. Every representation in terms of number entails that there are others than Him. This is idolatry. For this reason, it is not wrong to speak of God in both the male and female gender, mindful that He is both far and near, both similar and incomparable. On this, see Murata, *The Tao of Islam.*

[3] Quran, 2:255. The translations from the Quran are taken from Arthur J. Arberry, *The Koran Interpreted*, adapted to reflect the author's preferred rendering of certain terms in the Arabic original. [Translator's note: The quotations from the Recitation included in the Bosnian original were generally given in the author's own rendering.] The standard system of reference is used, with the first number referring to the chapter or *surah* and the second to the verse or *ayat.* The Arabic noun *Quran* was translated as *Učenje* throughout the Bosnian original. [Translator's note: after discussion with the author, it has been decided to use Recitation, as a generally accepted English equivalent, though Discourse, Learning, Lesson, or Teaching might have been more in keeping with the Bosnian word, as the remainder of this footnote makes clear.] This has been done to introduce the relevant concept into the semantic chains that bind the language in which this book is written. The concept of Quran refers generally to anything which is heard, seen, or in any other way comes to be known and transmitted in human discourse. All the revealed books, in their greater and lesser parts, are thus "Quran." The Quran is, at its broadest, the totality of existence—both visible and invisible worlds. When not otherwise

indicated, the Recitation refers to the Arabic Quran, in the sense of the Book sent down by God as His discourse through the Holy Spirit into the heart of His Messenger, who transmitted it to humanity. That which the Messenger received and transferred took the form of the Book. The same person never rereads the same text in exactly the same way. Moreover, because of the message it contains and the belief of those who accept it, the Recitation is the discourse of God, which is to be understood differently in accordance with the requirements of each new moment. In agreement with the fundamental message of this book, we have avoided reification or misleading rigidity in our use of concepts referring to our relationship with God, in particular *islam* (being-at-peace), *iman* (faith), *ihsan* (acting well and beautifully), and *din* (debt or obligation). This is why the reader will not find in this text the formulations "Islam says," "the Quran says," etc. To do so would be ideological reduction of Divine Discourse to a discourse on certain things, things which remain for the most part unclear and undetermined.

[4] See Quran, 2: 31-34.

[5] See Quran, 53:23, 28:65.

[6] See Bešlagić, *Kamene stolice srednjovekovne Bosne i Hercegovine.*

[7] Six settlements with the name Stolac are to be found in the *Rječnik naseljenih mjesta u Bosni i Hercegovini*, 269. This book is about one of them, which developed as a town over a long period on the banks of the River Bregava, in a valley encircled by hills, in the south of Bosnia, some 20 km from the shores of the Adriatic.

[8] On the destruction of Stolac and the expulsion of its inhabitants see *Crimes in Stolac Municipality* and Dizdar, *Suđeni Stolac.* The crime has been described in several indictments of the Hague tribunal. While the destruction of Stolac gathered pace at the end of the nineteenth century, its roots were already evident in the construction of the complex of houses known as the Begovina (The Bey's Manor). When this was built in the middle of the nineteenth century, it brutally disturbed the sacred unity of the valley and its built environment. The separation of a group of houses outside the town unit, drawing attention to themselves as particularly significant, served for more than a century to divert attention from the union of sacred doctrine and sacred art which imbues the valley of Stolac as a whole. One may say of these tasteless and isolated houses, outside and opposed to the town, that they provided and have remained grounds for the destruction of Stolac and for action against it based on ignorance of the whole. The position of the Begovina with regard to the Stolac *čaršija* as a whole corresponds to its builder Ali Pasha Rizvanbegović's program to break up the movement led by Husein, the Captain of Gradačac, the goal of which was to establish a united Bosnia. Just as Begovina is opposed to the integrity of Stolac, so Herzegovina was opposed to the integrity of Bosnia. Begovina was opposed to Stolac in order to deny its center and spread away from it. It casts a shadow over the whole and its parts, the unitary sacred cluster which extends from the *mihrab* of the *čaršija* mosque, towards which all the elements of the town are turned. Herzegovina was also separated by force from Bosnia and opposed to it. Before Ali Pasha Rizvanbegović's egomaniacal

and destructive project, Herzegovina was never separate or opposed to the whole. Thus, a framework for hindering and undermining a united Bosnia was already in place in the early nineteenth century. For more on Ali Pasha Rizvanbegović's role in the anti-Bosnian movement and on the non- and anti-Bosnian significance of Herzegovina, see Aličić, *Pokret za autonomiju Bosne od 1831. do 1832. godine* and Kapidžić, *Ali Paša Rizvanbegović i njegovo doba.*

[9] Al-Ayyashi narrates in his *Al-Tafsir* the following from as-Sadiq: "Abu Dharr said: 'O Messenger of God! What is the best of that which has been revealed to you?' He said: 'The verse of the "Chair". The seven heavens and seven earths in the "Chair" are but like a ring thrown in a vast open space.' Then he said: 'And surely the excellence of *al-Arsh* [the Throne] over the Chair is like that of the open space over the ring'" (cited after Tabatabaii, *Al-Mizan*, 4:163). The Chair in this quotation is the same as the seat in our translations. This tradition is also given in Kisai, *Adjaib al-Malakut*, 538, fol. 4 and Tabari, *Tafsir*, 3:7, 17 (cited in Wensinck, "The Ideas of the Western Semites Concerning the Navel of the Earth," 58).

A Note on Anthropological and Cosmological Premises

[1] Mak Dizdar (1917-1971) is known principally for his book *Kameni spavač/ Stone Sleeper*, a poetical discourse of humanity, the world, and God in the idiom of traditional Bosnian culture. For more on his poetic opus from the perspective of perennial philosophy, see Mahmutćehajić, *Across the River: On the Poetry of Mak Dizdar.*

[2] The translations of Dizdar's poetry used in the text are by Francis Jones, given in Dizdar, *Kameni spavač/Stone Sleeper* and for "Blue River" in Mahmutćehajić, *Across the River.*

[3] Quran, 22:18.

[4] It is the author's practice to refer to the Prophet Muhammad through the literal translation of the Arabic meaning of his name, "the Praised," in order to make clear his metaphysical and anthropo-cosmological significance as our guide in ontological totality, through whose example we learn the dignity of the human form of being as the focus of the praise directed by the cosmos at God. The designation "the Praised" corresponds to *Muhammad* and *Ahmad* in Arabic. The decision to translate these names in this way, which is not normal practice, is due to the need to understand the semantic fields which render the name of the Praised (Muhammad) inseparable from the concepts of "praising" (*hamd*), "to praise" (*hamida*), and the divine name the All-Praised (*al-Hamid*). By introducing the name into the semantic chain in this way we may "revive" the perennial significance of the name and the person of the Praised as the "seal of the prophets," "the finest example," "the mercy unto the worlds," "the shining lamp," the one who has been announced by all God's prophets who came before him. Only in the modern age has this perennial nature of the Praised been overshadowed by his historical aspect. Moreover, many reduce the Praised just to his historical aspect and so to his earthly death. In this way, they exclude the human need for a perfect example,

which the Praised is at all times and for each one of us. His presence does not depend on place or time. He is both present and near as the Messenger, though we may be absent and remote in so far as we take secular phenomena in our images of the world as ultimate and sufficient. Regarding this presence, the Messenger says: "I was the prophet when Adam was between clay and water" (Ibn Hanbal, 4:66). This includes his being a mercy unto the world, a shining lamp, and the finest example, without limitation by anything before or anything after. No historical phenomenon can magnify or undermine his being so from beginning to end. Each of us senses and knows our own highest moment, which is indelible, regardless of our condition. Our highest or perfect moment always exists within us: it is both within us and outside us; we take pleasure in it as we do in a created gift, but also as we do a gift of God. This is one meaning of God's revelation regarding the Praised, who dwells amongst us (see Quran, 49:7), but also in all existence as it praises God. This sublime human potential in all things is Truth and the Truth's ability to attract. Our desire to know the Truth of all creation and to be what we know is love for Him. And love is the desire for unification. There is only one way for us to realize this desire, through our own perfection and witness to Unity, by following the Praised as our eternal moment of sublimity, according to which we may realize ourselves and experience the bliss of Truth's love for us.

[5] Quran, 67:3.

[6] According to this holy tradition, God says through the Praised: "My heavens and My earth embrace Me not, but the heart of My believing servant does embrace Me." Although not confirmed by the exoteric rules used in confirming the reliability of tradition, it is accepted by the Sufis. It is cited by al-Ghazali in his *Ihya ulum ad-din*, 3:5.1.

[7] See Quran, 82:7.

[8] While the Prophet is the Praised, as the most praiseworthy example, God is the All-Praised as the object of all the love and praise that is in the cosmos. Creation is the circuit of praise from God as All-Praising to God as All-Praised through His praiseworthy creation.

[9] Quran, 33:72.

[10] Quran, 95:1-6.

[11] See Quran, 2:30.

[12] See Quran, 37:96.

[13] Bukhari, 8:336-37.

[14] Quran, 2:30.

[15] Quran, 2:30.

Locating Bosnia for the American Reader

[1] Mak Dizdar, *Stone Sleeper*, 100.

[2] Mak Dizdar, *Stone Sleeper*, 100.

1. *Philosophia Perennis*

[1] *Philosophia perennis*, or the perennial philosophy, refers: (a) to the metaphysics which admit the importance of the divine reality for the world of things, life, and consciousness; (b) to the psychology which finds in the self something similar or equivalent to the Divine real; and (c) to the ethics which consider our final purpose to be the knowledge of the essence or truth of all being. As such the perennial philosophy has existed always and everywhere. In spite of the differences between its manifestations at different times and in different cultures and languages, its essential content has always remained recognizably the same. "The debt of (up)rightness of being" (*al-din al-kayyim*) may be thought of as another name for what we also know as the *philosophia perennis*: humanity was originally created in most beautiful (up)rightness (*fi ahsani taqwimin*), which means that our original nature shows itself as absolute harmony that reflects the entire external world. Both we and the world were created by God the Upright (*al-kayyum*). This is why both we and the world reflect this one of His names: we are related to God through (up)rightness of being (*al-sirat al-mustaqim*). Only on this path, which is divine and leads to God, can we realize our authentic and original creaturehood. By violating that which was not to be violated and opposing our will to the Divine Will, we lost that original inner balance and fell to the lowest of the low places; our original and beautiful (up)rightness is an attainable goal, through the discovery of what we have lost, so long as we turn towards God, admit our debt to Him, and ascend upon the upright path to return to Him. The world and the self are sources of necessary, but not sufficient knowledge. Ascent presupposes that we accept the need for a third source of knowledge—that sent down by God to His prophets, which they passed on to us as doctrine, way, and virtue. By confessing our debt to God, we open ourselves up to receive and to realize in our own selves the Divine names. God is Wise, however, so each of us receives from Him the opportunity to become wise in that wisdom which drives us in love towards God and to return to Him. This is made possible by our original nature (*al-fitra*), which is indestructible, as the Spirit of God, breathed into each of us, is uncreated. Our ascent towards our original nature is liberation and resurrection. When we violated the inviolate center of the garden, we wounded ourselves. Liberation is the healing of this wound and the cleansing of its consequences. It entails a changed understanding of the world and ourselves, particularly with regard to the paradox of liberation: "Woe that day unto those who cry it lies, who cry lies to the Day of Debt; and none cries lies to it but every guilty aggressor. When our signs are recited to him, he says, 'Fairy-tales of the ancients!' No indeed; but that they were earning has rusted upon their hearts. No, indeed; but upon that day they shall be veiled from their Lord" (Quran, 83:10-15). The *philosophia perennis* is primarily concerned with the unity of the Principle and the principle of Unity. This is the question of God's reality as the essence of the manifold of being. This reality is such that it is manifest both mediately and immediately. The question of immediate knowledge of

the real is the heart of the perennial philosophy. That some individuals have such knowledge and that they pass it on to others as doctrine, ritual, and virtue may be accepted or rejected. Both responses have been made throughout the history of humankind. The rejection or forgetting of perennial philosophy as an important factor in human history may only be interpreted as evidence of human weakness stimulated and deepened by arrogance. As is evident from the now generally accepted name for this phenomenon, the *philosophia perennis* relates to wisdom or *Sophia.* Such wisdom has always existed at the core of the various religions and traditional philosophies. Wisdom is one, but it has found expression in different languages. The love of wisdom is the love of God as Wise, a love which leads away from separation, as He has no other. Given that human existence derives from God as Perfect, our goal can be nothing less than perfection. This is our potential. It does not depend, in principle, on the circumstances of our lives: it is a matter of the human mode of being as such. Circumstances may facilitate or hinder our discovery or distortion of our original perfection. They cannot, however, destroy or render entirely impossible the realization of the purpose of humanity. Accordingly, the perennial philosophy is not a matter of history or the future, which lie beyond the reality of any given self: it is, above all and beyond all, a matter of our individual self-realization. The ontology, metaphysics, cosmology, anthropology, and psychology of the perennial philosophy affect our self-realization in our highest moment—the discovery of ourselves as fully in God's image. On the history of the concept of the *philosophia perennis* in the west see: Schmitt, "Perennial Philosophy: from Steuco to Leibnitz." For more on this and the perennial philosophy itself, see the following works: Schuon, *Islam and the Perennial Philosophy*; Guénon, *Man and His Becoming according to the Vedanta*; *The Multiple States of Being*; Schmitt, *Studies in Renaissance Philosophy and Science*; Lings, *The Eleventh Hour*, *Symbol and Archetype*; Nasr, *Knowledge and the Sacred*; *Islamic Philosophy from its Origin to the Present*; Pallis, *The Way and the Mountain*; Perry, *A Treasury of Traditional Wisdom*; Burckhardt, *Fez: City of Islam*; *Chartres and the Birth of the Cathedral*; Smith, *Forgotten Truth*; Laibelman, *The Other Perennial Philosophy*; Chittick, *The Heart of Islamic Philosophy*; Veljačić, *Philosophia Perennis*; Huxley, *The Perennial Philosophy*; Schmidt-Biggemann, *Philosophia Perennis*; Shah-Kazemi, *Paths to Transcendence.*

[2] Through His mercy and His knowledge, God comprehends everything (Quran, 7:156, 6:80). By creating the heavens and the earth and everything between, God reveals Himself in His knowledge. Everything He dispersed in the worlds gathers in us. There is nothing in the heavens or the world or between them that does not have a place in us as a potential object of our knowledge: "We can perhaps envision the enlargement of the self diagrammatically as a series of constantly expanding concentric circles which symbolize the unplumbed sensitivity of the mind to embrace heaven, earth, and the myriad things. To enlarge oneself is therefore to purify, enlighten, and bring to fruition the ultimate capacity of the mind to 'embody' the cosmos. The self so conceived is not a static structure but a dynamic process. It is a *center* of relationships, not an enclosed world of private thoughts and feelings. It needs to reach out, to be in touch with other selves, and to communicate

through an ever-expanding network of human relatedness" (Wei-Ming, *Confucian Thought*, 133). On our path of expanding the self through knowledge, the Praised is our best perennial example. At once a-historical and historical, he prayed, in the Divine Revelation: "O my Lord, increase me in knowledge!" (Quran, 20:114).

[3] Bosnian unity-in-plurality is one of our key themes. The reader can find out more on this theme in Mahmutćehajić, *Bosnia the Good: Tolerance and Tradition*, *Sarajevo Essays: Politics, Ideology, and Tradition*, and *Learning from Bosnia: Approaching Tradition.*

[4] The normal term for a Muslim graveyard in Stolac is *harem*, a word which means a forbidden or inviolate area, which must not be profaned. This is the same word used to refer to the forbidden or private area of the house. The ordinary word for graveyard, *groblje*, is normally used to refer to Christian burial grounds. In Sarajevo, it is normal to refer to Muslim burial grounds as graveyards (*groblje*), while *harem* is used to refer to the area around the mosque.

[5] In this essay, tradition is used to refer to the relationship between human beings and God as the Highest Principle: "Tradition, because of its comprehensive character," says Marco Pallis, "is not easy to define; but a few indications may make it clearer. It embraces the whole of a civilization, in all its modes and departments, and tends to the obliteration of all antitheses, such as 'sacred and profane,' even 'Creator and Creation.' A truly traditional civilization has its roots fixed in a doctrine of the purely metaphysical order, beyond the limitations even of Personality. This doctrine gives to the whole, its principle or sufficient cause. The other constituents of the Tradition, whether ethical, social, or artistic, down to the most petty activities of daily life, all derive their authority from this doctrine, to be exercised within their prescribed spheres. Ideas of the metaphysical order are the cement which binds every part together. The whole body of thought must be viewed as a hierarchy, with a pure metaphysics at the head" (*Peaks and Lamas*, xvii). For further treatment of the concept of "tradition" see Mahmutćehjajić, *Learning from Bosnia.* The *philosophia perennis* provides a basis and framework for the meditations within this book. This means a focus on the relationship between prophecy and philosophy, a relationship that has been increasingly ignored in the west since the Middle Ages. The link between prophecy and philosophy is of crucial importance for any deeper consideration of the sources of western philosophy, "origins that western philosophy shares with Islamic philosophy but that have come to be understood in radically different ways by these two currents of thought as western philosophy has come to distance itself to an ever greater degree from both the perennial philosophy and Christian theology" (Nasr, *Islamic Philosophy from Its Origin to the Present*, 5).

[6] The concept of "tradition" is used in this text a little differently than is usual in contemporary discourse. Tradition is the awakening principle of a healthy society or the "prevenient idea" that underpins and inspires the entire life of a people. This principle is both supra-individual and individual. Through it, the individual and society are both constantly "connected" with the complex diversity of being, from the material to the spiritual, from the interpretation to the revelation. In such a relationship, neither the individual nor society can be imprisoned within

an image of the Real. They are called to reject each image for that of which it is an image.

[7] The concept of the "heart" is used in this text in accordance with its use in the Quran and the tradition whose source is the Revelation. The heart does not signify the sensitive or emotional aspect of human nature, but the center of consciousness and intellectuality. It is the human ability to comprehend God in the fullness of His revelation. According to Ibn Arabi, only the heart can know God or reality in a focused way, bringing together analytical understanding and supra-analytical revelation (see Chittick, *Ibn Arabi*, 25).

[8] The entire reason and purpose of humankind is to be found reflected in this sentence, which may be translated as: "No art without knowledge." This is true for every art and for every skill. Even architecture and poetry and music involve a truth they must express, "while others had begun to think, as we now think, of houses, and even of God's house, only in terms of construction and effect" (Coomaraswamy, "*Ars sine scientia nihil*," 229). From such a point of view, whose beginnings are referred to in the citation, knowledge and action must be separated, so that *ars* is separate and independent from *scientia*. When preference is given to action, knowledge may become even further degraded. Then, the source of knowledge and its range are determined by the one who takes action or has power. But knowledge properly understood does not belong to us. We receive it. Recognizing the Lord's claim against us is to recognize that knowledge, ritual, and virtue are inseparable and that coming-to-know is taking over or receiving That which is known, while ritual and virtue involve a ceaseless turning towards the Known. When this is not the case, action increases our sense of restlessness and our unsatisfied quest for "sweetness," awakening desire and emotion. "The notion and necessity of a μετανοια are inseparably bound up with the formulations of the *Philosophia Perennis* wherever we find them" (Coomaraswamy, "On Being in One's Right Mind," 39).

[9] On sacred art see the following: Coomaraswamy, *The Transformation of Nature in Art*; *Christian and Oriental Philosophy of Art*; Burckhardt, *Sacred Art in East and West*; *Art of Islam*; *The Universality of Sacred Art*; Lings, *Splendors of Quran Calligraphy and Illumination*; Kapikian, *Art in the Service of the Sacred*; Howes, *The Art of the Sacred*.

2. The Garden

[1] The holy city of Mecca lies in a desert valley, between harsh hills. It is mentioned in the Quran as Mecca once (48:24) and elsewhere as Becca (3:96). Muslim tradition also identifies the second form in Psalm 84, which mentions both sacred places, the Inviolate Mosque in Becca and the Further Mosque on Zion. There is a rich esoteric tradition in Bosnia about the relationship between the two phonemes /b/ and /m/. The phoneme /b/ is made with a gentle exhalation of breath which opens the lips, while /m/ is made by inhaling gently, so as to close the lips. In this way, Bosnian tradition knows a symbolic blossom comprising four Cyrillic letters /b/, which signifies the inseparability of Muhammad, Mary, the Messiah, and the

Mushaf (a bound copy of the Quran), which is to say the Praised, the Virgin, the Anointed, and the Book.

[2] The regularly shaped or conic hilltop signifies the heart as our innermost core—the cave is the inverse triangle. The hill is the clearest earthly sign of verticality or uprightness. After we violated the inviolate, the clarity of this sign in the external world remained as it had been. Our inner condition, however, changed: the heart was veiled, so that our self-realization became conditional on withdrawal into solitude and the seeking of mysteries. The *mihrab* is a sign of this inner condition and withdrawal. The cave is a place for the ritual of initiation or for gathering the community of the just. On the relationship between the mountain and the cave, see Guénon, "The Heart and the Cave" and "The Mountain and the Cave."

[3] Local tradition passed down amongst the Muslims of Stolac talks of the mosque at the top of the peak or Vrsnik as an old temple, about the raising of which nothing is known. There really are some old ruins on that spot, which rises like a peak from the valley. One should not forget that the peak of Visočica, the most important mountain in the spiritual geography of Bosnia, is also referred to as the Mosque, as are a number of other hilltop or mountain-top locations in Bosnia today.

[4] *Al-din al-haqq.* The Arabic word *din* is normally translated into English as "religion" and into Bosnian as *vjera.* In accordance with the views of such authors as Cantwell Smith, the author believes this translation is unhelpful as it tends to support the reification of faith and our relationship with God in and through institutional forms. In the worst cases, it can lead to the substitution of the form for the proper relationship itself. At the heart of our relationship to God is our debt towards Him, both on account of our creaturehood and as a result of our first ancestor's transgression in paradise. One of the meanings of the Arabic word *din* is "debt," whence the extended meaning "obligation." The author therefore translates it into Bosnian as *dug,* which is roughly equivalent to the English word "debt." It is perhaps also worth noting that the Latin word *religio* is thought by some to derive from the same root as "obligation," the verb *ligare* or "to bind." Religion is thus the establishment of an authentic relationship between parties to a contract in which one gives and the other takes. This is at heart a relationship of "confidence," as between a creditor and one under an obligation to that creditor, which is to say a debtor. As creatures, all that we are and all that we have we have received from the Creator. Returning the confidence the Creator has shown in us is to pay the debt of existence.

[5] *Al-din al-khalis.*

[6] *Al-din al-qayyim.*

[7] Quran, 48:28

[8] Quran, 39:2-3

[9] Quran, 12:40.

[10] The Inviolate Mosque in the valley of Becca or Mecca and the Further Mosque

in Jerusalem are both mentioned in the Recitation (17:1). For the meaning of the valley of Becca in Abrahamic tradition see Lings, *Mecca.* According to the historian al-Azraqi (Wüstenfeld, *Die Chroniken der Stadt Mekka*), an inscription with the following words was found in the foundations of the Kaaba: "I am God the Lord of Becca; I made it a sanctuary on the day when I created heaven and earth, sun and moon; on the day when I made these two mountains" (Cited after Wensinck, "The Ideas of the Western Semites Concerning the Navel of the Earth," 12).

[11] The reader should not be confused by this translation of the term *masjid.* Annihilation of the self or self-abnegation simply means liberating the self from appearance and from connection to unreality and so opening it up to the Real. By thus annihilating the unreal self, we become open to the Self. We neither have nor can have anything we have not received from that Self. And what do we want from that which we have received? Does anything befit us except the Self? Whatever level of being we may be on, when we annihilate the self or bring about its death, the possibility is always open to us that we be born to a higher level. This is the meaning of the frequently quoted verses of Rumi: "I died as mineral and became a plant, I died as plant and rose to animal, I died as animal and I was Man. Why should I fear? When was I less by dying? Yet once more I shall die as Man, to soar with angels blest; but even from angelhood I must pass on; all except God doth perish. When I have sacrificed my angel-soul, I shall become what no mind e'er conceived. Oh, let me not exist! For Non-existence proclaims in organ tones: 'To Him we shall return'" (Cited after Nicholson, *Rumi: Poet and Mystic*, 103).

[12] Bukhari, 4:383. According to this tradition, the Inviolate Place of Annihilation at the bottom of the "valley of tears" has existed since the beginning of the world. Its history, however, begins with the historical appearance of the Praised. From the seventh century on, construction began and has continued in the sacred area of that valley which should reflect consciousness of God as the Creator and of human existence and of what we do. On the buildings that have appeared within the valley and on the inviolate Mosque since the seventh century see Grabar, "Upon Reading al-Azraqi."

[13] Quran, 95:4-6.

[14] Quran, 2:144.

3. The Town

[1] The world and we are two inseparable sides of the manifestation of the One and the Same. We can no more be separated from the world than the world from us. It is expected of us that we discover and realize our original nature in being-at-peace, so that we may become the people of peace, and so that God may appear through us as Peace. The world is at peace before God as Peace and reveals Him as such. The world is therefore within us, just as we are within it. We and it are not two separate things. As we come to know ourselves, and are thus both knower and known, so our knowledge of the world as a whole can never be separated from our own selves. "Since the value of the human is not anthropocentric, the assertion that man is the measure of all things is not humanistic enough. To fully

express our humanity, we must engage in a dialogue with heaven because human nature, as conferred by heaven, realizes itself not by departing from its source but by returning to it. Humanity, so conceived, is the public property of the cosmos, not the private possession of the anthropological world, and is as much the defining characteristic of our being as the self-conscious manifestation of heaven" (Wei-Ming, *Centrality and Commonality*, 102).

[2] Quran, 3:31.

[3] Bukhari, 4:525-26.

[4] Bukhari, 2:157.

[5] Psalms, 84:5-7.

[6] Quran, 95:1-6. That the designation "the land of the faithful" (*al-balada amin*) is connected with the valley may be seen from the prayer of Ibrahim (Quran, 14:35-41); there the Inviolate Mosque (*al-masjid al-haram*) is referred to as the inviolate house (*bayt al-muharram*).

[7] We all enter this world from a form of pre-existence and bring with us as our innermost nature our original oath to God: "And when thy Lord took from the Children of Adam, from their loins, their seed, and made them testify touching themselves, 'Am I not your Lord?' They said, 'Yes, we testify'—lest you should say on the Day of Resurrection, 'As for us, we were ignorant of this'" (Quran, 7:172). From the gathering of all of us in pre-existence, God chose His prophets, 124,000 from all the peoples. Through these prophets, He sent down His messengers to all people and all nations, each in their own tongue. And God required of each of these prophets that they bear witness in pre-existence to the Praised: "And when God took compact with the Prophets: 'That I have given you of Book and Wisdom; then there shall come to you a Messenger confirming what is with you—you shall believe in him and you shall help him; do you agree?' He said. 'And do you take My load on you on that condition?' They said, 'We do agree.' God said, 'Bear witness so, and I shall be with you among the witnesses.' Then whosoever turns his back after that—they are the ungodly" (Quran, 3:81-82).

[8] Ibn Hanbal, 4:66.

[9] See Quran, 7:157.

[10] Quran, 9:120.

[11] See Bukhari, 2:391, and Lings, *Muhammad*, 336.

[12] See Quran, 53:13-18.

[13] Sophrony, *St. Silouan the Athonite*, 448-49, quoted from "Adam's lament" in the liturgical manual *The Lenten Triodion*, "The Sunday of Forgiveness Vespers"; according to Patton, "Howl, Wail, and Moan, and Bring It Back to God," 262-63.

[14] Revelation, 22:1-4. The "lamb" is the symbol of the prime creation or the Praised. The lamb knows its mother amongst thousands of others: it is the incarnation of the confession that for him there is no mother but his own. This image

corresponds to the confession that there is no god but God and that we, as God's servants, are expected to recognize Unity in the manifold and to confess that there is no provider but the Provider. The perfect principle of this knowledge is the Praised: he is as such God's servant and Messenger. The Lamb is beside the Lord on His throne. This name is normally associated with Jesus. It may, however, refer to any of the prophets. Their confession that there is no god but God signifies the restitution to all things of the Reality through which they were created. Just as the lamb unerringly finds its mother amongst the multitude of similar sheep, so the prophet knows that all provision comes from God: "Surely God is the All-Provider, the Possessor of Strength, the Ever Sure" (Quran, 51:58). God sent down his command to the Praised: "Say: 'Shall I take to myself as Protector other than God, the Originator of the heavens and of the earth, He who feeds and is not fed?'" (Quran, 6:14). Regarding this, Jesus said: "Take no thought for your life, what ye shall eat, or what ye shall drink; nor yet for your body, what ye shall put on. Is not the life more than meat, and the body than raiment? Behold the fowls of the air: for they sow not, neither do they reap, nor gather into barns; yet your heavenly Father feedeth them. Are ye not much better than they?" (Matthew, 6:25-26).

4. The *Mihrab*

[1] *Sahifa*, 250.

[2] In talking of the *musafirhana*, the *mekteb*, and the mosque, we should make clear that understanding the *čaršija* and the surrounding area requires consideration of the institutions of the *waqf* or Islamic endowment. There are more than two hundred such *waqf*s in and around the Stolac *čaršija*. The surviving endowments make clear the town's inhabitants' awareness of their responsibilities towards it and life in it and the intimate connection between their personal welfare in this and the other world and the welfare of the town overall. One is left with the impression that these endowments reflect individual and group consciousness, which is closely related to the *čaršija* itself. The *waqf* endowments include the mosques and *mekteb*s, the *musafirhana* and the clock tower, the graveyards and certain houses, shops, and bridges, mills and gardens, books and funds. Over the centuries, people have left their property in the belief that they were prolonging their life in the world they were in fact leaving behind and so sending before them some good to find them in the other world and be accounted to their benefit on the Day of Debt.

[3] In the notes to his book of poems, *Kameni spavač,* Mak Dizdar mentions the legend that "good people," saints who lost their lives in the fight against the evils of their times, are buried under the stones of the medieval Bosnian necropolises. Sacred Bosnian tradition maintained and maintains an awareness of these good folk and their legacy is a living one even today. The survival of both the *stećci*, or decorated medieval tombstones, and the *nišani*, or decorated muslim tombstones, is a single story. They stand guarantee for each other. So long as their heirs look after them, the sky will care for them and the places they are to be found, so that they are not affected by hail or sickness. During the dog days of summer, folk visit these plinths under which the good people lie, these *stećci* and *nišani*, as places

that bear witness of human perfectibility, to pray for rain. Mak Dizdar claimed to have taken part during his childhood in such processions to the graveyards in Stolac to make such prayers, graveyards which contained both *stećci* and *nišani*. According to the same legend, Dizdar says "The Just One is buried under one of the *stećak*s near Stolac, in the vicinity of medieval Vidoška [the old name for Stolac Fort], though which one nobody knows. He was so called because he was killed in a persecution, a massacre." The poet goes on to say: "His voice flies up to heaven and will continue to fly until it is heard. That voice can sometimes be heard, but only in places where the hubbub of the world does not drown out all else, in the silence, and it can be made out only by those who prefer in their thoughts, and words, and deeds that justice be done in this world" (Dizdar, *Kameni spavač/ Stone Sleeper*, 192; see also Dizdar, *Stone Sleeper*, 117). This story is to be found in many variants in the oral tradition of Stolac. It has been attached to many good people from different periods of history. They serve to focus our memories and dissolve the differences between people as we travel together towards perfection. It is always possible for good people to be born, so that every human search for self-realization is at the same time a quest for such people. They find reasons for their journey towards perfection everywhere around them and in their own selves. When these stories refer to Veli-Dede, the good man after whom the hill, cave, and mosque within Stolac Fort are named, they recount that he could read the confession that the Praised is the Prophet on every leaf of every tree and hear it in every song of every bird and in the whispering of the wind. He could demonstrate how every page of the holy Gospels made reference to the Praised. And he would carry them it with himself everywhere, and whenever he read them, tears would stream down his face and chin. He would carry a staff as tall as himself and would shout out, "We are waiting for him, and welcome him!"

[4] Quran 21:1-3.

[5] The verb "to realize," the noun "realization," and the adjective "real" are key concepts for this discourse. The "real" corresponds to the Arabic *haqq*, which may also mean "true," "suitable," "appropriate," "right," and "just." The divine name *Al-Haqq* may be translated as the Real, the Truthful, or the True.

[6] Quran 62: 9-10.

[7] Quran, 62:11.

[8] Quran, 22:18.

[9] The *mihrab* symbolizes the navel of the world or the heart. It is the place in which we attempt to bring together what is separated and to transcend the dualism of body and Spirit, earth and heaven. This dualism is signified by earth and heaven or the Inviolate and the Further Mosque. The navel of the world may sometimes be signified by the rosebud. The Praised is both the rosebud and its blossoming. Any encounter with a rose recalls this link to the Praised.

[10] *Nahjul Balagha*, 486.

5. From Left to Right

[1] See Quran, 25:53.

[2] Quran, 7:40.

[3] See Quran, 59:23.

[4] Quran, 2:186.

[5] See Quran, 12:53.

[6] See Quran, 6:14.

[7] This tradition is cited widely in Sufi texts. It is given by Al-Ghazali in his *Ihya ulum al-din.* See Chittick, *The Sufi Path of Knowledge*, 107.

[8] The Stolac *dershana* is mentioned by Bećirbegović in her *Prosvjetni objekti islamske arhitekture u Bosni i Hercegovini.* The data cited on its age are inconclusive. They fail to take into account the Stolac tradition of the *dershana*'s great age, which puts it even earlier than the Stolac *hammam.*

[9] Quran, 89:27-28.

[10] *Nahjul Balagha*, 521-2. Our sojourn at the bottom of the valley, in full awareness of the insult to the inviolate, entails the turn to the original height (Ar. *tawbah*, Gk. *μετανοια*) and involves the vision of hell, as the underside of the valley floor, and of paradise, as its opposite. The Inviolate Mosque at the bottom of the valley marks the depth, from which we may choose either the fall into hell or the ascent to heaven. The Further Mosque marks our ascent. The prophets and their followers are gathered in life and death around the Inviolate Mosque, or, to put it more fully, around the axis which joins the centers of existence at all levels—the seven heavens and the seven earths (see note 1 to the Foreword). According to Azraqi, "Every prophet, after his people had perished, would establish himself at Mecca; there he and his followers with him used to perform worship till he died" (cited in Wüstenfeld, *Die Chroniken der Stadt Mekka*, vol. 1, 363, 9; cited after Wensinck, "The Ideas of the Western Semites Concerning the Navel of the Earth," 28). The congregation of the prophets and their followers about the Kaaba, which marks the depth from which we turned towards the height, entails an identical congregation around the Rock in Jerusalem, as the sign of the height. This pair, the valley and the mount, are, as we say in Bosnian tradition, like a tureen and its lid, like an open grave and the earth waiting to fill it, like the valley and the sky. The lid is crowned by the bud of the rose or lotus whose image is to be found at the bottom of the tureen. This bud is the kernel of the world, the universal desire to return from the depth to the original height, from the many to the One. "On the authority of Malik b. Anas it is said: 'Paradise is longing after Jerusalem and Jerusalem after paradise. And Jerusalem is the navel of the earth'" (Nuwairi, *Nihayat al-Arab*, 89; cited after Wensinck, "The Ideas of the Western Semites Concerning the Navel of the Earth," 36). Once we know that the Rock at Jerusalem and the Kaaba at Mecca are two signs of one and the same principle, manifest on the world-axis, there is nothing obscure in the claim that the Kaaba is the "navel of the

world" (Kazwini, *Kitab Athar al-Bilad*, 75, 10; cited after Wensinck, "The Ideas of the Western Semites Concerning the Navel of the Earth," 36). Both the Rock in Jerusalem and the Kaaba in Mecca are the navel or bud of all existence. The navel and the bud are signs of the heart, so it is hardly surprising that both Jerusalem and Mecca are referred to as the heart of the world (see Wensinck, "The Ideas of the Western Semites Concerning the Navel of the Earth," 46).

6. The Call

[1] See Revelations, 17:18: "And the woman which thou sawest is that great city, which reigneth over the kings of the earth." The Book of Revelations is a thread woven into the long history of Bosnian spirituality. See Hamm, "Apokalipsa bosanskih krstjana."

[2] Quran, 6:163.

[3] The valley of Mecca is referred to as "infertile" in the Recitation (14:37).

[4] In the Recitation, God tells the Praised (68:4): "Verily of an immense magnitude is thy nature."

[5] Quran, 68:52.

[6] See Quran, 26:194.

[7] Quran, 6:92.

[8] See Quran, 59:23.

[9] Quran, 4:58.

[10] Quran, 4:135.

[11] As may be seen at other points in this exposition, the number 19 is a key symbol within the *čaršija* complex. The *čaršija* mosque has 19 pillars. This corresponds to the 19 divisions of the hand, with four bones for each of the four fingers and three for the thumb. The meaning of the open raised hand is "nineteen." Nineteen is the numerical value of the divine name of the Only (*Al-Wahid*), one of the most beautiful names of God. The significance of saluting by raising the open hand is as an expression of witness to the Only as Outer and Inner, as First and Last, throughout existence. This confession is for us the reason and purpose of everything that is. Without this confession, no meaning can be discerned in it.

[12] Quran, 5:3.

[13] Quran, 6:125.

[14] Quran, 61:7.

[15] The claim that the number nine refers to the heavens may seem in disagreement with previous references to the seven heavens. In certain symbolic representations, the number seven is framed, giving nine. The framing prime and finial signify substance as the principle which is at once the beginning and the end of all things. If

we allow that one is the principle for the manifestation of all seven heavens, but also their extremity, then we may be able to understand why the number nine is used to symbolize the heavens. For more on the number nine as a symbol for the heavens in the various traditions, see Schimmel, *The Mystery of Numbers*, 164-79.

[16] Quran, 56:8.

[17] Bukhari, 8:336-37.

7. The Hour

[1] We have frequently used in this discourse the terms "the most beautiful height/sublimity" and "most beautiful (up)rightness of being." Some explanation of them may help understanding of the text as a whole. Existence has a countless number of levels. Each of these levels is revealed in the form of difference or dispersion, albeit in a manner that its particularities and the whole both retain a connection to the levels above and below. This connectivity runs through all of being, from essence and unity as its first revelation all the way to ultimate dispersion at the lowest level of existence. The terms "most beautiful height" and "most beautiful uprightness of being" correspond to or translate the content of 95:4-6 in the Recitation: "We indeed created Man in the most beautiful uprightness of being, then We restored him the lowest of the low—save those who believe and do righteous deeds: they shall have a wage unfailing." As may be seen from the citation, we exist between two extremes—"the most beautiful uprightness of being and the most beautiful height" and "the lowest depth." This distinction within us corresponds to a distinction that runs throughout existence. The most beautiful height is our highest moment or condition, the best we can be with regard to God as the Creator and Ruler of all existence. The closer we approach our highest moment, the more clearly the things in the world appear to us as signs of the Creator. The further we remove from Him, the deeper we go into the depth, the darker and less clear the things of the world appear, so that they obscure both the self and the world. We take ourselves as sufficient, requiring no external authority and responsible to none for our acts. Nonetheless, it is in our nature that we may exit the depth to find our authentic condition and shape ourselves to it. Our doing so is conditional, as is clear from the citation given above, on belief and the doing of good deeds. Belief or faith is our manner of relating to God as the Faithful. It may, consequently, be distinguished into two elements—knowledge and love. As the Creator, God offered this relationship with Him to us, as His creatures. God embraces everything with His knowledge. Our knowledge is always little. The totality of existence is presented to us as a revelation of God's love to be known. Through this revelation of God to us, it is offered to us that we supplement our little knowledge with love for Him whom that knowledge reveals. We have accepted this relationship: everything within the horizons of the world or our own selves reveals the One who sees and hears us at all times, who loves us. Our love for God is our desire through that which we know to become that which we know and so to unite with the Beloved. Love of the Known and knowledge of

the Beloved require us to be in a way that corresponds to this knowledge and this love. This is virtue or the doing of good deeds. Such an orientation towards the Known and His love requires will. This is the capacity to turn from the false to the true. To do so, we must accept that the entire manifold is the reception of Peace in movement through the ages. Then, as recipients of Peace, we confirm our relationship to Him through being-at-peace. Our best example is the Praised, the perfect man: he is always already our fullest potential and our guide on the steep path that leads from the lowest depth to the most beautiful height. Our relationship with God is contained in His call to follow the Praised, if we love God, so that God may love us. We received our creaturehood and our guidance from the Creator, so that they represent our debt towards Him. If we are to return this debt to the original owner, we must first recognize it. Recognition of this debt to God is our turning towards Him, our assumption of (up)rightness of being. It is recognition that everything within the scope of our knowledge is a sign that points to the vertical connection between us and our Creator. How we may best find the truth of our creaturehood and our guidance is indicated by the terms: "the Day of Resurrection" (*yawm al-qiyama*), "the upright path" (*sirat al-mustaqim*), "the debt of uprightness" (*al-din al-qayyim*). These terms mark our relationship as creatures "in most beautiful (up)rightness of being" (*fi ahsani taqwimin*) with God the Upright (*al-Qayyum*).

[2] Quran, 16:125.

[3] Quran, 23:73-74.

[4] See Quran, 33:6.

[5] Quran, 28:88.

[6] Quran, 28:88.

[7] Quran, 17:50-52.

[8] See Quran, 99:7-8.

[9] See Quran, 22:62.

[10] Quran, 6:32.

[11] Quran, 56:1-12.

[12] Quran, 27:88.

[13] Quran, 53:43.

[14] Quran, 67:2.

[15] Quran, 6:1.

[16] See Chittick, "Weeping in Classical Sufism," 138.

[17] See Quran, 24:35.

[18] See Quran, 6:1.

[19] Quran, 14:1.

[20] See Quran, 21:107.

[21] See Quran, 7:156.

[22] On the weeping of the All-Praised, see Chittick, "Weeping in Classical Sufism," 132.

[23] Quran, 18:110.

[24] See Quran, 50:16.

[25] See Quran, 42:11.

[26] God says in the Recitation (29:45): "Recite what has been revealed to thee of the book, and perform the prayer; prayer forbids indecency and dishonor. God's remembrance is greater; and God knows the things you work."

[27] Quran, 2:115.

[28] Quran, 10:25.

[29] John, 5:28.

[30] Quran, 6:31.

8. The Guest

[1] Quran, 25:7.

[2] Quran, 6:151-52.

[3] Abu Daud, 3:215.3221.

[4] Bayhaqi, *Al-Sunan al-Kubra*, 4:92.

[5] Malik, *Al-Muwatta*, 452. See also Bukhari, 8:321.

[6] The Prophet was asked: "Messenger of God, tell me, if I come to a man who gives me no entertainment and hospitality and he afterwards comes to me, shall I give him entertainment or treat him as he treated me?" He replied, "No, give him entertainment" (Tirmidhi, 4248).

[7] See Bukhari, 3:110.

[8] Quran, 47:38.

[9] Imam Ali said: "These hearts are vessels" (*Nahjul Balagha*, 521).

[10] Quran, 20:114.

[11] Mark, 8:35.

[12] Bukhari, 8:99.

[13] Bukhari, 1:19.

14 Quran, 45:23.

15 Quran, 33:6.

16 Muslim, 1:31.

17 Tirmidhi, 161.

9. The Market-Square

1 Activity in the *čaršija* was inseparable from spiritual chivalry (*futuwwa*). There is no human skill or art which does not demonstrate our original perfection. The confession that there is no god but God places us at every moment on the cusp between the false and the true, urging us to cleave to the true. Doing so always and everywhere is the path that embraces our life and our journey towards the Most Beautiful. This path is exemplified in the perfect individual, expressed in the confession that the Praised is the Messenger of God. These two admissions place us in a chain that binds us permanently with the Praised. Each act or abstention from action is in principle a response to the call to act in the most beautiful way and so to join with God as the Beautiful and the Lover of the Beautiful. One could become involved in the *čaršija* in two ways. The first was to join one of the smaller or larger groups of people who carried out their business there. The other was to come there to meet one or other of our needs. All those who carried out their business in the *čaršija*, whether all the time or from time to time, could do so because of a general process of initiation. What they did as craftsmen was only one small part of what was expected of them as individuals initiated into these activities—to know their responsibilities to themselves and to others, to society and the world in general. As such, they were responsible for the order in which their own selves were constantly reinforced and their guests felt, both before and after their being in the *čaršija*, that they had been well received, well served, and well escorted (see Sulami, *The Book of Sufi Chivalry* and Aščerić-Todd, "The Noble Traders"). Doing business in the *čaršija* involved one in the world of spiritual chivalry. Each participant in the *čaršija* passed through degrees of preparation and training to be inducted into the community of the trained. Official initiation was conducted through a public ritual of "fitting the apron." The Grand Master (*ahubaba*) or his deputy would say to the initiate: "My son, listen with all your heart and receive this advice: do not transgress, even one step, the boundaries of the Sharia; yield not to passions nor to temptors; do not disregard prayers; respect the Masters and keep a civil tongue with the journeymen; betray not him who has given you bread; do not bear false witness; work with one hand for yourself and the other for the poor, for thus you may attain good in the other world; never fail to do what is good. Have you heard and do you accept this?" To which the initiate would reply: "I have heard and I accept." Then the Grand Master or his deputy would fit the apron, looking at him and saying: "Here are your articles. In this, may you prosper and keep yourself from that which is not permitted. If you can do so, do; if you cannot, then leave this craft, for I shall be your accuser before the world" (Kreševljaković, *Esnafi i obrti u Bosni i Hercegovini*, 63). Moreover, it is

worth mentioning that the *mihrab* is the center of the *čaršija*, which is a labyrinth through which each individual passes on his way towards that central point. All those who took part in the life of the *čaršija* were obliged to assist any individuals seeking this center, for in this way they assisted their own progress on the same path. Just as God did not create the world as a game or entertainment, neither is there anything in the *čaršija* that has not its point. Indeed, is not lack of seriousness in the *čaršija* the worst indicator of human irresponsibility towards the self, God, and the guest?

[2] On the division of the self into six stations of wisdom within perennial philosophy see Schuon, *Stations of Wisdom*; a comprehensive elucidation of this distinction from the perennial wisdom of humanity and its reception into the various ontological, cosmological, anthropological, and sociological discourses of the day is given in Perry, *A Treasury of Traditional Wisdom*. The figure of seven represents transcendence.

[3] Muslim, 1:2. On this distinction and progress through the degrees of wisdom—"being-at-peace" (*islam*), "faith" (*iman*), and "the realization of beauty" (*ihsan*) in the teaching of the Praised as the "Seal of the prophets" see Murata and Chittick, *The Vision of Islam*. The terms *muslim*, *islam*, and *salam* have transferred from Arabic into almost every other language in the world. Their meaning has changed over time: in modern ideological constructions, they have taken on aspects which not infrequently "extract" these terms from their original semantic fields. The Christian concept of God's incarnation, which has had multiple consequences for modernity, has both directly and indirectly affected the modern configuration of the term *islam*. The concept of the incarnation depends entirely on reported knowledge. The incarnation took place in history as a witnessed historical event, so that what we know of it depends upon the tradition and authority of the original historical witnesses and those to whom they passed it on. On the other hand, perennial wisdom does not depend on any such external event. Its source is human nature or the Spirit breathed by God into us. It cannot contain any contradiction between the divine revelation and human reason. Here, revelation and reason are two aspects of the One. Western modernity, by contrast, has seen a sharp split between these two forms of knowledge—intellectual, which does not depend on external sources or on tradition, and rational knowledge, which is entirely dependent on the manifold and our ability to compare the factors underlying its content. The Muslim tradition is very different in its approach to the incarnation as an intervention by the divine in history. "It is often assumed by both Muslims and non-Muslims that Islam began with the historical event of Muhammad and the Quran. There is some truth in this, of course, but the Quran paints a different picture, one that has had a deep effect on the way people have conceived of their religion. In this perspective, Islam begins with the creation of the world. In its broadest meaning, the word *islam* (submission, submittedness, surrender) designates the universal and ever present situation of creatures in face of the Creator. 'To Him is submitted everything in the heavens and the earth' (Quran, 3:83). This helps explain why the first and fundamental dogma of the religion is *tawhid*, which is

nothing to do with the historical facts of Muhammad in the Quran" (Chittick, *Science of the Cosmos, Science of the Soul*, 111). Accordingly, confession of the unity of God is the truth which comprehends all, all things and all time, all of creation and eternity (see Quran, 7:156). This is so, because everything is at peace with the One and Only God. It is true that we were created in God's image, so that we have free will. We may therefore reject being-at-peace and come into conflict with our own original nature and the totality of existence. Nothing in existence is originally corrupt or deficient. This certainly does not mean that the world is without evil. Free will is inconceivable without evil. We are expected to avoid evil on the basis of free will, to outflank it and prevent it, as we meet the claims of whatsoever is in existence. For everything in existence reveals the truth of the Creator as the one and absolute Truth. When we accept, discover, and realize being-at-peace as the means of relationship to the God of Peace, our selves become simply an alternative form of expression of existence as a whole. Then world and humanity become an organic unity through which God reveals himself. Then we are on the upright path and follow the Praised to whom all of God's prophets, all 124,000, bore witness and announced. In this way, anyone who has accepted any of God's prophets has accepted them all, including the Praised as "the first of the people of peace," whose truth and light are the first manifestation of God, as the Truth and the Light. Bearing witness to and following them includes, accordingly, their trans-historical truth, as well as their appearance in history. For this ahistorical truth to appear within history it had to take on determinate form. The confession that there is no god but God and that the Praised is His Prophet has shown itself in as many forms as there are prophets of God. There are as many ways of or possibilities for following these revelations as there are individuals, from the first to the last of us. Each one of us was created with this transhistorical witness. And each one of us is equally capable of forgetting that which forms the core of our being. The prophets call the people of each age and tongue to that which is already within their original nature. Once they have reminded us of this, it is up to us to recall what we have always known, but forgotten.

[4] Quran, 1:1-7. No discourse has meaning unless it confirms silence as the world from which it comes and to which it returns. Discourse is the opening of silence. The satisfaction of the self is the teaching in silence in which it will speak without utterance. There are three silences: the silence of the mouth, the silence of conscience, and the silence of the will. By opening ourselves to silence and allowing silence to open to us we gather ourselves for prayer. "The Opening" (*al-Fatiha*) is the first chapter in the Recitation. It involves the use of analytical reason, feeling, the will, and the imagination to elicit respect and devotion to God as the One and Only Self: "Praise belongs to God, the Lord of all Being, the All-Merciful, the Ever-Merciful, the Master of the Day of Debt. Thee only we serve; to Thee alone we pray for succor!" As is clearly evident, "the Opening" includes a decisive act of submission in which the self submits to the Self as its real essence, to the Self as near and manifest to all and as far and incomparable. In this act of submission and openness made in silence, the self submits to confidence in the Self, asking for

itself and for all others: "Guide us on the upright path, the path of those whom Thou first blessed, not of those against whom thou art wrathful, nor of those who are astray!"

[5] See Quran, 3:83.

[6] Ibn Maja, *Muqaddima*, 9.

[7] Quran, 7:147.

[8] See Muslim, 1:1-2.

[9] Quran, 4:125.

[10] Quran, 2:195.

[11] Quran, 7:56.

[12] Quran, 29:69.

[13] See Quran, 50:16.

[14] See Quran, 57:4.

[15] Quran, 12:76.

[16] See Quran, 20:114.

[17] Quran, 96:1-2.

[18] Quran, 2:31.

[19] Cited in Chittick, *Faith and Practice of Islam*, 45-46. This quotation is from the discussion in *The Rising Places of Faith* which William C. Chittick thinks was probably written by Sadr al-Din Qunawi, a Sufi teacher and writer who was a contemporary of Ibn al-Arabi and Jalal al-Din Rumi and corresponded with them both.

[20] Quran, 9:111.

10. The Book

[1] During the destruction of Stolac, which lasted more than a century, many books were destroyed, as were other written materials. Books form part of the city's sacred unity. More than 100 manuscripts produced in the town or owned by families from it still remain in the manuscript collections of the Herzegovina Archives in Mostar, the Gazi Husref Bey library in Sarajevo, the Yugoslav Academy of Sciences and Arts (formerly JAZU, now HAZU) in Zagreb, and of certain individuals. This is, however, only a small part of what was once in the town and destroyed. The oldest preserved book known to have been produced in the town is a copy of the Quran made in 1593 by Korkut Halifa, preacher and imam at the Sultan Selim mosque in Stolac (Hasandedić, *Katalog arapskih, turskih, i perzijskih rukopisa*, 209-10). It is worth noting that one of these surviving manuscripts is in fact the oldest known manuscript of the Quran in Bosnia. It was copied out by Šahin bin

Abdullah an-Naşiri, also known as al-Ašrafi, during Ramadan in 878 AH (January or February 1473 A.D.) (see Lavić, *Katalog arapskih, turskih, perzijskih, i bosanskih rukopisa*, fascicle 15:5). The life of the people of peace is inseparable from the activities of listening and memorizing, writing and reading the *Mushaf, Dala'il al-Khayrat*, and the many other books associated with the global confession that there is no god but God and that the Praised is His servant and His Messenger. On the death of these listeners, memorizers, writers, and students, the books were left to their heirs, that they might live their lives with them and by them. And when there were no longer any heirs, or when they were not worthy in their lives to receive the inherited books, they would be taken and deposited in the mosques or buried in graves. Books were also buried during periods of confusion and insecurity, when it seemed to their owners that they might fall into unworthy hands. As a result, the *harems* of Stolac are also graveyards of books. One can determine the years in which large quantities of books were buried in the Stolac graveyards: between 1875 and 1879, at the time of the great revolt and the Austro-Hungarian seizure of Bosnia; between 1917 and 1919, during the period of the creation of the Kingdom of Serbs, Croats, and Slovenes; between 1940 and 1954, during the Second World War and the initial period of Communist rule. The writer has collected reminiscences regarding the burial of books in the graves of their former owners from Muhamed Medar (b. 1936), Izet Rizvanbegović (b. 1923), Derviš Zilić (1915-2003), and Meho Turković (1917-1992). Muhamed Medar described book burials in all the Stolac graveyards. Izet Rizvanbegović had seen a number of such burials in the Great Harem as a child, and had heard of more as common knowledge. Derviš Zilić described a major burial of books, including very many manuscripts, at the southern wall of the Great Harem. The books were buried close to the surface, and many of them could be reached after shaking off a layer of earth. He had taken and kept one of them, a fine manuscript of the Quran. Meho Turković described how the books from his mother Fatima's (née Basarić) house had been loaded onto carts and taken and buried in the Great Harem. The books from the house where Šefkija Behman (1892-1974), the son of Muhamed and grandson of Alija, was born were first taken to the Uzinovići Mosque, and afterwards buried in its graveyard. Salih Hromić (d. 1943) buried his books shortly before his death under the hearth of the Uzinovići *mekteb*, which was then in ruins. According to the testimony of Salko Nurković (1923-1990) and Alija Pirija (b. 1924), books were on some occasions thrown into the winter flood of the Bregava River, to prevent them falling into "dishonorable and unclean hands."

[2] Quran, 22:67.

[3] See Quran, 12:1-3.

[4] The tradition on the Pen as the first of God's creation is found in a number of forms in Tabari, *Tarikh al-rusul wal-muluk* ("The History of al-Tabari"), 198-203.

[5] Existence is division into pairs which reveal unity. The bottom of the valley and the peak of the mount are two of the key signs of this division: the bottom of the valley is the symbol of the lowest depth and the peak of the mount is the sign of

the most beautiful height. The bottom of the valley is marked by the house, the sign of the attempt or ritual of return; the peak of the mount is marked by the rock or the transformation of the manifold into unification and solidity. The bottom of the valley is at risk of flooding, but the house marks the place of refuge, the ark of redemption. This ark crosses the sea, through the storms of the world, to the peak. This recalls the belief that at the end of times the House or Kaaba, as the center of the Inviolate Place of Annihilation, will come as bride to the Rock, as the center of the Further Place of Annihilation (See Grabar, "The Meaning of the Dome of the Rock in Jerusalem," 144; and Schimmel, *My Soul Is a Woman*, 101). This union of base and peak is a sign of the realization of both world and human being on the path back to God.

[6] See Quran, 7:172.

[7] Quran, 15:39-40.

[8] Quran, 17:65.

[9] Quran, 2:37

[10] See Quran, 33:72 and 7:172.

[11] See Quran, 2:28-39.

[12] Cragg, *The Mind of the Quran*, 142.

11. "Recite!"

[1] Quran, 96:1-5.

[2] Regarding the first divine revelation to the Praised see Ibn Ishaq, *Sirat Rasul Allah*, 104-107; and Lings, *Muhammad*, 43-45.

[3] See Quran, 2:152.

[4] Quran, 2:186.

[5] God reveals: "I am the Lord thy God, which have brought thee out of the land of Egypt, out of the house of bondage. Thou shalt have no other gods before me. Thou shalt not make unto thee any graven image, or any likeness of anything that is in heaven above or that is in the earth beneath or that is in the water under the earth: thou shalt not bow down thyself to them, nor serve them: for I, the Lord thy God, am a jealous God" (Exodus, 20:2-5).

[6] Quran, 1:2-4.

[7] Quran, 36:82.

[8] Veli Dede was, according to the tradition of the Muslims of Stolac, a good or holy man who lived at the time of and studied with Saltuk Baba, the fourteenth century Muslim spiritual master from Bulgaria. Although originally from a noble family, he lived as a poor man and spent most of his life in a cave above Stolac. The mosque bearing his name was later raised above that cave. They say that he

walked with a stick and used to exclaim, "God is great (Veli), and the Paraclete is in you and with you!"

[9] The oral tradition into which the author was born and in which he grew up was fond of the sacred number seven. He would often hear oaths of the form, "By the seven sacred books and the seven sacred messengers, and the seven sacred mosques!" When he asked the old women who used these oaths which books and messengers and mosques they meant, he would get a variety of answers, including, "if you know one, you know them all." Another frequent oath was, "By the seven mosques of Stolac!" Again, on asking which mosques exactly, the lists would lack the name of at least one mosque. To resolve the conundrum, his informants would say, "The seventh mosque is wherever you happen to be in full awareness of God." Or they might say, "That is the one you carry with you always, but you must know how to find it." On rare occasions it was possible to get a list of seven names—the Čaršija, Uzinovići, Vrsnik, Veli-Dede, Podgrad, and the Ćuprija or Bridge mosques mentioned in the text and the Ošanići mosque, a little further from the town. Traces of all of them survive today, five having been restored after the destruction of 1993, while two, Veli-Dede and Vrsnik, are in ruins. The current Ošanići mosque developed out of a *mekteb*. There was an older one which was destroyed long ago, but its location is preserved in local oral tradition.

[10] The Podgrad, the Ćuprija, and the Uzinovići mosques, named for the part of the town they are in.

[11] Quran, 1:5-6.

[12] The description of the prophet's ascension to the lote tree of the furthest boundary is given in Muslim, 1:110. See also Quran, 53:16.

[13] Quran, 52:1-6.

[14] See Muslim, 1:102.

[15] These are the seven major attributes of God that are manifest in the human being as created in His image.

[16] Matthew, 5:3, 8-9.

[17] Matthew, 5:14.

[18] Matthew, 5:15.

[19] Chittick, *Science of the Cosmos, Science of the Soul*, 136.

12. The Scales

[1] Quran, 58:7.

[2] See Quran, 24:35.

[3] See Quran, 65:12.

[4] See Quran, 17:85.

[5] See Quran, 95:4.

[6] See Quran, 3:31.

[7] Our selves focus all the names, which is to say all the most beautiful names of God. Realizing our own humanity means discovering or finding those names in our self. God is the All-Praised (*al-Hamid*). He owes His being All-Praised to no one. His being All-Praised is manifest in all existence. All existence is praised, as the recipient of the praise given by God, as the All-Praised, to all things. When this praise is focused in a human being, then he is the Praised (Muhammad). What we have received, we can give. Praise binds us as praised with God the All-Praised. The perfect recipient of praise is the Praised (Muhammad), as the first and the last of existence, and so "the most beautiful example," "the burning candle," "a mercy unto the worlds," and "the seal of the prophets."

[8] The confession (*shahada*) means being present and not absent and both showing and speaking. The most important aspect of human presence is our direct and indirect vision that there is no god but God and that the Praised is His servant and His Messenger. Forgetting or denying this under any circumstances deforms our authentic nature. This is why this confession is a precondition for us to realize our original and final perfection. This confession contains the doctrine, the way, and the virtue required for our return to God. God is a witness of the visible and invisible (Quran, 6:73; 9:94, and 105), and we are called to be witnesses, for even though our knowledge is limited, it is enough for confidence. We are expected to form our nature to this confession (Quran, 3:19, 6:19, and 63:1). The full linguistic expression of this is, "I confess that there is no god but God, and I confess that the Praised is His servant and His Messenger" (*ashhadu an la ilaha illa Llah wa ashhadu anna Muhammadan abduhu wa rasuluhu*). This confession is not limited by time or space. It is always open to us: it is everything that is in the horizon of the world or our own selves, and so it may be expressed in all tongues. God calls us to it: "O believers, believe in God and His Messenger and the Book He has sent down on His Messenger and the Book which He sent down before. Whoso disbelieves in God and His angels, and His Books, and His Messengers, and the Last Day, has surely gone astray into far error" (Quran, 4:136). For a fuller interpretation of this confession in its doctrinal and historical context see Wensinck, *The Muslim Creed.*

[9] Quran, 4:135.

[10] Quran, 67:3.

13. The House

[1] See Quran, 68:4.

[2] See Quran, 21:107.

[3] One should note that the world was created in seven heavens and seven earths: "It is God who created seven heavens, and of earth their like, between them the Command descending, that you may know that God is powerful over everything

and that God encompasses everything in knowledge" (Quran, 65:12).

[4] Quran, 5:15-16.

[5] Quran, 6:127.

[6] Quran, 10:25.

[7] See John 14:1-6.

[8] As above, the concept of the mosque is translated by the author as the place of annihilation or self-abnegation. This is to stress that only the self which confesses its absolute poverty, which holds as naught all sufficiency that does not derive from the All-Sufficient, is open to receive the All-Sufficient. For only He can satisfy our desire for perfection. This is the way of existence: everything on earth and in heaven and between them prostrates itself before God in worship. This everything is the universal mosque or place of annihilation, for nothing is real except God. Once it is understood as the denial of anything beyond God, then "everything" reveals Him.

[9] Mufid, *Kitab al-Irshad*, 21. In our text, we have associated the name of Ali with the epithet "the exalted." This meaning of his name, which is no longer immediately present to the mind of the modern reader, speaks directly to the heart of this essay: the Praised is next to God, and those who follow him are next to him. The closer they are to the Praised, the closer they are to God. Ali, the exalted one, is the perfect example of how to follow the Praised.

[10] Psalms, 118:19-23. The Hebrew *Rosh Pina* is normally translated as the corner stone, but its proper meaning is the key stone. On this, see Guénon, "The Cornerstone."

[11] See Ibn al-Hibban, *al-Ihsan fi Taqrub*, 14:6914. The tradition that God sent down 124,000 prophets (*al-anbiya*), of whom 313 were messengers or apostles (*al-mursalun*), is given by Bayhaki, *Al-Sunan al-Kubra*, 9:4, (*hadith*, no. 17,489). It relates that Abu Dharr once asked: "Messenger of God, how many prophets have there been?", and the Messenger replied, "124,000." Then [Abu Dharr] asked, "How many of them were sent as messengers?", and he said "313." The testimony of all 124,000 prophets is contained in the Praised's own confession of his prophethood and his apostolic mission. The prophets are the friends of God, which means that friendship is how they relate to God the Friend (*al-Wali*). At no time have the prophets been without heirs. Accordingly, there are always at least 124,000 heirs or friends in the world of the 124,000 prophets of God (Ibn al-Arabi, *al-Futuhat al-makkiyya*, 3:208.14; after Chittick, *Ibn Arabi: Heir to the Prophets*, 14). How can one be the heir of one of these prophets? We simply do not know about the heirs of many of them. The answer to this question is: their legacy is contained in the prophecy of the Praised. His friends are the friends of all the prophets. Some of these prophets are mentioned in the Recitation, sent down by the Holy Spirit to the heart of the Praised and revealed through him to all the world. These limited references are given so that we might understand the common and perennial

content of the message God sent us through them. God says of this: "We sent Messengers before thee; of some We have related to thee, and some We have not related to thee" (Quran, 40:78).

[12] See Quran, 3:81.

[13] See Quran, 33:40.

[14] Muslim, 4:1235. This tradition is given in various forms. See Bukhari, 4:482-483. The keystone and the final brick have the same meaning: the completion of the building. They both symbolize the Messenger. He is both the keystone and the final brick, the beginning and the end of God's purpose in creation. No end is possible without the Messenger. Through him the builders of this world are admonished that there is a purpose before and beyond them through which their work may be perfected.

[15] Bukhari, 9:483.

[16] See Quran, 99:6-8.

[17] Quran, 22:26-28.

[18] See Quran, 2:115.

[19] See Quran, 55:26-27.

[20] The Inviolate Mosque (*al-masjid al-haram*) and the Further or Remote Mosque (*al-masjid al-aqsa*) are on a north-south axis. The Prophet's mosque (*al-masjid al-nabi*) lies between them. Rising from the depth towards the height can only take place through the Prophet: he is the guide on the path back to God. He embraces the world with his being, from its lowest depth to its highest height. This is the meaning of the ascent of the Praised from the Inviolate to the Further Mosque.

[21] Quran, 102:1-8.

14. Doors and Windows

[1] In a letter from Harun Softić of 29 June, 1907, sent to an unknown person by the name of Ivo, the following is written: "I asked a number of people in the cafe about what you ask me regarding the 99 windows and doors in Stolac. They are all aware of it, but none know the details. They said that there was a certain Ahmetaga or a certain Hasan who might know and whom they could call. But I did not have the time."

[2] See Quran, 7:187.

[3] See Quran, 7:40.

[4] The totality of existence is the revelation of God as the All-Merciful and Ever-Merciful. He says: "My mercy embraces all things" (Quran, 7:156). The name of God (*Allah*) gathers all of His names, while the dedication or introductory phrase, "In the Name of God the All-Merciful, the Ever-Merciful" includes two of those names, namely both those which express His mercy. His names gathered within

the name God are separated into two groups—strength and gentleness, or majesty and beauty, or mercy and wrath. The presence of two names denoting mercy within the name of God, which comprehends all the names, speaks to mercy as the principle according to which God governs all. Existence as a whole derives from His mercy and because of it. Mercy is the purpose in everything, as God says: "My mercy takes precedence over My wrath" (Bukhari, 9:483).

[5] An exception worth mentioning is Čelić's "Stolac *Čaršija*." In this text, the writer recognizes its integrity and importance, but entirely from the exoteric point of view of modern positivist science. The important meaning of the Stolac *čaršija* as a unity whose parts can only be understood from the point of view of perennial philosophy remains unclear to him. While the author attempts to make clear the non-sustainability of separating the whole and its elements from the totality of Bosnian history, he does not in general manage to transcend certain of the forms whereby the content of this and other Bosnian cultural forms are denied from the point of view of modern ideology. Čelić continues to apply the model of "Islamic Oriental" influence with regard to many of the forms of tradition in their Bosnian manifestation. In such an approach, "Islam" is reified and objectified as something "brought," "introduced," "imposed," and "added" to some presumably more important, older layer. Islam or being-at-peace is not, according to this or similar views, the perennial content of all human yearning for relationship with Peace as the principle, equally present in all forms of sacred tradition (Judaism, Christianity, etc). The epithet "Oriental" explicitly emphasizes the foreign nature of "Islam" seen in this way. This is a commonplace in all the anti-Muslim ideologies which have provided a framework for applying pressure on the Muslim population, with the support of church and national leaders, organizations, and their agents, as well as for the occasional lapse or occasion for murderous and destructive activities. Such images of "Islam," as something added from above to a "subordinated," "ancient," and "original" culture, are offered the support of archaeology as the decisive form of "proof": "Our antiquities" must exist in the layers beneath what can be seen on the surface, so the thinking in such ideological approaches goes. A similar case is the essay by Radovan Samardžić on Balkan cities or towns ("On Urban Civilization in the Balkans between the 15th and 19th Centuries"). Samardžić recognizes and elucidates the plural content of Balkan towns of the premodern period and their ideological representation in opposition to the country and peasant life as the locus of the revolutionary thought, reasons, and powers of the new age. Stolac is an example of an open and consequently cosmopolitan town, such as all Balkan towns were. But, these towns did not simply copy forms which were originally foreign. These towns were founded on an image of the world as the theater of human redemption and the discovery of our most beautiful potential. This is why one can say that these towns reflected the model of unity in differences. But, history and human models are normally no closer to each other than the earth is to heaven. Still, we are determined by our models.

[6] In Bosnian tradition, towers as the central part of family mansions normally had three storeys. The first floor or *izba*, which is partly below ground, corresponds

to the body; the second floor or *odaja* to the soul, and the third floor or *čardak* to the upper Spirit. This ascending order of *izba-odaja-čardak* (body-soul-Spirit) corresponds to another in the external world, namely earth-everything in between-heaven. The floors of the house were normally connected by trapdoors. Raising them meant opening the path by which one might ascend or descend.

[7] See Quran, 37:96.

[8] Quran, 6:35.

[9] Quran, 16:3.

[10] *Tabla*, from the Latin *tabula* (a tablet, board, picture), in Arabic *lawh* (tablet, board, inscription). God wrote down for Moses "on the Tablets of everything an admonition" (Quran, 7:145); God also says: "but it is a glorious Quran in a guarded tablet" (Quran, 85:21-22). The *tabla* brings together and comprehends the whole drinking of coffee. It is circular and yellow, and the circle is the declaration of its center. Any given center may serve a countless multitude of circles. In this way the *tabla* signifies unity in the manifold, expressed by the confession that there is no god but God. Unity does not depend on the many, but the many does depend on It. The totality of existence is all that which lies between two expressions of Unity—one internal, to which the center corresponds, and the other external, to which infinity corresponds. On the *tabla*, which is to say between the absolute interiority and absolute externality of Unity, are laid out or inscribed signs which should be read and experienced while drinking. The glass of water is the first inscription on the *tabla*. It signifies Unity and the purity of the Principle from which life derives. God says: "Of water We fashioned every living thing" (Quran, 21:30). This original Unity as purity is the goal of our path. Everything in the world is because of that goal. We are under an obligation to that purity: preserving our authentic nature, we guard the world; nowhere on our path is there anything which needs to be supplemented as lacking. Everything must be revealed in this authentic purity. Drinking water at the beginning means bearing witness to this authentic original purity of the world and of the human being as the two sides of God's revelation of His Self and our return to God as to our own source.

[11] *Findžan* is a word with a very complex etymology, leading one back from Bosnian through Turkish to Arabic and Persian. Even Greek is in the mix. A glance at the dictionary reveals that the ancient Persian word *pangan* then toured Persian, Arabic, and Turkish as *findžan*. Its roots lie in the Greek *pentix*, which means "a five sided cup." The fact that the *findžan* is associated with the number five suggests connection with the soul or the self: our position between the earth and heaven corresponds to the number five, while the realization or discovery of our authentic perfection corresponds to the number six. The word *findžan* means "soul" or "self." When the *findžan* is empty, that is the pure self. When it is full, that is the self darkened by action on the basis of the will without the Will. The academic etymologies of the words *tabla*, *findžan*, and *džezva* are not decisive for these teachings of the Bosnian Sufis regarding the ritual of drinking coffee.

[12] *Džezva* is from the Arabic *jadhwa* or *judhwa* or *jidhwa* (verbal root *j-dh-w*), meaning lamp, brand, or torch, a piece of wood with an ember or an actual flame at the end. Moses tells his companions: "Tarry you here; I observe a fire. Perhaps I shall bring you news of it, or a faggot from the fire (*džezvetin minennar*), that haply you shall warm yourselves" (Quran, 28:29). As such, *džezva* symbolizes our desire to subordinate light and fire to our power and to achieve independent monarchy over the world.

[13] All of existence is an image of the perfect human being, while the perfect human being is the epitome of all of existence. The relationship between the world in its fullness of order and the pure self is signified by this empty and pure vessel placed in front of us: it is the sign of our perfect inception and our perfect original nature and the possibility of a perfect return to God from the world and through it. This is why, in the teaching of the Praised, knowledge of the self is indivisible from knowledge of the cosmos. For more on this see Nasr, *An Introduction to Islamic Cosmological Doctrines.*

[14] John, 4:14.

[15] Quran, 2:17.

[16] It may occur to someone to ask: "And what about the sugar?" The illustration given here includes the basic symbols: the tray, the water glass, the empty cup, and the vessel full of coffee. This contains the full teaching. It may be embellished considerably, whether through knowledge or ignorance, but little can be added to the clarity of the lesson regarding the three symbols on the tray. As happens in most traditional teachings, people embellish out of ignorance, disguising the original clarity. Bitter coffee is an experience one might expect in the effort to turn and return to original purity, while sugar is an attempt to reduce or hide that bitterness. This is the desire that one may participate in ritual without hardship or pain. But one cannot return without passing the narrow hilly path. Consequently, this is the answer to those who ask about sugar: "This ritual is not for those who cannot participate in it as a sacrifice in which we find what is lost."

[17] Arabic *lawh al-mahfuz* ("the well-preserved tablet"). See Quran, 85:22. This represents the first intellect or the treasury of all archetypes and pre-orderings.

[18] Arabic *umm al-kitab* ("the mother of the book"); here "mother" may mean "essence" or "source," while *kitab* is equivalent to the Greek *logos.* This is the book of origins, the Word. See Quran, 3:7, 13:39, and 43:4.

[19] As to the way in which evil entered the world, see Coomaraswamy, "Who Is 'Satan' and Where Is 'Hell'?"

[20] See Ibn al-Arabi, *Al-Futuhat al-makkiyya,* 1:31.4.

[21] Quran, 3:79.

15. The Labyrinth

[1] The following on the relationship of the "debt," as the link between human beings and God, and on our original nature, which allows us to fulfil this debt, was sent down through the Praised: "So set thy face to the debt, a man of pure faith—God's original upon which he originated mankind. There is no changing God's creation. That is the right debt; but most men know it not" (Quran, 30:30). The Prophet says: "Every child is born according to primordial nature (*al-fitra*); then his parents make him into a Jew, a Christian, or Magian" (Bukhari, 6:284).

[2] Translator's note: the point is made more strongly and more subtly in the original, as the Bosnian term for city or town, *grad*, which is cognate with garden, French *jardin*, and yard, is to be found in the term for a vineyard, namely *vinograd*. This allows a smoother transition from the idea of the city to the garden.

[3] Quran, 92:18-21

[4] Quran, 39:69.

[5] Quran, 10:61.

[6] The people of Stolac have preserved a saying of Veli Dede: "There is an enormous store of gold in the *mihrab*, so seek it!"

[7] *Nahjul Balagha*, 464-65.

16. The Valley and the Mount

[1] See Quran, 95:4-5.

[2] Quran, 17:1. All the prophets bore witness of the Praised in pre-existence (Quran, 3:81-82). By doing so, they recognized him as the best example to recall us to our authentic perfection. The creation of Adam and his placement in the garden, at the peak of the mount, was the first revelation of this confession. All the prophets after Adam went down to the bottom of existence, the bottom of the valley. Wherever they found themselves, the prophets were witnesses of the Praised. The two mosques, the one in the valley and the other on the mount, symbolized the process of descent and ascent, departure from the peak and return to it. Both processes unfold with the Praised. The return to the peak is, ultimately, our return to our authentic perfection as we stand before God. This is suggested by the words of the Prophet Isaiah (2:2): "And it shall come to pass in the last days, the mountain of the Lord's house shall be established on the top of the mountains, and shall be exalted above the hills; and all nations shall flow into it." Imam Ali also stresses this meaning of Jerusalem and the Further Mosque as the center or navel of the world on a horizontal axis from the low point in the valley towards the high point on the mount, or from earth to heaven: "The highest of all countries and the nearest to heaven is Jerusalem." (Halabi, *Sira*, 1:195, 5; cited after Wensinck, "The Ideas of the Western Semites Concerning the Navel of the Earth," 14). In this regard, it is worth mentioning one further element of Bosnian spiritual heritage, according to

which the *čaršija* is symbolized by a circle inscribed with a cross. When this sign is written or carved on a horizontal surface it signifies our search for the center or the gold in our heart. And when we find this gold, we straighten up and find ourselves between nothing and everything. Our self comprehends the earth and the heavens and everything in between. The outer edge of the circle corresponds to the Further Place of Annihilation (*al-masjid al-aqsa*), while the lower part of the circle represents the Inviolate Place of Annihilation (*al-masjid al-haram*). Then we display human perfection, which is announced by the heavens and the earth and everything in between.

[3] For the Prophet's sayings on the claims others have on us, see Wensinck, *Concordance*, 1:486. This tradition is given in Tirmidhi, 4:2413. Ali, the son of Husayn, wrote a more detailed discussion on rights and claims, on the basis of these commands of the prophet. See Zayn al-Abdin, "The Treatise on Rights (*Risalat al-Huquq*)."

[4] This tradition is frequently cited in Sufi texts; it is given by al-Ghazali in his *Ihya ulum al-din.* See Chittick, *The Sufi Path of Knowledge*, 107.

[5] Bukhari, 3:108.

[6] Quran, 33:72.

[7] Quran, 19:58.

[8] On the 2nd of August, known variously as Elijah's day and Ali's day, people held meetings throughout Bosnia, often in places with a sacred connotation in the popular mind. For more on such meetings, see Niškanović, "Ilindanski dernek kod turbeta Đerzelez Alije u Gerzovu"; Hadžijahić, "Sinkretistički elementi u islamu u Bosni i Hercegovini"; and the sources cited by these two writers. These are gatherings of both Muslims and Christians and the relationship between Elijah and Ali in sacred tradition is the key to understanding their meaning and place. One may state of the gatherings at Mile (Arnautovići near Visoko), at the mosque on Ocrtalje, at Elderberry Vale near Nevesinje, by the wells, *stećci*, and headstones at Zabrđe near Stolac, at Ali Đerzelez' tomb at Gerzovo, on Trebević in Sarajevo, and in other places the length and breadth of Bosnia that they embody the complex Balkan relationship between the different and the common in sacred tradition. These gatherings have a particular place in the Muslim understanding of God's prophets, who have revealed one and the same truth at different times and in different places. This single truth is the splitting of the Praised's original light into a multitude of forms, which are then gathered and confirmed in him, as the historical seal of all God's prophets. The question of Elijah, the Christ, and the Prophet stretches, it seems, over millennia. Moses spoke of the Prophet (Deuteronomy, 18:18-22) as like himself, but that he would not be raised in Israel (Deuteronomy, 34:10). The Christ, we are told, came from the House of David (Micah, 5:2). The Prophet Isaiah said of the Christ: "and there shall come forth a rod out of the stem of Jesse and a branch shall grow out of his roots" (11:1). It is worth noting that Jesse was the father of the Prophet David. While Jesus said of Elijah, as a prophet of God and destroyer of idols throughout Israel (1 Kings, 17-19), who was

raised up: "but I say unto you, that Elijah is indeed come, and they have done unto him whatsoever they listed, as it is written of him" (Mark, 9:13). Both Elijah and Jesus were raised in Israel and from it. But, Jesus said of the Praised: "but when the Comforter is come, whom I will send unto you from the Father, even the Spirit of truth, which proceedeth from the Father, he shall testify of me. And ye shall also bear witness, because ye have been with me from the beginning" (John, 15:26-7). The heralds of the Praised in the tradition of the people of peace are Moses, Elijah, and Christ. They take the Comforter mentioned by Jesus to be the same as the prophet mentioned by Moses, about whom Jesus' disciples asked. He cannot be separated from the Holy Spirit, as whatever he tells people comes to him from the Holy Spirit (Quran, 16:102). Ali is the human incarnation of the acceptance and following of the prophets—human perfection attained through following the Seal of the prophets. Ali is the flag-bearer of the Praised. Whoever knows Ali, knows the best that human beings are capable of when he is with Abraham, Moses, Elijah, Isaiah, or any of God's prophets, who were raised up from the time of the first man to that of the Praised. Elijah (Arabic: Ilyas, Greek: Eleias, Hebrew: Eliya) was a prophet and a messenger of God (Quran, 6:85, 37:123-132), as were Abraham, Moses, and Jesus. He and all of God's prophets swore an oath in pre-existence to God to accept the Praised (Quran, 3:81-82). According to Bosnian Muslim tradition, the Prophet Elijah came and confirmed his oath from pre-existence to the Praised in this world, who required of him that he first recognize Jesus as the Messiah and then stand under the banner of the Praised, held by Ali. This is the source of the old saying, "Until noon, Elijah, after noon, Ali." This tradition regarding the Prophet Elijah under the banner of the Praised, the Seal of the prophets, the banner borne by the model disciple Ali, was recorded as early as 1871 (see Hadžijahić, "Sinkretistički elementi u islamu u Bosni i Hercegovini", 322).

9 *Sahifa*, 247.

10 Quran, 20:105-7.

11 Quran, 17:79.

12 Ibn al-Arabi, *Al-Futuhat al-makkiyya*, 4:433.10.

17. Earth and Heaven

1 Gabriel asked the Praised, "What is the Hour?" (Muslim, 1:2). Buddha told his students to seize the hour; he would congratulate those who had "seized their hour" and express pity for those "whose hour had passed" (*Khanatita; Samyuta Nikaya*, 4:126, cited in Eliade, *Images and Symbols*, 82).

2 See Quran, 7:187.

3 See Quran, 2:255. As already discussed, the Seat and the Throne are part of a chain from above downwards: the first comprehends all of existence, but is itself comprehended by the other. See Burckhardt, *Mystical Astrology according to Ibn Arabi*, 14n4.

4 Quran, 11:56.

[5] Quran, 10:3.

[6] Quran, 19:93.

[7] Quran, 39:75.

[8] Quran, 2:30

[9] See Quran, 2:34.

[10] Tirmidhi, *Tafsir, Sura* 38, 2; Ibn Hanbal, 1:368

[11] Quran, 33:6

[12] Quran, 3:81.

[13] See Quran, 3:101, in which is said: "How can you disbelieve, seeing you have God's signs recited to you, and His Messenger among you?" The Arabic *fikum* can be translated as either "with you," "among you," or "within you."

[14] Quran, 3:84.

18. The Tree

[1] Quran, 2:35.

[2] The *čaršija* or "four sides" signify, as has been mentioned more than once in this book, the way in which the human being acts as a focus of the center the world. It is worth remembering the cosmological image of the tree at the center of the world. As the Praised has said: "There is a tree among the trees which is as blessed as the man of Peace!" (Bukhari, 7:259). It is revealed in the verse on the Light: "God is the Light of the heavens and the earth; the likeness of His Light is as a niche wherein is a lamp (the lamp in the glass, the glass as it were a glittering star) kindled from a blessed tree, an olive that is neither of the east nor of the west whose oil well nigh would shine, even if no fire touched it; Light upon Light; God guides to His light whom He will. And God strikes similitudes for men and God has knowledge of everything" (Quran, 24:35). Given this description, it would seem that the relief engraved into the wall of the Captain's house refers to the connection between the tree at the center of the world and the human being. The carving clearly shows an indentation for a lamp, above which is a tree; there are two birds by the tree, one to either side, and above it are two apples or suns. (For an interpretation of the verse of Light see Tabari, *Tafsir*, 18:98.4, ff.) As may clearly be seen from the image, the indentation and the tree are in the center along the vertical axis. If the images of the birds flying around the tree are read as angels circling the Throne, as creatures of light, and the two suns as representing east and west, then the picture as a whole may be read as a lesson on the human heart, which embraces the Throne of God. This centrality of the tree on the earth, which corresponds to the bottom of the valley and the peak of the mount, can only be understood in the context of the story of the garden and Adam before the fall. For, the beginning is always the end: the journey down begins from the tree, and so return is to the tree. Ali, the son of Abu Talib, refers to this transcendence of duality and cleaving to unity (Bukhari, 8:285): "The world is going backwards

and the Hereafter is coming forwards, and each of the two has its own children; so you should be the children of the Hereafter, and not the children of this world, for today there is action but no accounts, and tomorrow there will be accounts, but no deeds to be done." This call to turn from "this world" towards "the other world" corresponds to the relationship between the valley and the mount: we are expected to begin our ascent from the low point of existence, where the four cardinal points meet in unity. This high point of return is referred to in the Recitation: "No indeed; the book of the pious is in Illiyun; and what shall teach thee what is Illiyun? A Book inscribed, witnessed by those brought nigh" (Quran, 83:18-21). If we are to answer the question regarding the place called Illiyun with reference to its basic meaning, then, following most interpreters, it is the place of sublimity and glory. It is a place in the seventh heaven, the place of the lotus tree of the final boundary. This sublime location is also referred to by its other names: *al-darajat al-ula* (Quran, 20:75) and *janna aliya* (Quran, 69:22 and 88:10).

3 Quran, 7:181-2.

4 See Quran, 9:41.

5 Quran, 34:15-16.

6 Quran, 16:10-11.

7 This *hadith* is cited in Ibn Hanbal, *al-Musnad*, 4:183 (hadith no. 17679). The same collection of the *hadith* of the Prophet also contains the following: "It is related by Abu Said al-Khudri that a man once said to the prophet of God—peace and relations with the Lord be with upon him: 'O, prophet of God, blessed (*tuba*) be he who believes in you.' To which he replied: 'Blessed be he who has seen and believes in me, but thrice blessed is he who believes in me without seeing!' To which the man replied in question: 'And what is this "blessing" (*tuba*)?' 'The tree in the garden whose circuit lasts 100 years; for the clothes of the inhabitants of the garden are from its fruit.'" (Ibn Hanbal, *al-Musnad*, 3:71, hadith no. 11691).

8 Quran, 6:153.

9 Quran, 48:18.

10 See Quran, 19:23-6.

11 Quran, 3:37.

12 See Quran, 26:192-7.

13 Quran, 14:24-5.

14 Ibn al-Arabi, *al-Futuhat al-makkiyya*, 2:468.12.

15 Ibn al-Arabi, *al-Futuhat al-makkiyya*, 2:326.19.

19. Oblivion and Recollection

1 Çelebi, *Putopis*, 419. Given the absence of a full English version of the *Seyahat-name*, the translation here is made from the Bosnian translation of the sections

related to Bosnia.

[2] The original text in Turkish may be found in the Court Record of Ibrahim Vehbi, Qadi of Stolac, now in the possession of Rusmir Mahmutćehajić.

[3] Muslim, 1:2.

[4] Çelebi, *Putopis*, 419.

[5] See Quran, 25:63.

[6] See Quran, 95:4.

[7] Decree no. 08.1-6-915/03 of 6 May 2003.

[8] Matthew, 4:4.

[9] Quran, 21:47.

[10] Quran, 29:25.

[11] Quran, 73:8-9.

[12] Quran, 16:90.

[13] Ibn al-Arabi, *al-Futuhat al-makkiyya*, 2:641.21, cited in Chittick, *Ibn Arabi: Heir to the Prophets*, 65.

Afterword

[1] Stolac is a "city of the Spirit" and "a sacred city" and has been such since it was first built, but also a place in which the perennial love for wisdom has always been recognized, so that individuals there have always sought and delineated the uncreated essence within themselves, finding harmony with nature and building on that. Even today it remains a city of the Spirit, but one that has sustained heavy wounds and much damage. We will here note only some of the main aspects of the destruction carried out in ways too difficult to count, affecting both individual aspects and the overall natural and built environment of the town. The worst assaults on Stolac and damage to it took place between the end of the nineteenth and the end of the twentieth century. This began with the demolition of a great part of the fortress and the Veli Dede mosque at the end of the nineteenth century, as well as the construction of the Poprati-Stolac road through the graveyards at Radimlja and Gorica with their *stećci* and Muslim headstones. Between 1918 and 1939, the following buildings were destroyed: the *mekteb* (1924), the clock tower (1936), the graveyards at Ratkovina (partly in 1909 and entirely in 1938) and at Muftićevina (1939). Between 1948 and 1993 the Podgrad mills were destroyed (partially in 1955 and fully in 1961); followed by the Old, Great, and Podgrad graveyards (1949), the *muselimat* (1966-67), the Šarić demesne with its summerhouse (1948-49), the *tepa* pavilion over the scales (1972), the Šarić family house (1971), and the buildings of the Muftić, Tatarević, Šarić, and Šabić *hans* or inns (1938, 1956, 1956, and 1975-76, respectively), the *dershana* and the Sumbulović

Oriole (1970), the Great Graveyard (1949), and the shops by it (in part in 1939, entirely in 1955). Additional damage was done by the construction of buildings which did not respect the sacred character of the valley and its built heritage: the reshaping of the street from Podgrad to Zągrad and the destruction it entailed (1952); the straightening of the riverbed and imposition of an unnatural course (1955-56); the widening of the roads in front of and behind the Mufliz Bridge and the demolition of many shops in that part of the town (1955-56); the cutting of a road through the center and through the gardens at Križevac (1975); and the road from Šljivin *sokak* through the gardens on the slopes of Komanje hill to Bokulja (1987); the cutting of a road above Luka (1975); the construction of many unsuitable buildings in the gardens between the *hammam* and Šljivin *sokak*, at Ratkovina, at Luka, and under the road to the fort, and the building of schools, storage facilities, kindergartens, and shops where there had once been graveyards, and of industrial facilities in residential parts of the town, particularly Vidovo *polje* (1948-70); the construction of unsuitable shops on top of the Old Graveyard (1982-85); the construction of a supermarket on top of previously demolished shops (1973-75); the construction of a new weighing station on part of the Old Graveyard (1982-85); and the destruction of the old dam and its replacement with an unsuitable concrete weir (1977-78).

The entire *čaršija* was leveled in 1993, when more than 2000 houses in the town were destroyed and the entire Muslim population expelled. The individuals responsible set up a spit in the center of the valley on the location of the *čaršija* mosque and roasted a pig, in imitation of the old Crusader custom of "nullifying" Muslim presence. Following that criminal act, crosses were placed along the road to the fort, and a cross was placed above the ruins of Veli Dede mosque to make clear the reason for and purpose behind the destruction of the town.

[2] The graveyards were largely destroyed after 1948. A school and sports hall were erected on part of the Great Harem or Graveyard, in which there had been more than 1000 inscribed headstones. First a town park and then a series of shops were built on the Old Harem, an extension of the *čaršija harem* towards Uzinovići. Storage facilities were built on part of the Podgrad graveyard. Some minor graveyards had been destroyed earlier, at the beginning of the twentieth century. These include the *harems* at Ratkovina and Muftićevina. The school building, to the east of the *čaršija* mosque, and a residential building, to the west, were built with the express purpose of overtopping the minaret, in an attempt to negate its fundamental symbolic meaning.

[3] Quran, 2:37-39.

[4] See Quran, 37:96.

[5] Quran, 67:3-4.

[6] See Quran, 68:3-4.

[7] Quran, 20:114.

8 See Quran, 15:85.

9 Quran, 20:50.

10 Wensinck, *Concordance*, 1:486. This tradition exists in various forms. See for example Buhkari, 8:101-102. In the version of the tradition given here, one should note the order of self, Lord, and guest. Starting from the self indicates the importance of bearing witness and knowledge in the self. This knowledge does not depend on anything external. It is Spirit which God breathed into us, the learning of all the names which God gave to us, and intellect as the first creature and the heart as the house of God. Everything in existence, whether visible or invisible, all the prophets and all the books, are merely an *aide-mémoire* to the knowledge we already have in our hearts because God gave it to us without mediation. This is why the human self is powerful and so made that it may know itself, and consequently that it may know its Lord. The prophet said: "He who knows himself knows his Lord." (On this well-known *hadith* see Chittick, *Sufi Path of Knowledge*, 250-52). The Praised is the perfect example of self-realization through knowledge of God, as he says: "I was sent with the all-comprehensive words" (Bukhari, 4:140). Following the Praised is the perfect way for each of us to love God, and it is why the Praised is closer to each one of the faithful than their own selves (see Quran, 33:6). This is the case because the Praised is the perfect servant of God: as this servant he was given the mission to act as the seal to all prophecy. The human self is always somewhere between nothing and the Self, between earth and Spirit. If one were to represent this being "between" of the self in terms of a circle two diameters of which make a cross, then that circle is a perfect revelation of the unquantifiable center that corresponds to the human heart or spirit. Only the irradiation of the Spirit or Light, which takes place constantly, maintains and renews the life of the circle. The presence of the center is felt at every point on it. This is the meaning of the *čaršija* as a sign of the human being between nothingness and God. We return to Union from this state of being between, from the multitude of phenomena which belong to us and to which we belong. Any form of learning takes place in and through the self. There is no knowledge outside of the self. But knowledge both changes and magnifies the self. As it grows in knowledge, it approximates its higher potential. The self of the Praised fully realized the confession that there is no self except the Self. This is why the self of the Praised is the most precious thing to any of the faithful. The way back to God is through him. The change in the relationship from the self-Lord to Lord-self is a clear indication that God is both at the center and the edge. We, however, are always somewhere "between." This is the case, because God is both First and Last, both Inner and Outer.

11 Quran, 9:24.

12 See Buhkari, 4:73-74.

Images of the *Čaršija*

1 Quran, 2:144.

[2] Quran, 3:96.

[3] Quran, 2:156.

[4] Quran, 5:114.

[5] Quran, 96:1-5.

[6] Quran, 6:127.

Post Scriptum: My Ruins

[1] Lings, *Muhammad*, 317.

[2] Ibn Sad, *Kitab at-Tabaqat al-Kabir*, 88-89. Cited in Lings, *Muhammad*, 327.

[3] Cited in Lings, *Muhammad*, 327.

[4] The New Mekteb was built at the end of the nineteenth century. It was called "new" because an Old Mekteb already existed as part of the Čaršija Mosque complex. The Old Mekteb was demolished in 1924, while the New Mekteb was stripped of its functions in 1952. There were a further two *mekteb*s in Stolac, the Čuprija or Bridge Mekteb and the Uzinovići Mekteb. A number of other public and private buildings were used for the same purposes.

Existence has two aspects, the visible and the invisible. The boundary between them is what gives form to the visible, which comprehends all phenomena as signs revealing Unity or the One, whether in descending or ascending order. The revelation of Unity through this duality renders it both infinitely far and entirely near. This Unity is manifest in the vast multitude of pairs, while always remaining what it is—the source and destination of everything. Each human being is an epitome of all existence, and so we too are this duality of visible and invisible. Our sense of self is split between the flesh and the Spirit. We and the world, with our visible and invisible aspects, both present the two sides of one and the same revelation of God. As a result, we find ourselves in an unbreakable relationship with ourselves, God, and everything in existence. As we discover ourselves, we come to know the world, and *vice versa*—as we discover the world, we come to know our own selves. Neither the world nor human beings are their own beginning or end. The process whereby we come to know ourselves and the world is quite simply coming to know God through His creation and His self-revelation. Our core is of that same uncreated, universal essence whereby God taught us the names of all things, which He breathed into us as His Spirit. One of the names for the uncreated core of the human being is Prime Intellect. It was through this same core that God revealed to us the Call and the Book. The Call and the Book are always one and the same discourse, but they have appeared in history as various Books, the Torah, the Psalms, the Gospels, and the Quran. These various Books, which reveal One and the Same God, act as foci for people, who are consequently "People of the Book." There are as many peoples of the book as there are languages. Each of these peoples is centered upon its Book as its connection to its prophet. Each prophet reminds or admonishes those around him of their original oath to God and the Praised as the highest example of humanity: "He has sent down upon thee the Book with the truth, confirming what was before it, and He sent down the Torah and the Gospel aforetime, as guidance to the people, and He sent down the Salvation" (Quran, 3:3-4). Connection with any of the prophets is at the same time connection with the Praised. This is because all of the prophets have sworn an oath to God to recognize him. This is because he is the seal of prophecy and so for each of the prophets: there is no path to God except through the Praised. The Book as the focus around which the people are gathered makes it impossible for any discourse of one of the false prophets to take root amongst a people sharing the same tongue. God sent down the Book to people through His prophet. It reaches them in their own language, but it's proper and full interpretation remains with God. The number of people the Book reaches is the number of its interpretations. No one can claim absolute or complete interpretation, and we are all called to participate in furthering our interpretations, and so our own selves, on the path back to God. The Book sent down, in which everyone is admonished equally, becomes the touchstone of everything in existence and so distinguishes between human will and failure of will. Each of us is under an obligation to confess the centrality of the Book in our individual and collective life. We are all gathered around the Book as the unquestionable authority, from our first steps in the world to our last, as we exit it. This responsibility we each have to gather around the Book cannot be relinquished to any political authority or be rendered conditional on any external social circumstances. It is consequently understandable why every modern ideology involves hostility towards the revealed Book as a focus around which people gather, necessarily with equal rights and duties, dignity and responsibilities, capacity and openness towards the interpretation of the Book, in the infinite, various, and constant flow of interpretations. We relate to the Book through the sacred arts of listening, discoursing, writing, and reading. These four arts focus the essence of humanity as the Recitation and the most sublime and most mighty nature of the Praised. These acts are passed on and received everywhere—in nature, at home, at the mosque, or in the building actually designated for that purpose. The name of that building is the *mekteb*. The Communist authorities in Bosnia made a final decision to close the *mekteb*s. They made their demand of leading individuals within the religious community. Under the reformist ideologies of the nineteenth century, the political authorities in countries where Muslims lived tried to subordinate the *mekteb* to the political order and their indirect authority. All such attempts shared the essential requirement that the mediate nature of the Quran and the open nature of its interpretation be supplemented by the contents of modern educational systems. It was not easy to find grounds for opposing the *mekteb*, so the quest for them was like feeling one's way around a labyrinth. Closing the *mekteb*s entailed a complete inversion of the picture of the world as revelation of Unity focused by the human self and consequently known in its uncreated essence through the process of self-revelation. Fazlija Alikalfić (1910-2004), one of the Communist heroes who helped rid Bosnia of the *mekteb*, dealt with doubts about the *mekteb*s in 1952 in the following way: "In considering this issue, to strike only at the hygienic and non-educational aspect would be purely palliative, as they may easily respond: 'If the *mekteb* is not hygienic, we will paint it!' This is one aspect of the problem, but we are here to deal with its essence. . . . Muslims conscious of their position must make peace with the fact that the *mektebs* are an evil and that those who suffer from it by far the most are the Muslims themselves" ("Minutes of the Joint Session of the Waqf Council Board and the Ulema of the Islamic Community," held on the 28th of February, 1952; from a copy held in the Gazi Husref Bey Library in Sarajevo). The *mektebs* were *de facto* closed, even though this was concealed for a time by moving them into the mosques. The irreconcilability of these two images of the world, the traditional and the ideological, is clear in this situation. According to the traditional image, the indirect authority of the Community cannot be assumed by any interpretation of the world, and so by any individual or group. In contrast, every ideology is based on the determination of an authority which it is right to impose on all people. According to Halid Hadžimulić of Sarajevo, when the Bosnian *mektebs* were banned in 1952, Mustafa Merhemić (1876-1959) said that it would have done less harm "had they destroyed all the mosques, including the Bey's." And the Bey's Mosque is the most important and most visible symbol of the existence of Bosnian Muslims. For further on this, see note 8.

[5] A school was built on the site of the Great Harem. Its front, facing the *čaršija*, was made of dressed stone, some of which had been transferred from the fortress. The transfer of stone was halted after a worker, Mujo Hodžić, son of Avdaga, was killed. Shattered headstones from the great and the old graveyards were built into the foundations and walls of the school. They were covered over by earth and mortar. On 20 April, 2007, when repairs were being carried out to the school roof, one of the workmen, Ahmed Zubović, discovered that the inside of the wall, which had not been plastered in the attic, had been built largely from broken headstones. That same day, in the attic twilight, Amer Medar inspected a part of these walls and found hundreds of pieces of broken-off headstones. It seems reasonable to conclude, in line with this evidence, that the outer school walls were largely put together from the remnants of shattered headstones, which were then plastered over both internally and externally. A large number of these headstones had inscriptions which had been defaced "because of the school." Many such inscriptions from the shattered headstones now lie hidden within the walls. When the entire Stolac *čaršija* was destroyed and all the Muslims of the town driven away, in 1993, crosses were introduced into the classrooms of the school and placed, together with nationalist symbols, on the walls in front of the Catholic schoolchildren, to whom the school was now allocated as their exclusive birthright.

[6] In a letter from the Waqf Office of the Islamic Religious Community of 23 October, 1955 (number 2782/55) to the Expropriation Committee of the Executive Council of the People's Republic of Bosnia and Herzegovina, to which is appended the illegible signature of the Director, one finds the following: "as early as 1949, the . . . People's Committee in Stolac had usurped, without any legal basis or the agreement of the representative bodies of the Islamic Religious Community, the real property of the Waqf, the graveyards, on which were built silos, warehouses, a park for children, and a school." This letter was written six years after the destruc-

tion of the three above-mentioned graveyards (Podgrad, the Old, and the Great graveyards), as part of the later legalization of the crime.

[7] According to certain of my relatives, the first members of my family to settle in Stolac were a father and son. They came there from Unđurovina. Their ancestors had previously lived in the area between Skadar and the Neretva. Their graves were in the Great Graveyard. Whenever members of my family visited that graveyard, as instructed by their elders, they always prayed first for the souls and the memory of those two. Also in that graveyard amongst the graves of my ancestors were Ibrahim, Mahmud, and Salih, military officers and officials (Serdars and Ćehaja) of Stolac, and their many male and female descendants. It was not possible to separate the stories of their lives, so eloquently put before us by their graves and headstones, from love and passion, hope and suffering, and the expectation of the Guided One, who will fill the world with justice and beauty, in place of injustice and corruption.

[8] Derviš Mahmutćehajić (1864-1959), son of Mehmed and Hasnija (née Muftić) and grandson of Mustafa and Fatima (née Bakšić), had seven sons: Mahmut (1900-1926), Azim (1906-1938), Džemal (1907-2000), Mustafa (1912-1982), Zulfikar (1915-2000), Mehmed (1920-2000), and Remzija (1929-1987). While Džemal, Mustafa, Zulfikar, and Mehmed were respected and influential members of the anti-fascist movement and played significant roles in the new government, they were powerless to prevent the killing of two of their close relatives. Muhamed, son of their brother Mahmut and his wife Ramiza (née Kemura), born in 1927, was summarily executed as a member of the partisan movement in 1944. Šućrija, the son of Ćamil and Munta (née Serdarević), born in 1921, was killed in 1945, also without trial. Both killings were carried out by the Communist authorities. In 1995, when my brother Mirsad revisited Stolac for the first time, escorted by members of the International military forces in Bosnia, he found his own two houses and my one house there burnt, along with hundreds of others. My father's house, in which he and his brothers had been born, as had the children of his brother, Azim, and his own children, had not been burned down. It is possible that the criminals knew that this house had been the repository of the family's and the town's cultural treasures, gathered over centuries, and so they had put off its destruction in order to search for its "hidden" treasures. When Mirsad visited the house, there was practically nothing left, no manuscripts or books, no medallions, no pictures, no archives, no furnishings of value. The floors and walls had been dug up. No doubt, the criminals had supposed them to contain the valuables they were searching for. Somewhere in this great rubbish heap, amongst the ruins of dug-up floorboards and the things the criminals had not carried away, he found a broken portrait of grandfather Derviš. When the wreckers had smashed the beautiful wooden frame of the picture, they had rent the canvas right through the old man's face. Back in Sarajevo, we had stared in dumbfounded silence at this torn picture, from which the old man in the fez had looked down with his mild smile on us, all his heirs in that house built in 1911. Even in this torn picture, the mild but clear eyes of this old man, the son of Mehmed-aga and the grandson of *hajji* Mustafa,

looked as they had looked on us all, as his children, and on the people of his town. The destruction of his house and his entire legacy, and even the desecration of his own portrait, had failed to extinguish the mild but encouraging smile of that warm old man. When his only immediate kin had, at the end of the nineteenth century, given in to pressure and moved east, he had decided to stay and borne witness through his life to his belief in the inviolate right and the indelible obligation of both the living and the dead to remain by the graves of their generations and never to accept that to do so is impossible, as so many have said. Every aspect of his life bore witness to the grounds for trusting in the meaning of the world, the human being, and the Book. As far as he was concerned, everything in this world began with the Call, "In the name of God, the All-Merciful, the Ever-Merciful!" just as it ended with the exclamation, "Praise be to God!"

[9] The destruction of the Muslim graveyards was only one expression of the great anti-Muslim movement. During both the nineteenth and twentieth centuries, all the Muslims of the Balkans suffered systematic persecution and killing. Their cultural heritage was cruelly destroyed. This persecution and murder was an element in all Balkan national programs and their realization. There was no attempt to establish a national state in the Balkans that did not involve the persecution, killing, and baptism of Muslims and the destruction of their cultural heritage in the areas supposed to be that nation's territory. This suffering was of terrible proportions. Even during periods of respite, this fear still reaches deep in the Muslim soul, because no attempt to establish a national program is possible, in its "pure" ideological form, so long as Muslims remain within the body of the nation. Because of their individual and collective trauma, they remain incapable of formulating a response to the suffering they have borne. The promises of communism provided a frame for these processes. They carried as their secret content the continuation of the old nationalist programs to deal with the "Muslim question" by persecution, killing, baptism, and the destruction of Muslim cultural heritage. Consequently, with the Muslim experience of suffering during the Second World War still fresh, the new Communist order established a framework for new forms of trauma and a continuation of the destruction of the Muslim people in Bosnia. Immediately following the end of the war, violence against key symbols of Muslim cultural identity continued (*mekteb*s, mosques, *tekke*s, *harems*, etc.). Such actions had a terrible psychological impact, particularly as these people had not yet come to terms with the extent of their suffering during the just finished war (more than 100,000 or around 8% of this group had been killed—according to the research presented in Žerjavić, *Gubici stanovništva Jugoslavije u drugom svjetskom ratu*, and Kočović, *Žrtve Drugog svetskog rata u Jugoslaviji*). The new Communist government took no account of the traumatized condition of the Muslim people and allowed it no psychological breathing space under the new circumstances. The authorities passed a series of laws allowing and, in fact, promoting the destruction of Muslim cultural heritage, while implementing a number of measures designed to increase fear and the sense of insecurity. The brutal punishment meted out to the members of the "Young Muslims" movement was intended, as the state prosecutor of the

time, Enver Krzić, himself said, "to freeze the blood in anyone who might ever think of such a thing again" (cited by Alija Izetbegović in Trhulj, *Mladi muslimani*, 62). This same prosecutor had, in 1948, told Ismet Serdarević (accused and convicted of being a member of the organization): "Between your conviction and your paradise, you will live through 1,000 hells" (*Mladi muslimani*, 46). The social and political circumstances in which all this took place were permeated by the maintenance of ancient and the imposition of new fears of everything Muslim as unacceptable and dangerous. Political and legal measures taken by the new government were strictly opposed to the reality that the Muslim personality is determined by the effort to realize the self through the confessions that there is no god but God and that Muhammad is His Messenger. These confessions are essentially ahistorical. They were manifest in history, but cannot be understood outside the metaphysically-grounded image of the world. Their ahistoricity is denied by the modern ideologies, which endeavor to reify Islam, excluding it to the periphery of history, while presenting this reification and exclusion as a historical phenomenon. Both these confessions are available to every individual through transferred or received knowledge. They are, however, also present in each of us as our authentic and original nature and as the Spirit breathed into us by our Creator. Received knowledge only serves the discovery and the realization of knowledge which already exists in us as our most profound nature, the knowledge of the names which God taught to Adam, and so to all of his children, at the end of Creation, when it was focused within us. This is why every individual and social act includes the desire for self-discovery and self-realization of that inner knowledge received from God. When a child is born, it is given a name by the most prominent member of the family or the community. That individual takes on the role of the Praised by calling us to confess the truth and claim of everything in existence and so to realize our own self in relationship with God, in particular through the highest moment of humanity, represented by the Praised as the Messenger of God. For, the Praised was at the beginning of all creation, as all the prophets and through them all those who have followed them have borne witness. That individual carries the child in his arms, which is to say symbolically at the prophet's breast, and recites the Call (*azan*) into his or her right ear and the Resurrection (*ikamat*) into the left. Then, he speaks out his or her name, which should, in principle, express the desire that the human being develop in beauty and goodness (see Mulahalilović, *Vjerski običaji muslimana u Bosni i Hercegovini*, 16). This Muslim tradition of introducing the name becomes unacceptable in the new ideological environment. Individuals from a Muslim background, included in the ideological apparatus, avoid such names, so that authentic Muslim names become scandalous. The circumcision of male children, as a symbol of our original covenant with God as the only source of the reality of all that is in existence, also became unacceptable, so that, in the aftermath of the Second World War, most Muslims carried it out in secrecy and fear. Teaching children sections of the Recitation, which is the principal expression that the human soul cannot be based upon individual willfulness, also became unacceptable and an act of opposition to the promises of "progress" and the scientistic ideology. The institution of the *mekteb*, as the place in which one first learns the use of the pen and the Book, is of decisive importance in the formation of the Muslim sense of self. Young children are gathered around the Book that God revealed as a mercy unto the worlds. Their teacher approaches the Book with the same rights and responsibility as they do. The Book is an authority that binds us all to the Praised as the perfect example and God as the source and destination of everything. It signifies our relationship to the Word and Its manifestation through phenomena, speech, and writing. Through this general relationship with the divine revelation, we find ourselves constantly affirming ourselves as "a people of the Book." Gathering around the Book has a greater symbolic than essential significance. In this way, the child is immunized against any authority which is not supra-individual and which mediates the child's relationship with God the Creator, so that ethical behavior with regard to other individuals and the admission of claims derive from our relationship with God the Creator and Governor of all existence and not from subordination to any secular authority which lays claim to some absolute right. The Book turns and orients the child towards the Creator who reveals Himself through the world, us, and the Book. In this way, the diversity of the world—the heavens and the earth and everything between—is connected with Unity as the Principle, while our ability to realize and discover this Unity within ourselves is confirmed. Because the Communist authorities outlawed the *mekteb*, the Recitation was displaced from its central position within Muslim society, as the decisive factor in the creation of the individual self. In its place, the new authorities introduced the new ideologically determined authority, whose defining characteristic was force and which was focused on the person of the leader, represented in terms of the new Communist ideology, and embodied in the party apparatus, with the State as its means. In 1952, the operation of the *tekke*s or dervish lodges was forbidden by order of the *ulema* of the Islamic community. (This decision was published in the *Gazette of the Supreme Islamic Council of Elders of the Federal People's Republic of Yugoslavia*, Sarajevo, 1-4 (1952): 199). In this way, religious life as a whole was reduced to the role of the "imams at the mosque." The role of the "imam at the mosque" is doctrinally just leading common prayer and may be carried out by any adult individual. Given that the nomination and installation of an imam did not require any particular conditions of spiritual initiation, therefore, it became part of a structure entirely under the oversight of the political authorities. According to Osman Ćimić (1927-2002), a senior official within the Communist police, most of the imams so appointed were linked with the security apparatus of the Communist authorities and followed their orders. They were, as such, frequently deeply involved in the destruction of Muslim society. This was not, however, the worst consequence of this reduction of the doctrinal unity of Islam, which ensures a balance between received and intellectual knowledge, without which no traditional image of the world can survive, and on which and through which human salvation through self-realization is based. Once the imams had been securely established in this subordinate position, under the authorities' surveillance, they were then drawn into the hierarchical network of an exoteric apparatus, entirely managed by the authorities. This was, however, only one of the degrees whereby traditional unities were transformed into ideologies which locate human salvation in political and lucrative action. With the full involvement of the ideological elite, the religious organizations were then transformed into a supreme value used to justify violence against individuals and their inclusion or exclusion, depending on the degree to which they accepted the authority of the ideological elite, which lorded over the apparatus as the authority elected by the elite as supreme. Human salvation through the realization of the Unity of God and the imitation of the Praised as the most beautiful example was suppressed, in favor of respect for an apparatus which had taken the place of the Unity of God and the apostolate of the Praised. Confession of the Unity of God was replaced by the inviolate unity of the people. Following the Messenger was now located within history and replaced by the inviolate nature of the leader and the leadership as the conditions of "progress." According to Arkoun, Islam was reoriented as "a means of disguised behavior, institutions, and cultural and scientific activity, inspired by purely western forms, which had been ideologically rejected" (*Rethinking Islam*, 13). Given that the participants in the apparatus are acting in accordance with the forms of ideological modernity, dressed up in traditional garb, and that God, as the transcendent and always present authority, is excluded or reduced to a framework for the instrumental rationality of the elite, it can hardly be confirmed except by the constant offering of new forms and the destruction of the old. According to such a point of view, the old is regressive, the new progressive. The standard bearers of the new know, or so they claim, the goal towards which history is leading and the ways it will do so. The "imams" and their apparatus had a significant position amongst the destroyers of Islamic cultural heritage during the modern period. They felt ill at ease with the old, inherited cultural unities, as they tried to present themselves as separate from the old and loyal to the new. (For more on this see the above-mentioned work by Arkoun; see also Mahmutćehajić, "Fundamentalizam nasuprot tradicijske intelektualnosti".) Such circumstances provided the perfect conditions for the destruction of endowed or *waqf* property, a crucial factor in providing Islamic culture with staying power. According to the researches of Amer Medar, there were more than 200 *waqf*s or endowed trusts in and around Stolac. He has confirmed the existence of 421 land registry entries for *waqf* properties. *Waqf*s are assets whose owners have excluded any possibility of alienation to ensure that any income accruing from them is used for the purpose of confirming the Unity of God and the apostolate of the Praised. In wills made to dedicate a property for such purposes, one frequently finds reference to the obligation to do good, in the expectation of relief on the Day of Judgment. Such endowments also frequently cite the Prophet's message: "When a man dies, his acts come to an end, but three—lasting charity, beneficial knowledge, and a pious son, who prays for him" (Muslim, 3:867). Only a few of the deeds of endowment (*waqfnama*) from Stolac have come down to us. A list of the ones preserved in the Gazi Husref Bey library in Sarajevo was published by Fajić in "Popis vakufnama iz Bosne i Hercegovine koje se nalaze u Gazi Husrev-begovoj biblioteci u Sarajevu," 291-293. For more on the *waqfnama* from Stolac, see Trako "Vakufnama hadži Mehmeda sina hadži Mahmudova Mehmedbašića Stočanina iz 1734. godine," 38-45; and Rizvanbegović, "Vakufname i vasijetname Ali-paše

Rizvanbegovića Stočevića." A review of the majority of the *waqfnama* from Stolac allows one to conclude that the endowment or property being left by an owner to his heirs or the community might include a shop, a house, a water cistern, land (gardens, meadows, an orchard, or pastureland), a mill or mill wheel, a washing area, books, livestock, furniture, or money.

[10] A large number of educated people have been born in the city of Stolac, in comparison to other Bosnian towns of a similar size. A number of them have had a significant influence on events in the country, and even outside. Here we will mention only some: Sulejman Šarac (1850-1927), a theologian and the Reis-ul-ulema or official head of the Bosnian Islamic Community (a unique post created by the Austrian authorities), Mehmed Šarić (1852-1920), a painter and politician, Adem Bise (1887-1957), a teacher and essayist, Dimitrije Mitrinović (1887-1953), poet, essayist, and philosopher, Mustafa Golubić (1889-1941), writer and general of the NKVD (Narodnii Komissariat Vnutrennikh Del/The People's Commissariat for Internal Affairs of the USSR), Šefkija Behmen (1892-1974), lawyer and politician, Mahmud Behmen (1894-1937), journalist and politician, Asim Behmen (1899-1924), essayist and official on the executive committee of the Communist Youth International in Moscow, Safet Burina (1907-1977), poet, Hamid Dizdar (1907-1967), poet and journalist, Džemal Mahmutćehajić (1907-2000), a delegate at the ZAVNOBIH (The National Anti-Fascist Council of the People's Liberation of Bosnia and Herzegovina) and AVNOJ (Anti-Fascist Council of the People's Liberation of Yugoslavia), Huso Salčić (1911-1942), writer, Mak Dizdar (1917-1971), writer and journalist, Asim Stranjak (1930-1984), economist, Alija Isaković (1932-1997), writer, Emir Buzaljko (1952-1992), architect and essayist. In spite of the fact that these citizens of Stolac were involved in various social, cultural, and political activities at home and abroad, as may be seen from their biographies and their works, the dimensions and the savagery of the treatment meted out to their own town and their country failed to find a place in their discourses or their writings.

[11] On this phenomenon in Persia during the twentieth century, see Nasr, *Islamic Philosophy*, 251ff.

[12] Chittick, *Science of the Cosmos, Science of the Soul*, 10-11.

[13] Đikić, "Povodom obustavljanja rada u mektebima," 27.

[14] For more on this subject, see Shayegan, *Cultural Schizophrenia.*

[15] Wei-Ming, *Centrality and Commonality*, 102.

[16] If an individual or some group ascribes its own misfortunes or the misfortunes of its country to the presence of a Muslim element in that country or community, and if it suggests that the situation be resolved or dealt with by depriving those Muslims of some of their rights, humiliating them, forcing them to accept apartheid, expelling them from the country, or simply doing away with them, then we say that that individual or group has anti-Islamic or anti-Muslim opinions. When these opinions are transformed into a systematic ideology, then the conditions

are ripe for the creation of an elite-ideology-organization-agency complex, as the framework for potential genocide.

[17] Few were the houses in Stolac which did not contain collections of manuscript or printed books. On the basis of conversations with a number of witnesses, the existence of such collections has been confirmed in the following families: Alihodžić, Basarić, Baščaušević, Behmen, Bukić, Buro, Buzaljko, Ćelić, Čerkez, Čohodarević, Dervoz, Dizdar, Duman, Đulepa, Elezović, Gačo, Grebiđela, Grljević, Hajdarević, Halilagić, Heko, Hrle, Hromić, Jašarbegović, Kadribegović, Kohnić, Korkut, Ljubović, Mahmutćehajić, Mehmedbašić, Mešak, Muftić, Opijač, Pašalić, Pirija, Prndelj, Repak, Rizvanbegović, Sarajlić, Stranjak, Sumbulović, Šarac, Šarić, Šehić, Šemić, Šljivo, Škoro, Trklja, Zekić, Žujo. These collections were, for the most part, destroyed during the twentieth century. A few hundred manuscripts, connected in one way or another with Stolac, have been preserved in the Gazi Husref Bey library in Sarajevo. For the content of one of these collections, which gives some idea of the forms of knowledge which were formative of traditional Stolac, see Nametak, "Rukopisna zbirka Habibe Mehmedbašić," 181-200. This collection was in the owner's house and disappeared during the war against Bosnia (1991-1996).

[18] For the destruction of the holy territory of Mecca, see Fattah, "The Profane Crowding Out the Sacred in Mecca," and Irfan, "The Destruction of Holy Sites in Mecca and Medina."

[19] Quran, 5:30-31.

[20] Quran, 25:63-76.

[21] See Quran, 37:96.

[22] Quran, 47:38.

[23] Quran, 35:15.

[24] *Nahjul Balagha*, 254.

[25] *Nahjul Balagha*, 375.

[26] Ibn al-Arabi, *al-Futuhat al-makkiyya*, 2:447.8.

[27] See Quran, 20:50.

[28] See Quran, 67:3.

[29] Peace is one of the beautiful names of God. See Quran, 59:23. This name is the most common form of salutation between people.

[30] Quran, 8:13.

[31] See Quran, 3:9 and 4:140.

[32] See Quran, 3:83.

[33] Luke, 17:20-21.

[34] Matthew, 7:7.

[35] Quran, 2:256.

[36] Quran, 63:3-4.

[37] During the nineteenth and twentieth centuries, there has been a systematic ruination of the Muslims in Bosnia and her eastern neighbors. This destructive process was completed in the areas to the north and west of Bosnia during the eighteenth century. On the killing and persecution of Muslims and the destruction of their culture during the nineteenth century, see McCarthy, *Death and Exile: The Ethnic Cleansing of the Ottoman Muslims 1821-1922*, Kanic, *Srbija, zemlja i stanovništvo*, and Dedier, *Genocid nad Muslimanima 1941-1945*.

[38] See Pfeiffer, *Meister Eckhart*, 114.

[39] See Quran, 15:29 and 32:9.

[40] Quran, 36:78-80.

[41] Quran, 23:35-38.

[42] *Nahjul Balagha*, 247-8.

[43] Burckhardt, *Alchemy*, 58ff.

[44] Quran, 10:22-23.

[45] See Quran, 37:96.

[46] For this decisive period in the history of Bosnia and the surrounding countries, see Banac, *With Stalin against Tito*. The ideological framework for Muslim inclusion in anti-Muslim activities cannot be understood unless one sees how it relates to the nationalist question and nationalism. On this see Banac, *The National Question in Yugoslavia*.

[47] See Quran, 2:286.

Glossary

avlija (gk. *avli*): a walled garden.

Becca: an alternative name for Mecca, used in the Quran.

čaršija (tur. *çarşi*; pers. *charsu*): the central public area of a town, the market place.

ćuprija (tur. *köprü*; gk. *géphyra*): bridge.

ders (tur. *ders*; ar. *dars*): a lesson.

dershana (pers. *dershane*): a place for holding lessons, a classroom.

din (ar. *din*): the basic term for our relationship with God. Its essential meaning is debt or obligation. Our debt to God arises out of our creaturehood and the fact that we disobeyed His one command. It consists of following the path of uprightness. It is often translated as religion, a usage which tends to reify what is a personal relationship to God.

džamija (ar. *jami*): a place for the congregation of Muslims for ritual purposes.

ghazal (tur. *gazel*; ar. *gazal*): a lyrical poem with 7-12 couplets.

haqiqa (tur. *hakikat*; ar. *haqiqa*): truth, the correct state of affairs, essence.

hammam (ar. *hammam*): a bathhouse.

han (var. khan, tur. *han*; old Turkish *hang*, *vang*): a title for a ruler or a name for an inn.

harem (ar. *haram*): an inviolate, forbidden, or sacred place, esp. a graveyard.

ihsan (ar. *ihsan*): doing what is good and beautiful; one of the dimensions of *din*.

imam (ar. *imam*): the leader in prayer; an exemplary model.

iman (ar. *iman*): faith or belief; one of the dimensions of *din*; our relationship as faithful (*mumin*) with God as Faithful (*Mumin*).

islam (ar. *islam*): our relationship as people of peace with God as Peace.

Kaaba (ar. *kaba*): the cubic structure at the bottom of the valley of Becca/Mecca.

kiraethana (tur. *kiraethane*; ar. *qiraa* + pers. *hane*): a reading room, derived from *kiraet* (ar. *qiraa*): reading; originally the recitation aloud of parts of the memorized or written Book; reading and learning are two related aspects of the approach to the Book.

kitab (ar. *kitab*): book.

marifa (ar. *marifa*): knowledge, gnosis.

mekteb (ar. *maktab*): the place of the Book; the place for studying the Book, and for listening, memorizing, speaking, and writing; the place of initiation into knowledge of the Book sent down to bind us to God.

mesdžid (ar. *masjid*): the place of prostration and worship; any place where one decides to participate in the universal worship of God as the Truth; any place from which we ascend towards God and return to our most beautiful sublimity. As such it is the place of annihilation or abnegation of the self in the face of our witness of God.

mihrab (ar. *mihrab*): the most sublime area within the *mesdžid*; a niche in the *mesdžid* wall facing the Kaaba; a sign that the worshipper is standing on the border of the material world and his or her determination to cross it; a place of anger, excess, and war in which we confess our determination to realize ourselves in relation to God as the Real.

mujezin (ar. *muadhdhin*): muezzin; the caller, the individual who calls to prayer from the minaret or some other place.

minaret (ar. *manara*): the place of fire, the *mesdžid* tower on which fires are lit as a sign of faith, love of God and the Praised, and of warmth and knowledge regarding them (enlightenment); the tower from which the muezzin issues the call and announces a short message on God, the Praised, relation to them, and salvation through them; the tower that speaks of the connection between earth and heaven, body and spirit, and our always being less than we are capable of.

musafirhana (tur. *misafirhane*): the guesthouse, derived from *musafir* (ar. *musafir*): guest.

muselimat: the administrator's offices or town offices, derived from *muselim* (ar. *musallim*): local administrator.

muslim (ar. *muslim*): one who has established an active relationship with God and His signs through being-at-peace, so as to have realized or discovered God as Peace within his or her own nature.

mutevelija (tur. *mütevelli*; ar. *mutawalli*): the administrator of a *vakuf* or *waqf*.

nišan (tur. *nisan*; pers. *nisan*): the Bosnian term for the Muslim gravestone, which normally takes the form of a pillar with a turban for a male and a blade for the female, both bearing inscriptions.

reis (ar. *rais*): leader.

reis-ul-ulema (ar. *rais al-ulama*): the leader of the scholars; in Bosnia the elected leader of the official Islamic Community, a position created by the Austro-Hungarian authorities to provide themselves with a counterpart equivalent to a patriarch or primate in the Christian churches.

sahat-kula (tur. *saat kulesi*): clock tower, derived from *sahat* (ar. *saa*): hour, clock.

satan (ar. *shaytan*, heb. *śatan*): any form of human or supernatural enemy; whatever turns us from the Real; the devil.

sedžda (ar. *sajda*): prostration, the culmination of worship, annihilation of the self before the face of God.

sharia (ar. *sharia*): literally the way to the water hole; the true system, whose main sources are the revealed Word of God, the life and acts of the Praised, and the procedures of legal process; exoteric way.

sheik (ar. *shaykh*): an elder, a leader, a spiritual master.

shirk (ar. *shirk*): association unto God, idolatry.

sofa (tur. *sofa*; ar. *suffa*): a porch.

sura (ar. *sura*): a form or image which contains a surplus connected to the multitude of signs, whether in the form of things on the earth and in the heavens or what lies between, or in the form of the human self, or in the form of the Book or its works.

stećak (pl. *stećci*): medieval tombstones whose form is derived from the ancient roman sarcophagus. They take various forms, but are generally shaped like houses to symbolize transition to our new home. Others are in the shape of crosses and upright stones. They are often decorated with carved motifs whose symbolism is related to the beliefs of the independent Bosnian church. They not infrequently bear inscriptions addressing the passer-by.

tariqa (ar. *tariqa*): the way or the path; the way of life which is determined from without by the *sharia* and from within by additional knowledge and ritual; esoteric way.

tepa (tur. *tepe*): a platform in the middle of the *čaršija*, with a covered area for weights and measures.

turban (tur. *tülbent*): a scarf wrapped around the head; it symbolizes the winding sheet and the crown of God's vicars on earth.

ulema (ar. *ulama*): the scholars.

waqf (ar. *waqf*): property entailed by its owner; an endowment, especially for religious purposes or to fund a mosque, public kitchen, or other good work.

waqfnama (tur. *vakıfname*): the charter of endowment.

For a glossary of all key foreign words used in books published by World Wisdom, including metaphysical terms in English, consult: www.DictionaryofSpiritualTerms.org.
This on-line Dictionary of Spiritual Terms provides extensive definitions, examples and related terms in other languages.

Bibliography

Abu Daud, al-Sidjistani. *Al-Sunan.* Cairo: Mustafa al-Babi al-Halabi, 1952.

Aličić, Ahmed. *Pokret za autonomiju Bosne od 1831. do 1832. godine.* Sarajevo: Orijentalni institut, 1996.

Arberry, Arthur J. *The Koran Interpreted.* London: George Allen & Unwin, 1980.

Arkoun, Muhammad. *Rethinking Islam: Common Questions, Uncommon Answers*, trans. Robert D. Lee. Boulder: Westview Press, 1994.

Aščerić-Todd, Ines. "The Noble Traders: The Islamic Tradition of 'Spiritual Chivalry' (*futuwwa*) in Bosnian Trade-guilds (16th-19th centuries)." *The Muslim World*, 97/2 (2007):159-173.

Banac, Ivo. *With Stalin against Tito: Cominformist Splits in Yugoslav Communism.* Ithaca/London: Cornell University Press, 1988.

———. *The National Question in Yugoslavia: Origins, History, Politics.* Ithaca/London: Cornell University Press, 1984.

Bayhaqi, Abu Bakr al-Khusrawdjirdi, al-. *Al-Sunan al-Kubra*, 10 vols. Beirut: Dar al-Kutub al-Ilmiyya, 1994.

Bećirbegović, Madžida. "Prosvjetni objekti islamske arhitekture u Bosni i Hercegovini." *Prilozi za orijentalnu filologiju*, 20/21 (1970/71):223-359.

Bešlagić, Šefik. *Kamene stolice srednjovjekovne Bosne i Hercegovine.* Sarajevo: Akademija nauka i umjetnosti Bosne i Hercegovine, 1985.

Bukhari, Imam, al-. *Sahih al-Bukhari*, 9 vols., trans. Muhammad Muhsin Khan. Beirut: Dal al-Arabia, 1985.

Burckhardt, Titus. *Alchemy: Science of the Cosmos, Science of the Soul*, trans. William Stoddart. Louisville, Kentucky: Fons Vitae, 2006.

———. *The Universality of Sacred Art.* Colombo: The Sri Lanka Institute of Traditional Studies, 2001.

———. *Chartres and the Birth of the Cathedral.* Ipswich: Golgonooza Press, 1995.

———. *Fez: City of Islam.* Cambridge, UK: The Islamic Texts Society, 1992.

———. *Mystical Astrology according to Ibn Arabi*, trans. Bulent Rauf. Gloucestershire: Beshara Publications, 1977.

———. *Art of Islam: Language and Meaning*, trans. J. Peter Hobson. London: World of Islam Festival Trust, 1976.

———. *Sacred Art in East and West: Its Principles and Methods*, trans. Lord

Northbourne. Pates Manor, Bedfont: Perennial Books, 1967.
Chittick, William C. *Ibn Arabi, Heir to the Prophets.* Oxford: Oneworld, 2007.
———. *Science of the Cosmos, Science of the Soul: The Pertinence of Islamic Cosmology in the Modern World.* Oxford: Oneworld, 2007.
———. "Weeping in Classical Sufism." In Patton, *Holy Tears*, 132-144.
———. *The Heart of Islamic Philosophy: The Quest for Self-Knowledge in the Teachings of Afdal al-Din Kashani.* New York: Oxford University Press, 2001.
———. *Faith and Practice of Islam: Three Thirteenth Century Sufi Texts.* Albany: State University of New York Press, 1992.
———. *The Sufi Path of Knowledge: Ibn al-Arabi's Metaphysics of Imagination.* Albany: State University of New York Press, 1989.
Coomaraswamy, Ananda K. "On Being in One's Right Mind." In Coomaraswamy, *What is Civilisation?*, 33-41.
———. *What is Civilisation?* Ipswich: Golgonooza Press, 1989.
———. *Selected Papers: Traditional Art and Symbolism*, ed. Roger Lipsey. Princeton: Princeton University Press, 1977.
———. "*Ars sine scientia nihil.*" In Coomaraswamy, *Selected Papers: Traditional Art and Symbolism*, 229-232.
———. *Selected Papers: Metaphysics*, ed. Roger Lipsey. Princeton: Princeton University Press, 1977.
———. "Who Is 'Satan' and Where Is 'Hell'?" In Coomaraswamy, *Selected Papers: Metaphysics*, 23-33.
———. *Christian and Oriental Philosophy of Art.* New Delhi: Munshiram Manoharlal, 1972.
———. *The Transformation of Nature in Art.* New York: Dover Publications, 1956.
Cragg, Kenneth. *The Mind of the Quran.* London: George Allen & Unwin, 1973.
Crimes in Stolac Municipality. Sarajevo: DID, 2001.
Čelebi, Evlija. *Putopis: Odlomci o jugoslovenskim zemljama.* Sarajevo: Veselin Masleša, 1973.
Čelić, Džemal. "Stolačka čaršija." *Slovo Gorčina*, 1982:42-49.
Dizdar, Mak. *Stone Sleeper*, trans. Francis R. Jones. London: Anvil Press Poetry, 2009.
———. *Kameni spavač / Stone Sleeper*, trans. Francis R. Jones. Sarajevo: DID, 1999.
Dizdar, Mehmed. *Suđeni Stolac.* Sarajevo: DID, 1996.
Dedier, Vladimir and Antun Miletić. *Genocid nad Muslimanima 1941-1945: Zbornik dokumenata i svjedočenja.* Sarajevo: Svjetlost, 1990.

Đikić, Hasan. "Povodom obustavljanja rada u mektebima." *Glasnik Vrhovnog islamskog starješinstva u FNRJ*. Sarajevo, 1-4 (1952):25-31.

Eliade, Mircea. *Images and Symbols: Studies in Religious Symbolism*, trans. Philip Mairet. Princeton: Princeton University Press, 1991.

Fajić, Zejnil. "Popis vakufnama iz Bosne i Hercegovine koje se nalaze u Gazi Husrev-begovoj biblioteci." *Anali Gazi-Husrev-begove biblioteke*, 5-6 (1978):245-302.

Fattah, Hassan M. "The Profane Crowding Out Sacred in Mecca." *International Herald Tribune*, March 7, 2007.

Ghazali, Muhammad, al-. *Ihya ulum al-din*. Cairo: Matbaat al-Amirat al-Sharafiyya, 1908-1909.

Goldstein, Ivo. *Croatia: A History*. Montreal: McGill-Queen's University Press, 2000.

Grabar Oleg. "Upon Reading al-Azraqi." In Grabar, *Early Islamic Art, 650-1100*, 57-68.

———. *Early Islamic Art, 650-1100: Constructing the Study of Islamic Art*. Aldershot: Ashgate Variorum, 2005.

———. "The Meaning of the Dome of the Rock in Jerusalem." In Grabar, *Jerusalem*, 143-158.

———. *Jerusalem: Constructing the Study of Islamic Art*. Aldershot: Ashgate Variorum, 2005.

Guénon, René. *Fundamental Symbols: The Universal Language of Sacred Science*, trans. Alvin Moore, Jr. Cambridge, UK: Quinta Essentia, 1995.

———. "The Heart and the Cave." In Guénon, *Fundamental Symbols*, 145-148.

———. "The Mountain and the Cave." In Guénon, *Fundamental Symbols*, 148-151.

———. "The Cornerstone." In Guénon, *Fundamental Symbols*, 187-197.

———. *The Multiple States of Being*, trans. Joscelyn Godwin. New York: Larson Publications, 1984.

———. *Man and His Becoming According to the Vedanta*, trans. Richard C. Nicholson. New Delhi: Oriental Book Reprint Corporation, 1981.

Hadžijahić, Muhamed. "Sinkretistički elementi u islamu u Bosni i Hercegovini." *Prilozi za orijentalnu filologiju*, 28/29 (1978/79):301-329.

Halabi, Umar al-Kahiri, al-. *Uyun al-Insan* (*al-Sira al-Halabiyya*), 3 vols. Cairo: Al-Manba al-Azhariyya, 1329-1330.

Hamm, Josip. "Apokalipsa bosanskih krstjana." *Slovo*, 9-10 (1960):43-104.

Hasandedić, Hivzija. *Katalog arapskih, turskih i perzijskih rukopisa*. Mostar:

Arhiv Hercegovine, 1977.
Hoare, Marko Attila. *The History of Bosnia: From the Middle Ages to the Present Day.* London: Saqi Books, 2007.
Howes, Graham. *The Art of the Sacred.* London/New York: I.B. Taurus, 2007.
Huxley, Aldous. *The Perennial Philosophy: An Interpretation of the Great Mystics, East and West.* New York: Harper Collins, 2004.
Ibn al-Arabi. *Al-Futuhat al-makkiyya*, ed. Osman Jahija. Cairo: Al-Haya al-Misriyya al-Amma lil-Kitab, 1972.
Ibn al-Hibban. *Al-Ihsan fi Taqrub* (*Sahih ibn Hibban*). Beirut: Shuayb al-Arnaut, 1988.
Ibn Hanbal, Ahmad. *Al-Musnad.* Beirut: Dar Sadir, n.d.
Ibn Ishaq. *Sirat Rasul Allah* (*The Life of Muhammad*), trans. Alfred Guillaume. Karachi: Oxford University Press, 1980.
Ibn Maja. *Al-Sunan.* Cairo: Dar Ihya al-Kutub al-Arabiyya, 1952.
Ibn Sad, Muhammad. *Kitab at-Tabaqat al-Kabir*, 9 vols. Leiden: E.J. Brill, 1904-1940.
Irfan, Ahmad. "The Destruction of Holy Sites in Mecca and Medina." *Islamica Magazine*, http://www.islamicamagazine.com, issue 15, November 11, 2007.
Judah, Tim. *The Serbs: History, Myth and the Destruction of Yugoslavia.* New Haven: Yale University Press, 2009.
Kanic, Feliks. *Srbija zemlja i stanovništvo: Od rimskog doba do kraja XIX veka*, 2 vols. Belgrade: Rad, 1985.
Kapidžić, Hamdija. *Ali-paša Rizvanbegović i njegovo doba.* Sarajevo: Akademija nauka i umjetnosti Bosne i Hercegovine, 2001.
Kapikian, Catherine. *Art in Service of the Sacred.* Nashville: Abingdon Press, 2006.
Kočović, Bogoljub. *Žrtve Drugog svetskog rata u Jugoslaviji.* Sarajevo: Svjetlost, 1990.
Kreševljaković, Hamdija. *Izabrana djela II.* Sarajevo: Veselin Masleša, 1991.
———. "Esnafi i obrti u Bosni i Hercegovini (1463-1878)." In Kreševljaković, *Izabrana djela II*, 7-381.
Laibelman, Alan M. *The Other Perennial Philosophy: A Metaphysical Dialectic.* New York: University Press of America, 2000.
Lavić, Osman. *Katalog arapskih, turskih, perzijskih i bosanskih rukopisa*, Fascicle XV. Sarajevo: Gazi Husrev-begova biblioteka, 2006.
Lings, Martin. *Splendors of Quran Calligraphy and Illumination.* Liechtenstein: Thesaurus Islamicus Foundation, 2005.
———. *Mecca: From before Genesis Until Now.* Cambridge, UK: Archetype, 2004.

———. *Symbol and Archetype: A Study of the Meaning of Existence.* Cambridge, UK: Quinta Essentia, 1991.

———. *Muhammad: His Life Based On the Earliest Sources.* London: Allen & Unwin, 1988.

———. *The Eleventh Hour: The Spiritual Crisis of the Modern World in the Light of Tradition and Prophecy.* Cambridge, UK: Quinta Essentia, 1987.

McCarthy, Justin. *Death and Exile: The Ethnic Cleansing of Ottoman Muslims 1821-1922.* Princeton, New Jersey: The Darwin Press, 1995.

Mahmutćehajić, Rusmir. *Learning from Bosnia: Approaching Tradition.* New York: Fordham University Press, 2005.

———. "Fundamentalizam nasuprot tradicijske intelektualnosti." *Dijalog,* 3-4 (2005):218-240.

———. *Sarajevo Essays: Politics, Ideology, and Tradition.* New York: State University of New York, 2003.

———. *Bosnia the Good: Tolerance and Tradition.* Budapest: Central European University Press, 2000.

Malcolm, Noel. *Bosnia: A Short History.* New York: New York University Press, 1996.

Malik ibn Anas, Imam. *Al-Muwatta,* trans. Aisha Abdarahman at-Tarjumana and Yaqub Johnson. London: Diwan Press, 1982.

Mazower, Mark. *The Balkans: A Short History.* New York: Modern Library, 2002.

Mufid, Shaykh, al-. *Kitab al-Irshad* (*The Book of Guidance into the Lives of the Twelve Imams*), trans. I.K.A. Howard. New York: Tahrike Tarsile Quran, 1981.

Mulahalilović, Enver. *Vjerski običaji muslimana u Bosni i Hercegovini* Sarajevo: el-Kalem, 1989.

Murata, Sachiko and William C. Chittick. *The Vision of Islam: The Foundations of Muslim Faith and Practice.* London: I.B. Tauris Publishers, 1996.

Murata, Sachiko. *The Tao of Islam: A Sourcebook on Gender Relationships in Islamic Thought.* Albany: State University of New York Press, 1992.

Muslim, Imam. *Sahih Muslim,* 4 vols., trans. Abdul Hamid Siddiqi. Riyadh: International Islamic Publishing House, n.d.

Nametak, Fehim. "Rukopisna zbirka Habibe Mehmedbašić." *Anali Gazi Husrev-begove biblioteke,* 11-12 (1985):181-200.

Nasr, Seyyed Hossein. *Islamic Philosophy from its Origin to the Present: Philosophy in the Land of Prophecy.* Albany: State University of New York Press, 2006.

———. *An Introduction to Islamic Cosmological Doctrines: Conceptions of Nature and Methods Used for Its Study by the Ikhwan al-Safa, al-Biruni, and Ibn Sina.* Albany: State University of New York Press, 1993.

———. *Knowledge and the Sacred.* Albany: State University of New York Press, 1989.

Nahjul Balagha: Sermons, Letters, and Sayings of Imam Ali. Qum: Ansariyam Publications, 1989.

Nicholson, Reynold A. *Rumi: Poet and Mystic.* London: Allen and Unwin, 1950.

Niškanović, Miroslav. "Ilindanski dernek kod turbeta Đerzelez Alije u Gerzovu." *Novopazarski zbornik*, 2 (1978):163-168.

Nuwairi, Shihab al-Din Ahmad, al-. *Al-Nihaja al-Arab*, 34 vols. Beirut: Dar al-Kutub al-Ilmiyya, 2004-2005.

Pallis, Marco. *The Way and the Mountain.* London: Peter Owen, 1991.

———. *Peaks and Lamas.* Oxford: Woburn Press, 1975.

Pavlowitch, Stevan. *Serbia: The History of an Idea.* New York: New York University Press, 2002.

Patton, Kimberly Christine and John Stratton Hawley. *Holy Tears: Weeping in the Religious Imagination.* Princeton/Oxford: Princeton University Press, 2005.

———. "Howl, Weep, and Moan, and Bring it Back to God: Holy Tears in Eastern Christianity." In Patton, *Holy Tears*, 255-273.

Perry, Whitall N. *A Treasury of Traditional Wisdom.* Cambridge, UK: Quinta Essentia, 1991.

Pfeiffer, Franz. *Meister Eckhart*, trans. C. de B. Evans, 1 vol. London: John M. Watkins, 1924.

Rječnik naseljenih mjesta u Bosni i Hercegovini. Sarajevo: Zemaljska vlada za Bosnu i Hercegovinu, 1910.

Rizvanbegović, Izet. "Vakufname i vasijetname Ali-paše Rizvanbegovića Stočevića." *Prilozi za orijentalnu filologiju*, 52/53 (2004):295-338.

Samayuta Nikaya (*The Book of the Kindred Sayings*), 5 vols., trans. C.A.F. Rhys Davids and F.L. Woodward. Lunchester: Pali Text Society, 1917-1930.

Samardžić, Radovan. *Ideje za srpsku istoriju.* Belgrade: Jugoslavijapublik, 1989.

———. "O gradskoj civilizaciji na Balkanu XV–XIX veka." In Samardžić, *Ideje za srpsku istoriju*, 79-89.

Schimmel, Annemarie. *My Soul Is a Woman: The Feminine in Islam.* London: Continuum, 1997.

Schmitt, Charles B. *Studies in Renaissance Philosophy and Science.* London:

Variorum, 1981.
———. "Perennial Philosophy: From Steuco to Leibnitz." *Journal of the History of Ideas*, 27 (1966):505-532.
Schmidt-Biggemann, Wilhelm. *Philosophia Perennis: Historical Outlines of Western Spirituality in Ancient, Medieval, and Early Modern Thought.* Dordrecht: Springer, 2004.
Schuon, Frithjof. *Stations of Wisdom.* Bloomington: World Wisdom Books, 1995.
———. *Islam and the Perennial Philosophy.* London: World of Islam Publishing Company, 1976.
Shah-Kazemi, Reza. *Paths to Transcendence: According to Shankara, Ibn Arabi, and Meister Eckhart.* Bloomington: World Wisdom, 2006.
Shayegan, Daryoush. *Cultural Schizophrenia: Islamic Societies Confronting the West*, trans. John Howe. London: Saqi Books, 1992.
Smith, Huston. *Forgotten Truth: The Common Vision of the World's Religion.* New York: Harper Collins, 1992.
Sophrony (Sakharov), Archimandrite. *St. Silouan the Athonite.* Crestwood, New York: St. Vladimir's Press, 1991.
Stavrianos, Stavros L. *The Balkans since 1453.* New York: New York University Press, 2000.
Sulami, Muhammad ibn al-Husayn, al-. *The Book of Sufi Chivalry: Lessons to a Son of the Moment, Futuwwah*, trans. Sheikh Tosun Bayrak al-Jerrahi al-Halveti, London: East West Publications, 1983.
Tabatabai, Muhammad Husayn, al-. *Al-Mizan: An Exegesis of the Quran*, 4 vols., trans. Sayyid Saeed Akhtar Rizvi, Tehran: WOFIS, 1982.
Tabari, Ali. *The Book of Religion and Empire: A Semi-Official Defence and Exposition of Islam Written by Order at the Court and with the Assistance of the Chalijah Mutawakkil (a.d. 847-861)*, trans. Alphance Mingana. London: Bernard Quaritch, 1922.
Tabari, Abu Jafar Muhammad b. Jarir, al-. *Tafsir*, 30 vols. Mior: al-Manba al-Maymaniyya, 1901-1903.
———. *Tarikh al-rusul wal-muluk* (*The History of al-Tabari*), 1 vol, trans. Franz Rosenthal. Albany: State University of New York Press, 1989.
Tanner, Marcus. *Croatia: A Nation Forged in War.* New Haven: Yale University Press, 2001.
Tirmidhi, Muhammad b. Isa Abu Isa, al-. *Al-Jami al-Sahih wa huwa Sunan al-Tirmidhi.* Cairo: al-Maktabat al-Islamiyya, 1938.
Trako, Salih. "Vakufnama hadži Mehmeda sina hadži Mahmudova Mehmedbašića Stočanina iz 1734. godine." *Glasnik Rijaseta Islamske zajednice u SFRJ*, 3 (1990):38-45.

Trhulj, Sead. *Mladi muslimani.* Sarajevo: OKO, 1995.

Veljačić, Čedomil. *Philosophia Perennis,* 2 vols., translated and edited by Goran Kardaš. Zagreb: Demetra, 2003/2004.

Wei-Ming, Tu. *Centrality and Commonality: An Essay on Confucian Religiousness.* Albany: State University of New York Press, 1989.

———. *Confucian Thought: Selfhood as Creative Transformation.* Albany: State University of New York Press, 1985.

Wensinck, Arent J. *Studies of A.J. Wensinck.* New York: Arno Press, 1978.

———. "The Ideas of the Western Semites Concerning the Navel of the Earth." In Wensinck, *Studies of A.J. Wensinck,* 1-65.

———. *The Muslim Creed: Its Genesis and Historical Development.* Cambridge, UK: University Press, 1932.

Wensinck, Arent J., J.P. Mensing, and J. Brugman. *Concordance et indices de la tradition musulmane.* Leiden: E.J. Brill, 1936-1969.

Wüstenfeld, Ferdinand. *Die Chroniken der Stadt Mekka,* 1 vol. Hildesheim: Olms, 1981 (reprint of the 1857 edition).

Zayn al-Abidin, Ali ibn al-Husayn, Imam. *Sahifa: The Psalms of Islam* (*al-sahifat al-kamilat al-sajjadiyya*), trans. William C. Chittick. Qum: Ansariyam Publications, 1987.

———. "The Treatise on Rights (*Risalat al-Huquq*)." In Zayn al-Abidin, *Sahifa,* 279-292.

Žerjavić, Vladimir. *Gubici stanovništva Jugoslavije u drugom svjetskom ratu.* Zagreb: Jugoslavensko viktimološko društvo, 1989.

Acknowledgments

This book is an expanded chapter from an unpublished manuscript, *The Čaršija Mosque: Language and Meaning*. The author and the Zagreb publisher of the original, Albert Goldstein, had long discussions about the manuscript, during which the idea of expanding this chapter into a separate book came up. Work on the book profited in various ways from the help of Miralem Brkić, Medina Hadžihasanović-Katana, Amra Hadžimuhamedović, Safet Hadžimuhamedović, Šeima Hodžić, Mujo Koštić, Ognjen Materić, Amer Medar, Hazim Numanagić, Irena Šaravanja, Aida Šunje, Asim Zubčević, and most of all, Halida Mahmutćehajić. The author owes them all his gratitude. It is due to the kind determination of Simona Goldstein to carry out the will of her father, who died in June 2007, before the book was finished, that the original of this book reached the press.

On first encountering the book, Desmond Maurer suggested to the author that it should be translated into English. It was as a result of this that this translation was completed in the summer of 2010. Cooperation with the translator and discussion on many of the topics in the book and others related to it proved examples of the values which the open margins of any manuscript demand. The author is both grateful and indebted to him and to everyone at World Wisdom publishers, particularly Michael Fitzgerald, Mary-Kathryne Steele, and Clinton Minnaar. The author also owes his sincere gratitude to his dear friends and respected colleagues Ivo Banac and Seyyed Hossein Nasr for their contributions to presenting this book to a wider world public.

Post scriptum

The author is the owner of all the drawings and photographs presented in this volume. The photographs on pages 139 and 144 were taken by Leopold Goldstein in or around 1870. It is not known who the photographs on pages 135, 140, 145, 193, and 195 are by. Judging by the look of the buildings and the town, they date from the late nineteenth or early twentieth centuries. The photographs on pages 138, 142, 151, 196, and 198 were taken for this book. The drawings represent the town as it looked before 1878. It is not known who drew them.

Biographical Notes

RUSMIR MAHMUTĆEHAJIĆ is a Bosnian academic, author, and former statesman and is considered one of the country's leading intellectuals and public figures. He served as Vice-President of the Government of Bosnia from 1991 to 1993; for the past twelve years, he has been President of International Forum Bosnia. He is the author of twenty books and several hundred academic articles and essays which have been translated into multiple languages, including *Learning from Bosnia: Approaching Tradition* and *Bosnia the Good: Tolerance and Tradition.* He lives in Sarajevo, Bosnia and Herzegovina.

SEYYED HOSSEIN NASR is University Professor of Islamic Studies at the George Washington University. The author of over fifty books and five hundred articles, he is one of the world's most respected writers and speakers on Islam, its arts and sciences, and its traditional mystical path, Sufism. Among his publications are *Knowledge and the Sacred* (the 1981 Gifford Lectures), *Religion and the Order of Nature* (the 1994 Cadbury Lectures), and *The Heart of Islam: Enduring Values for Humanity.*

IVO BANAC is Emeritus Professor at the Department of History at Yale University. He is also Professor of History at Zagreb University's Faculty of Philosophy and was the President of the Croatian Helsinki Committee on Human Rights. His publications include: *The National Question in Yugoslavia: Origins, History, Politics*, *With Stalin against Tito: Cominformist Splits in Yugoslav Communism*, and *Acta turcarum.*

DESMOND MAURER graduated in Classics from the University of Edinburgh. He has lived in Bosnia since 1995, where he has worked for the UN, taught in the English department of the University of Sarajevo, and been an author, editor, and translator of publications on economic, political, and literary topics. He also translated Rusmir Mahmutćehajić's book *On the Other: A Muslim View.* He is currently chairman of the Center for the Study of History at the International Forum Bosnia.

Index

Other Titles on Islam by World Wisdom

Art of Islam, Language and Meaning: Commemorative Edition,
by Titus Burckhardt, 2009

Christianity/Islam: Perspectives on Esoteric Ecumenism,
by Frithjof Schuon, 2008

Introduction to Sufi Doctrine,
by Titus Burckhardt, 2008

Introduction to Sufism: The Inner Path of Islam,
by Éric Geoffroy, 2010

Introduction to Traditional Islam, Illustrated: Foundations, Art, and Spirituality,
by Jean-Louis Michon, 2008

Islam, Fundamentalism, and the Betrayal of Tradition: Essays by Western Muslim Scholars,
edited by Joseph E.B. Lumbard, 2004

Men of a Single Book: Fundamentalism in Islam, Christianity, and Modern Thought,
by Mateus Soares de Azevedo, 2010

The Mystics of Islam,
by Reynold A. Nicholson, 2002

The Path of Muhammad: A Book on Islamic Morals and Ethics by Imam Birgivi,
interpreted by Shaykh Tosun Bayrak, 2005

Paths to the Heart: Sufism and the Christian East,
edited by James S. Cutsinger, 2003

Paths to Transcendence: According to Shankara, Ibn Arabi, and Meister Eckhart,
by Reza Shah-Kazemi, 2006

The Sacred Foundations of Justice in Islam:
The Teachings of 'Ali ibn Abi Talib,
edited by M. Ali Lakhani, 2006

A Spirit of Tolerance: The Inspiring Life of Tierno Bokar,
by Amadou Hampaté Bâ, 2008

The Sufi Doctrine of Rumi: Illustrated Edition
by William C. Chittick, 2005

Sufism: Love and Wisdom,
edited by Jean-Louis Michon and Roger Gaetani, 2006

Sufism: Veil and Quintessence,
by Frithjof Schuon, 2007

Understanding Islam,
by Frithjof Schuon, 2011

Universal Dimensions of Islam: Studies in Comparative Religion,
edited by Patrick Laude, 2010

The Universal Spirit of Islam: From the Koran and Hadith,
edited by Judith and Michael Oren Fitzgerald, 2006

Unveiling the Garden of Love:
Mystical Symbolism in Layla Majnun and Gita Govinda,
by Lalita Sinha, 2008

Wisdom's Journey: Living the Spirit of Islam in the Modern World,
by John Herlihy, 2009